D1161400

Melting Pot of
MENNONITE
COOKERY
1874-1974

Compiled by Edna (Ramseyer) Kaufman
Sketches by Avis Brandt and Esther Foth

Published by
Bethel College Women's Association
North Newton, Kansas 67117

MENNONITE CENTENNIAL SERIES

In commemoration of the Mennonite Centennial a number of pertinent publications are in preparation dealing with the coming of the Mennonites to the Prairie states and provinces of North America. The following are the first to appear:

Leonhard Sudermann, *From Russia to America: Spying Out a New Land.* Translated by Elmer F. Suderman. Derksen Publishers: Steinbach, Manitoba.

Elmer F. Suderman, *What Can We Do Here?* A book of centennial poetry. St. Peter, Minnesota: Daguerreotype Publishers, Box 66.

Melting Pot of Mennonite Cookery. Prepared and published by the Bethel College Women's Association, North Newton, Kansas.

First Edition 1974
Second Edition 1975
Second Edition, Third Printing 1983

Printed in U.S.A.
Mennonite Press, Inc.

North Newton, Kansas 67117

Dedicated to the
Mennonite Pioneer Women

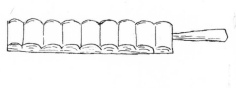

COOKBOOK COMMITTEE

Miss Honora E. Becker
Mrs. Leo Brandt (Mildred Haury)
Mrs. Waldo Brandt (Avis Unruh)
Mrs. A. J. Brubacher (Clara Hirschler)
Miss Eva E. Cooprider (Yoder)
Mrs. August Epp (Helen Peters)
Mrs. Walter Foth (Esther Krehbiel)
Mrs. P. E. Frantz (Marie J. Regier)
Mrs. Helmut Friesen (Gertrude Regier)
Mrs. Arnold Funk (Edna Loganbill)
Mrs. Herman Graber (Selma Voran)
Mrs. Isaac S. Harms (Helen Harms)
Mrs. Ed G. Kaufman (Edna Ramseyer)
Mrs. Harry L. Miller (Orpah Wagler)
Mrs. Arnold Regier (Helen Buhr)
Mrs. Lewy J. Schmidt (Neva Dyck)
Mrs. Herbert Schmidt (Mariam Penner)
Mrs. Virgil P. Schmidt (Doris Mendel)
Mrs. W. F. Unruh (Pauline Schmidt)
Mrs. W. W. Wagler (Alma Nisley)
Mrs. Henry R. Van Der Weg (Grietje Pyl)
Mrs. John Van Der Werf (Martha Dam)

E. Foth

5

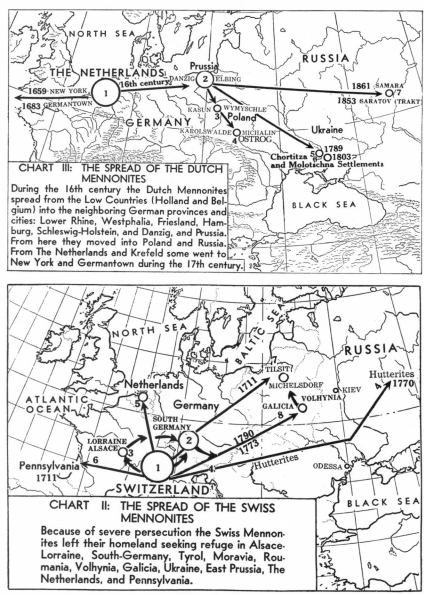

CHART III: THE SPREAD OF THE DUTCH MENNONITES

During the 16th century the Dutch Mennonites spread from the Low Countries (Holland and Belgium) into the neighboring German provinces and cities: Lower Rhine, Westphalia, Friesland, Hamburg, Schleswig-Holstein, and Danzig, and Prussia. From here they moved into Poland and Russia. From The Netherlands and Krefeld some went to New York and Germantown during the 17th century.

CHART II: THE SPREAD OF THE SWISS MENNONITES

Because of severe persecution the Swiss Mennonites left their homeland seeking refuge in Alsace-Lorraine, South-Germany, Tyrol, Moravia, Roumania, Volhynia, Galicia, Ukraine, East Prussia, The Netherlands, and Pennsylvania.

Courtesy MENNONITE LIBRARY AND ARCHIVES

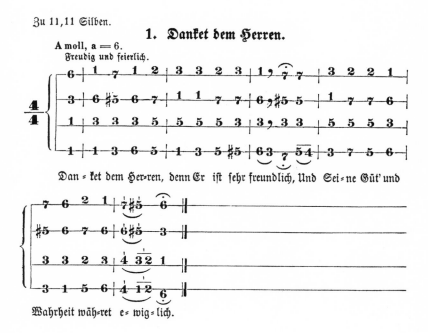

Zu 11,11 Silben.

1. Danket dem Herren.

A moll, a = 6.
Freudig und feierlich.

Dan = ket dem Her=ren, denn Er ist sehr freundlich, Und Sei=ne Güt' und

Wahrheit wäh=ret e = wig=lich.

All ethnic groups had their church services in the German language. Most churches did not have organs or pianos. They did not even have many songbooks, so several men were chosen to be *Vorsaenger*. This position was a great honor. The *Vorsaenger* would recite part of a song, then the audience would sing until all (ten) verses had been sung.

The pioneers celebrated each fall with an *Ernte Dankfest*, or Harvest Festival. They were truly thankful that God had led them to this country. A favorite with them was, *Nun danket alle Gott* — Now Thank We All Our God.

Prayers

*Komm Herr Jesu, sei unser Gast, und
segne was Du uns bescheret hast. Amen.*

Come Lord Jesus be Thou our Guest, and
may our daily bread be blessed. Amen.

*Segne Vater diese Speise, uns zur
Kraft und Dir zum Preise. Amen.*

7

Alle Guten Gaben
Alles was wir haben
Kommt von Dir, O Herr
Dank sei Dir dafuer. Amen.

Muede bin ich geh zur Ruh,
Schliesse meine Augen zu.
Vater lass die Augen dein
Ueber meinem Bette sein.

Hab' ich Unrecht heut getan,
Sie es lieber Gott nicht an,
Deine Gnad und Christi Blut
Macht ja allen Schaden gut.
Amen.

501. Jerem. 33, 11. Danket dem Herrn Zebaoth, daß Er so gnädig ist und thut immerdar Gutes.

1. Dankt dem Herrn! mit fro-hen Ga-ben Fül-let Er das gan-ze Land! Al-les, Al-les, was wir ha-ben, kommt aus Seiner Va-ter-hand.

2 Dankt dem Herrn! Er giebt uns Leben,
Giebt uns Nahrung und Gedeih'n.
O wer wollt' Ihn nicht erheben
Und sich Seiner Güte freu'n.

3 Dankt dem Herrn! vergiß, o Seele,
Deines guten Vaters nie!
Werd' Ihm ähnlich und erzähle
Seine Wunder spät und früh.

G. N. Fischer.

8

Foreword and Acknowledgements

When an idea is born it should be shared with others to check whether or not the idea has merit.

The idea was a *Cookbook* including typical old recipes of the various Mennonite cultural groups who have settled in Kansas and surrounding states within the last one hundred years.

The response from listeners was exhilarating and positive. "Just what I have been looking for," "Now is the time to prepare such a book," "There are already so many cookbooks, but women always want another if it is different."

The Bethel College Women's Association of North Newton, Kansas, accepted the Cookbook as their 1974 project and chose the name *Melting Pot of Mennonite Cookery*.

Selected women representing the ten cultural groups together planned, collected, and prepared the typical recipes, folk stories, and histories.

As the committee worked together, they became aware of their differences as a result of varying migrations and home countries, but, even more important, discovered a oneness, a unity, from the standpoint of a common faith and heritage. A beautiful fellowship and a deeper appreciation of each other and of the groups represented were important by-products of this endeavor.

Foods, with different names reflecting a certain country, were basically the same. The early pioneers, being mostly rural, made good use of foods from the garden, orchard, and dairy. Much creativity and resourcefulness are expressed in the many recipes for you to enjoy.

Special thanks should be given to:

Dr. Cornelius and Hilda (Wiebe) Krahn for the many hours given in guiding the committee, reading and preparing some of the materials;

Members of the Mennonite Press for their patience and helpfulness;

Avis (Unruh) Brandt and Esther (Krehbiel) Foth for the original and delightful drawings found within the book;

Each committee woman, whose name appears in the beginning of the book, for the many hours spent in collecting recipes, writing histories and stories;

9

The families of committee members for their patience and encouragement in the preparation of this book;

Each person who contributed a recipe, gave suggestions, did typing, etc.

May you find within the following pages a dedication to our common Anabaptist-Mennonite background and to the art and joy of food preparation.

On behalf of the
Bethel College Women's Association,

Edna (Ramseyer) Kaufman, President

Introduction

With interest, we have watched the development and production of the *Mennonite "Melting Pot" Cookbook* based on personal cooking experiences as well as the resources of the Mennonite Library and Archives. It was exciting to watch its emergence in discussion groups, in the practical "try-out" of the recipes, and the reading of the introductions of the various Mennonite ethnic backgrounds of the groups of Mennonites that came to North America a century ago.

It was only natural that the framework of the "century" was kept flexible. After all, the collectors had to reach far back into the history of cookery of each of the ethnic groups of which Switzerland, South Germany, and the Netherlands were the major backgrounds. The melting pot of recipes, however, really originated in West Prussia which at times belonged to Germany and at other times to Poland whence Mennonites spread into the interior of Poland and ultimately to Russia. Similarly, some of the Swiss and South German Mennonites and Amish and Hutterites spread to Russian Poland and Russia. Here most of them accepted *Borscht (Borshtsh)*, the symbol of the melting pot, in one or another variety.

If all participants and contributors to the *Cookbook* were not always quite in agreement as to the amount of "this" or "that" ingredient that goes into a dish of cooked or baked items, there was even less agreement in regard to the spelling of the name of the dish. After all, the development of a recipe can be perfect because of a practice in cooking, but the pronounciation of the name of this foreign dish, not to speak of its spelling, is another story. Consequently the careful reader may, even after much proofreading, discover slight variances. But after all, "What's in a name (or its spelling)? A rose by any other name would smell as sweet."

The Bethel College Women's Association and particularly Edna Kaufman and her many co-workers must be congratulated on their achievement in presenting this unique *Melting Pot* to many eager cooks and their families who will enjoy the art of cooking during this Centennial year and in the years to come.

Cornelius Krahn

11

Table of Contents

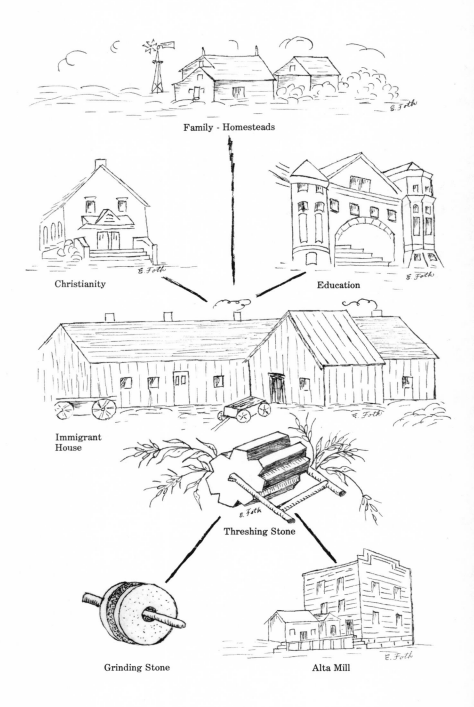

Family - Homesteads

Christianity

Education

Immigrant House

Threshing Stone

Grinding Stone

Alta Mill

1

Pennsylvania German Amish/Mennonites

HISTORY

The Pennsylvania German (Dutch) Mennonites came during the 18th century from Switzerland and the Palatinate *(Pfalz)* to Pennsylvania where other German Protestant groups settled. The Mennonites and the Amish were of the same Swiss-Anabaptist background. Ultimately these Pennsylvania Mennonites spread into Ontario, Virginia, Kansas and other western states. Many of the Amish have rejoined the Mennonites, and the Mennonites are primarily affiliated with the (Old) Mennonite Church or the General Conference Mennonite Church. The old Swiss culture has been best preserved by the Amish. (The following paragraphs were written by Melvin Gingerich and published in *Mennonite Encyclopedia,* Vol. IV, 142.)

Pennsylvania-German Culture

The ethnic group known as the Pennsylvania "Dutch" (from *Deutsch)* has left an indelible impress upon the American way of life. They are a group of people (of Swiss, Alsatian, and Palatine origin) who earlier shared and still share to a certain extent a common High-German Palatine dialect, and who settled mostly in Pennsylvania in the 18th century and later. Religiously there are three general types of Pennsylvania Dutch: (1) "Church People" so called because the adherents belonged to established state churches (Lutheran and Reformed) when they came to this country; (2) the Moravians; and (3) the "plain people".

15

Among the "plain people" (so named because of their plainness in dress) are the various groups of Mennonites, Amish, Dunkards or Church of the Brethren, Zion's Children, Brethren in Christ, and earlier the Schwenckfelder group. The Amish are currently photographed and popularized so much that there is a common mistaken notion that all Pennsylvania Dutchman are "plain". The plain people probably number not more than 10-15 per cent of the total dialect-speaking population; there are about a half million in North America who can speak or understand the Pennsylvania-Dutch dialect.

The Pennsylvania Germans preserved many of the finer features of the group culture which they brought with them from the Old World. Here will be discussed their contributions to the broader scope of American life, with occasional reference to elements of their ethnocentric culture, which of itself is a fascinating field for the sociologist.

Agriculture: Few persons will disagree that these people always have been among the best farmers in America. Accustomed to the intensive cultivation of their fields, they did not adopt the plantation system of the southern states or devote vast acreage to grazing. The farmstead became a fairly self-sufficient economic unit.

Nature is a stern disciplinarian and those who seek her rewards must learn the disciplines of life. The Mennonites, Amish, and other members of the plain people have integrated these disciplines with their spiritual and economic life.

The Pennsylvania Germans are credited with the introduction of the willow tree, many varieties of fruit, especially apples, the prevention of soil erosion, the balanced rotation of crops, the building of "bank" barns, the Conestoga wagon, prairie schooner of pioneer days, several types of fences, and numerous other elements found in modern agriculture.

Kitchen Culture: The excellence of Pennsylvania-German cooking is acknowledged by most people. Housewives are little concerned with calories and vitamins but are ever alert to the virtues of cleanliness, taste, and the complete banishment of hunger from the domains over which they rule. They contributed to our national pantry such delicacies as cottage cheese, scrapple, various types of sausages, pretzels, cole slaw, and, of course, sauerkraut.

Crafts: Every ethnic group has its own peculiar *Volkskunde;* that of the Pennsylvania Germans is of especial interest because of its expertness and the vestiges of Renaissance lore which survived the centuries in a new world. Early craftsmen included cabinetmakers, whose workmanship is attested to this day by antique collectors, weavers, potters, stone masons, wheelwrights, wain-wrights, carpenters, smiths, millers, coopers, and processors of farm products.

The young lady of the household filled the dower chest (perhaps one made by a relative and decorated by a friend) with linens made of flax which she spun and embroidered. Her mother quilted bed coverings, braided straw for the making of hats, and cut and sewed cloth to furnish garments for her family. Some of these handicrafts are still employed on farmsteads in Mennonite-Amish communities.

As a result of the Homestead Act of 1862, many Mennonites and Amish from the East came to Kansas. This act granted to United States citizens the title to 160 acres or less of some unappropriated land, provided he would live on and cultivate the land for a five year period. In 1871, the Kilmer family of Elkhart, Indiana, and R. J. Heatwole from Virginia and Illinois located in the south-eastern part of McPherson County and Canada, Kansas, north of Hillsboro. In 1873 the Henry G. Brunk family, from Virginia, traveled by covered wagon to Marion Center. Other families came during this early period.

Adversity was experienced by many—death as a result of drinking impure water, grasshoppers devouring all vegetation, scarcity of wood for building homes, and great distances from the source of important and necessary supplies. A furrow was plowed between the settlements, running east and west along the south edge of the present site of Hillsboro. There was nothing to break the monotony of the journey save flocks of prairie chickens and herds of antelope.

The first Amish settler in Kansas was Eli N. Yoder, who moved to Reno County from Pennsylvania in 1874. He was responsible for the establishment on his farm of a small station of the Missouri Pacific Railroad and had a post office and store in his own home. Many other Amish families moved from eastern states. Some left because of cheaper land; others sought a more spiritual environ-ment. Nisley, Mast, Miller, and Wagler are a few of the common names of the settlers.

The first years in Kansas were financially difficult; but, with the introduction of Turkey Red wheat and the feeding of steers, the settlers were able to make a good living.

Some of the Amish worshipped in churches, but others held their religious services in homes.

MENU

Breakfast
    Cooked cereal - oatmeal or cracked wheat served with
        milk and sugar
    Apple sauce
    Coffee

Dinner
    Chicken and noodles
    Cabbage slaw
    Bread and butter
    Apple butter
    Milk for the children
    Iced tea for adults

Supper
    Bean soup made with milk
    Crackers
    Fruit pie

BREADS

KUM ESSE!

"Cornbread and beans
Fit for kings and queens."
Anon.

Cornbread

Mix together:
    1 3/4 c. cornmeal   1/4 c. sugar
    1/2 tsp. salt   3/4 c. flour
    3/4 tsp. soda

Add 1/2 c. sour cream and 1 egg, beaten.
Add enough sour milk (about 1/2 c.) to make a soft dough,
like for a cake.
Bake at 450° for 20 minutes.

Cornbread

    1 c. sour cream   1 tsp. salt
    1 c. buttermilk   2 eggs, beaten
    1 1/2 tsp. soda, dissolved   cornmeal, enough to
        in the milk   make a firm batter
Bake at 425° for 20 minutes or until done.

Fried Bread

(A way to use old bread)

Beat:
        1 egg   1/2 c. milk
        salt and pepper to taste

Dip slices of dry bread into mixture.
Fry in shortening until brown.
Turn to brown the other side.
Serve with butter and syrup.

Overnight Pancakes

Sift together:
    2 c. flour   1 tsp. salt
    1 tsp. baking powder   1 tbsp. sugar

Add:
    1 egg, lightly beaten   2 c. buttermilk

Beat well. Let stand overnight.
Next morning add: 1 tsp. soda dissolved in 2 tsp. hot water.
Beat well. Bake on hot, greased griddle or skillet.
Serve with butter and syrup.

Communion Bread

(Unleavened Bread)

Sift together:
    6 c. flour
    1/2 c. sugar
    1 tsp. salt

Cut in:
    1 pound butter

Add 2 1/4 c. milk, gradually, to make a dough of pie crust consistency.

Divide into 4 parts, and work each part until it blisters. Then roll out fairly thin. Place dough on a baking sheet. Cut into 1 inch strips. Perforate each strip, from end to end, with a fork. Bake at 450° until lightly brown (8 to 10 minutes).

Place baked strips on a plate. A portion, about 1 inch, is broken off to serve each communicant.

Makes approximately 760 wafers.

Bread

(Yield one loaf)

1 pkg. dry yeast   2 tbsp. sugar
  (2 tsp. granulated yeast)   2 tsp. salt
2/3 c. warm water   1 1/2 tbsp. shortening
2/3 c. scalded milk   3 1/2 to 4 c. flour

Sprinkle yeast over warm water in small bowl. (Water warm, not hot.)

In a large mixing bowl, add sugar, salt, and shortening to the scalded milk. Cool till mixture is barely warm.

Combine yeast solution and milk.

Add 2 c. of flour. Beat till smooth. Then add about 1 1/2 c. more flour to make dough easy to handle.

Kneading is very important. To knead, round the dough into a ball. Plunk it onto a floured board and mix with hands. Push dough away from you with your palms, gather it up, give it a quarter turn and push again. Keep this up for 8 to 10 minutes. At first, dough is sticky, then gradually takes on a satin finish and doesn't stick to the hands. Round it to a ball, grease and place in bowl to rise to twice its size. Cover and set in a draft-free place, about 80-85°.

Punch down with fist, spanking out the air with palms of hands. Cover and let rest 10 minutes.

Shape into a loaf, place in greased pan. Let rise till doubled in size.

Bake at 350° for 1 hour until nicely browned and the loaf sounds hollow when tapped on the bottom.

Cool on a rack or cloth.

Hints For Bread Making

— from 1 to 4 cakes compressed yeast may be used to one cup of liquid. Two tbsp. to one c. of liquid yeast will yield one loaf of bread.

— for one c. of liquid use approximately three c. of flour.

— a good bread flour will take up more liquid than poor flour.

— good bread flour rubbed between the fingers has a granular feeling. It will not hold its shape when pressed in the hand.

— the handling of the dough, not the proportions of ingredients, is the secret.

— temperatures most satisfactory for bread to rise is between 75° and 95°.

— for a soft crust, rather than crisp, butter the top and sides of the loaf after removing from oven.

— to test for doneness, a hollow sound when tapped, or loaf shrinks away from sides of the pan.

— sugar hastens activity of yeast.

— scalding the liquid kills all organisms that spoil the dough.

Spook Yeast Bread

Spook yeast is a liquid. To make it, take 1 cake of "Yeast Foam" and soak it in 1 c. of warm, unsalted potato beer, which is the water drained off cooked potatoes and is quite concentrated. Add 1 tbsp. sugar. Set this liquid in a very warm place, just warm enough so it doesn't scald. Stir now and then, if it doesn't foam within 5 hours, throw it out and start over.

In 24 hours the liquid is ready to use. Add 3 c. of potato beer about noon with 3 tsp. of sugar. Stir off and on during afternoon.

Before going to bed, you are ready to stir the bread. Mix 3 c. of slightly warmed water, 1 tbsp. salt, 1 tbsp. lard, and 3 c. of the yeast. (Seal the remaining c. of yeast in a jar and set in very cool place.)

Take a large size dish pan to mix dough. Stir in flour to make a soft dough. Then knead in more flour to make a dough that is elastic and doesn't stick to the fingers.

Turn the dough onto a flat floured surface and work it with the palms of the hands. Let the dough stand in the bread pan overnight.

Early the next morning knead the bread down and form into 5 loaves. Place loaves in greased pans. Let rise 3-4 hours until very light. Bake 1 hour in hot oven.

CAKES AND COOKIES

Church Cookies

Cream together:
        2 c. white sugar   1 c. shortening
        2 c. brown sugar
Add:
        3 eggs, beaten
Sift together:
        2 c. flour   3 tsp. baking powder
        3 tsp. soda   1/2 tsp. nutmeg (optional)
        1 tsp. salt
Mix with creamed mixture
Combine:
        1 c. cream   1 tsp. vanilla
        1 c. milk

Add liquids alternately with 8 1/2 c. more flour, making a soft dough. Set in a cool place or refrigerator overnight.
    Drop by spoonful onto lightly greased baking sheet. Bake at 400° until lightly browned.

Old Fashioned Sugar Cookies

Cream:
        1/2 c. shortening   1 c. sugar
Add:
        1 egg, lightly beaten
Sift:
        3 c. flour   3 tsp. baking powder
        1/4 tsp. salt
Add to creamed mixture alternately with 1/2 c. milk.
    Add 1 tsp. vanilla. (For special flavor add 1 tsp. nutmeg, 1 tsp. almond extract.)
    Mix well. Chill.
    Roll out fairly thin. Cut in desired shapes. Lift with spatula to lightly greased pans.
    Bake 375° for 8-10 minutes. May be iced.

Filled Cookies

Cook together filling:

    2 c. raisins (or prunes,   3/4 c. sugar
       dates, figs cut up)   3/4 c. water

Add, if desired, 1/2 c. chopped nuts. Cool filling.

Dough:

    1 c. sugar   3 tsp. baking powder
    1/2 c. lard   1 tsp. soda
    1 egg   Flour (approx. 2 1/2 c.)
    1/2 c. sweet milk   to make soft dough

Roll out and cut dough in shapes. Place one piece of dough on lightly greased baking sheet. Place a spoonful of filling in center and top with a second piece of dough. Press edges together. Bake at 400° for 8-10 minutes.

Oatmeal Cookies

    1 1/2 c. brown sugar   3/4 tsp. soda dissolved in
    3/4 c. butter   2 tbsp. hot water
    3 eggs   1 c. oatmeal
    pinch of salt   2 tsp. cinnamon
    2 c. flour, scant   1/2 c. raisins
    2 tsp. vanilla   1/2 c. nuts

Cream shortening and sugar. Add eggs and beat until fluffy. Sift dry ingredients. Add oats and soda and mix well. Add vanilla. Mix dry ingredients into creamed mixture. Fold in chopped nuts and raisins. Drop in small balls on greased pan. Bake at 350° for 12 to 15 minutes.

Grandma's Cookies

    8 c. brown sugar   4 c. shortening
    4 c. buttermilk   12 eggs
    flour to roll out   8 tsp. baking powder
    (approx. 10-12 c.)   8 tsp. soda

Cream sugar and shortening. Add well beaten eggs. Sift dry ingredients and add alternately with the milk. Add enough flour to make a soft dough which can be rolled out. Cut with a cookie cutter. Put on greased pans. Bake at 350° until a light touch of finger on cookie top, leaves a slight indentation.

Roman Apple Cake

1/2 c. brown sugar	2 1/4 c. flour
1 c. white sugar	2 tsp. baking powder
1/2 c. butter	2 eggs
3/4 tsp. cinnamon	1/2 c. milk
1 tsp. soda	4 c. raw apple slices
1 tsp. salt	

Cream sugar and butter for 2 minutes. Add beaten eggs. Sift dry ingredients and add alternately with the milk. Blend well and add the apples. Pour into greased pan. Bake at 325° for 40 minutes or until done.

Topping:

1/2 c. sugar	1/2 tsp. cinnamon
1/2 c. chopped pecans	

Mix and sprinkle on top of hot cake.

Sour Milk Gingerbread

Sift together:

2 1/3 c. flour	2 tsp. ginger
1/2 tsp. salt	

Mix:

1 c. sour milk	1 c. molasses
1 3/4 tsp. soda	4 tbsp. melted shortening

Beat the flour mixture into the liquid mixture, until batter is smooth. Bake in a greased 9 inch square pan at 350° for 25 minutes or until done.

Chocolate Buttermilk Cake

3 c. flour	1 tsp. salt
2 tsp. soda	2 tsp. vanilla
3 tbsp. cocoa	2 c. buttermilk
2 1/2 c. sugar	3/4 c. melted butter
1 tsp. baking powder	2 eggs

Sift dry ingredients together. Put in a mixing bowl, and make an empty space in the middle. Put all the liquid mixture in empty space, then beat together. Pour into greased pans. Bake at 350°. Makes 3 layers.

Oatmeal Cake

1 1/4 c. boiling water	2 eggs
1 c. oatmeal (uncooked)	1 1/2 c. flour
1/2 c. butter or shortening	1 tsp. soda
1 c. sugar	1/2 tsp. salt
1 c. brown sugar	3/4 tsp. cinnamon
1 tsp. vanilla	1/4 tsp. nutmeg

Pour boiling water over oats. Cover and let stand 20 minutes.
Beat shortening till creamy; gradually add sugar and beat.
Blend in vanilla and eggs. Add oatmeal. Mix well.

Sift dry ingredients together. Add to creamed mixture. Mix.
Pour into well greased and floured 9 inch square pan.

Bake at 350° for 50-55 minutes. Do not remove cake from pan.

Frosting:

1/4 c. melted butter	1/2 c. brown sugar
3 tbsp. light cream	1/3 c. chopped nuts
3/4 c. coconut	

Mix, then spread on cake. Place cake in oven to broil until frosting
becomes bubbly. Serve warm or cold.

Milkless, Eggless, Butterless Cake

1 c. brown sugar	1 tsp. cinnamon
1 c. water	1/2 tsp. cloves
1 1/2 c. raisins	1/2 tsp. nutmeg
1/3 c. lard	pinch of salt

Boil these together 3 minutes. Cool.

Add 1 tsp. baking soda dissolved in 1 tbsp. hot water.

Beat in 2 c. flour to which has been added 1/2 tsp. baking powder.

Bake in greased loaf pan at 350° until toothpick comes out clean,
about 45 minutes.

Nuts make splendid addition, especially black walnuts. May be
cooked in the evening and baked next morning.

CANDY

Sour Cream Candy

Combine:

2 c. brown sugar

1/4 tsp. cream of tartar

1/2 c. sour cream (or sour
milk plus 1 tbsp. butter)

Boil to soft ball stage. Add 1 tbsp. vanilla. Cool.

Beat till creamy. Pour into buttered pan. Cut while soft. Store in covered container.

Pop Corn Balls

Have 4 quarts of freshly popped corn.

Boil together to a soft ball stage:

1 c. syrup

1/2 c. sugar

1 tsp. cream of tartar

Add:

1 tbsp. butter

1/4 tsp. soda

Stir well and pour over freshly popped corn. Form into balls. Yield: 12 large balls.

Taffy

3 lbs. or 3 pts. sugar

2 lbs. or 3 c. syrup

1/3 layer paraffin

3/4 c. water

1 tbsp. butter

Boil until syrup forms a soft ball in cold water.

Add 1/2 tsp. gelatin soaked in 1 tsp. water.

Continue boiling until it cracks in cold water.

Add 3/4 c. nut meats; also 1 tsp. vanilla.

Pour out onto a flat greased pan.

Take a portion with buttered hands and pull till ropes of taffy are white.

Lay on a greased pan.

Crack the ropes into pieces.

Store in a covered container.

Falle is nix, abers ufschte.
To fall is nothing — but to get up!

CHEESE

Cottage Cheese

Use 2 gallons of sweet milk. Add 1 c. of sour milk to hasten curdling.
Heat slowly to 75-80°. Let set over night.
Then heat the curds slowly, about an hour, to 120°. (Set the container of milk into a pan of hot water to heat.)
Cut curds in the stirring process to insure thorough heating.
Drain in a colander and rinse curds with cold water.
Mix curds with salt and pepper and sweet cream.

Schmierkaese

Take 1 bucket of skim milk. Let it sour. Then scald to 120°. Drain off the whey. Tie the curds in a cloth and hang up to dry.
Then add 1 tbsp. soda to curds. Mix well.
Add 1 tbsp. salt and put into a double boiler.
Add 2 beaten eggs to 2 c. of milk.
Pour over the curds. Cook until smooth. Pour into a pan to harden. Slice to serve.

Egg Cheese

2 qts. milk	1 qt. buttermilk
6 eggs	1 tsp. salt

Scald milk. Add the buttermilk and well beaten eggs and salt. Continue heating over low heat until curds are separated from the whey. Strain through a fine sieve or cheesecloth bag.
Delicious served with fresh maple syrup.
(A delicious cheese from Ontario, Canada.)

Hund as gautze beisse net.
A barking dog seldom bites.

DESSERTS

Apple Betty

Cover bottom of pan with thinly sliced apples. Sprinkle with 1 c. sugar and 1 1/2 tsp. cinnamon.
Mix the following with fork or fingers to make coarse crumbs:

1/4 c. butter	1 c. flour
1/2 c. brown sugar	1/4 tsp. salt

Sprinkle crumbs over sliced apple mixture and bake at 350° for 30-40 minutes.
Serve with cream.

Apple Dumplings

Peel and core 6 apples. Fill apples with raisins, brown sugar, butter, and a bit of cinnamon.

Prepare a dough:

3 c. flour	6 tbsp. lard
1 1/2 tsp. baking powder	9 tbsp. water or milk
1/2 tbsp. salt	

Mix gently as for biscuits. Roll out one-half inch thick and cut into squares. Place an apple in each square, pinching corners together over top of apple.
Place on buttered pan. Bake at 350° for about 40 minutes.

Chocolate Bread Pudding

2 squares chocolate (grated)	1/2 tsp. salt
	1 rounded tbsp. butter

Stir into 1 1/2 pints of hot milk. Pour over 2 c. bread cubes. Let cool.
Beat 2 eggs.

Add:

2 c. sugar	1/2 c. nuts
1/2 c. raisins	

Stir eggs, sugar, raisins, nuts into the milk and crumbs. Bake in a greased pan at 350° for 45 minutes.
Serve warm or cold with or without whipped cream.

Grandma's Baked Apples

6 nice apples   1/8 tsp. salt
1 c. sweet cream   3 tbsp. flour
1 c. sugar

Peel and core apples. Cut each into 8 slices and place in casserole. Mix other ingredients and pour over apples and bake at 350° for 1 1/2-2 hours.

Custard

9 eggs   6 1/2 c. lukewarm milk
1 1/2 c. sugar   1/4 c. cream
3 level tbsp. flour   or 6 3/4 c. whole milk

Preheat oven to 450°.

Beat eggs well, add sugar. Beat again. Add flour and beat. Add milk and cream. Stir to mix. Pour in a 9 inch by 13 inch pan. When brown, turn off fire. Leave in oven until set.

Honey Custard

Heat in a double boiler:
    4 tbsp. honey   2 c. milk
Beat until thick:
    3 egg yolks   1/8 tsp. salt

Add hot milk to yolks and return to boiler to finish cooking. When mixture coats silver spoon, remove from heat.

Add 3/4 tsp. vanilla or dash of cinnamon or nutmeg.
Chill before serving.

Rhubarb Crisp

Mix:
    3 c. rhubarb, cut into   1/4 tsp. mace
        small pieces   3/4 c. sugar
    1 egg, beaten   2 tbsp. flour

Put into a greased baking dish. Cover with crumb mixture.
Mixture:
    1/4 c. butter   2/3 c. flour
    1/3 c. brown sugar

Bake at 350° for 30 minutes until done.

E. Foth

Short Cake

Sift together:
    2 c. flour   3/4 tsp. salt
    2 1/2 tsp. baking powder   2 tbsp. sugar
Cut in:
    5 tbsp. shortening
Stir in with fork:
    1/3 c. milk

Divide into 2 parts. Roll each into a circle, 1/4 inch thick. Put first circle into 8 inch round pan.

Butter top of first layer. Place second layer on top. Bake at 450° for 20 minutes.

To serve, separate layers; put strawberries between and on top.

Birchermuesli

6 tbsp. oatmeal	3 peaches or pears
12 tbsp. water	1/3 c. raisins
4 medium apples	1/3 c. walnuts or almonds
1 lemon, peel and juice	3 tbsp. sugar
3 bananas	5 tbsp. cream
3 oranges	

Soak oatmeal for 30 minutes in water. Grind apples with peels; add ground lemon peel and juice. Stir frequently. Slice remaining fruits; add raisins, chopped nuts, sugar, and oatmeal mixture. Mix well.

Just before serving, add the cream.

Yield: 4 servings.

This is a light summer lunch or supper dish.

Cornstarch Pudding

1 pint of milk
2 eggs, separated
3 tbsp. sugar

2 tbsp. cornstarch dissolved in 2 tbsp. water

Heat milk to boiling point.

Beat egg yolks and sugar. Add dissolved cornstarch to eggs and sugar. pour into boiling milk, stirring constantly, until thickened. Remove from heat.

Beat egg whites until stiff and fold into pudding. Add 1 tsp. flavoring, vanilla or lemon.

Serve cold.

DUMPLINGS

Ham Dumplings

Cook a ham bone, with some meat, till tender. Take the bone out and see that the meat and broth is boiling. It is now ready to put the dumplings in.

Dip a spoon in the broth, then get a spoonful of dumpling dough and put it in the broth. Repeat till dough is used up. Let it cook 10 minutes. Taste for salt.

Dumpling Dough

2 c. flour   1 egg

Just enough water so you can stir it together.

Homemade Noodles

1 c. flour   2 eggs or 2 yolks plus
1/2 tsp. salt   2 tbsp. water

Mix salt and flour together in a bowl. Make a well in center of flour mixture and add eggs. Mix thoroughly, beating with fork. Knead dough on a floured surface. Roll very thin and cut in lengthwise strips, 2 1/2 inches wide. Stack strips on top of each other and slice thinly. Separate noodles and let dry on a dry cloth.

Buttered Noodles

"Schmeldtzde Nudelen"

Cook as many noodles as are needed in salted water. Drain. Put noodles in serving dish and pour browned butter over them. Scatter croutons over the top.

Dumplings
(Never Fail)

To be cooked in either meat broth or fruit juice.
Sift into mixing bowl:

    1 1/2 c. flour   1/4 tsp. salt

       1 heaping tsp. baking
          powder

Add:

       1 egg, lightly beaten   3/4 c. sweet milk

Beat well.

Drop by spoonful into boiling broth. Cover closely and cook 5 minutes. Then uncover and cook 5 minutes longer or until done.

Beef broth containing small pieces of meat and potatoes cooked done make a good "bed" on which to cook dumplings. Also fruit with juice such as cherries, blue plums, prunes makes a delicious dish.

FOWL

Pressed Chicken

Dress as many chickens as desired. Cut into pieces. Cover with water and season with salt and pepper. Boil until tender, removing scum as it forms. Remove meat from bones and cut into very small pieces.

Reheat liquid and simmer 15 minutes.

Pack meat into a crock, and pour "boiled-down" broth over meat. Press down and put a plate over mixture. Put a weight on the plate.

Set in a cool place (refrigerator).

When cold turn out on a platter and slice. This was a "Special" for Sunday company.

MEATS

Meat Loaf

4 pounds veal   2 pounds beef
2 pounds fresh pork

Season with salt and pepper. Cook each separately until very tender. Grind separately. Place a layer of each in a mold or pan. Mix broths and boil down. (Add 1 pkg. of plain gelatin if desired.) Pour broth over the layered meat. Press down with heavy plate. Set in cool place. Serve cold in slices.

Meat Balls

Mix together well:
  1 1/2 lbs. ground beef   1 tsp. pepper
  1 onion chopped fine   2 slices of bread soaked
  1 tsp. salt   in water to moisten
    dash of paprika
Add:
  1 egg, well beaten
Mix in:
  5 tbsp. uncooked rice

Form into balls 1 1/2 inches in diameter.

Drop meatballs into 1 quart of boiling tomato juice or canned tomatoes. Cover and simmer for 1 hour.

Scrapple
"Pon Haus"

Separate one hog's head into halves. Remove and discard the eyes and brains. Scrape and thoroughly clean the head. Put into large, heavy kettle and cover with 4 or 5 quarts cold water. Simmer gently for 2 to 3 hours, or until meat falls from the bones. Skim grease from the surface; remove the meat, chop fine and return to the liquid in the kettle. Season with salt and pepper to taste and cook. This may be served on cornmeal mush or a slice of bread.

Or — sift in granulated cornmeal, stirring constantly, until the mixture is thickened to the consistency of soft mush. Cook over low heat 1 hour, stirring occasionally as it burns easily. When cooked, pour the scrapple into lightly greased loaf pans and cool. Cover and store in a cool place. To serve, cut into thin slices and fry in hot fat until crisp and brown. (Delicious, too, served hot from the kettle, on mush or on a slice of bread.)

MISCELLANEOUS

Cereal
Grape Nuts

3 1/2 c. whole wheat flour	1 tsp. soda
2 c. buttermilk	1/2 tsp. salt
1 c. brown sugar	

Mix all ingredients. Put into a greased pan and bake in moderate over, 350°, about 35 minutes, or until done.

Remove from pan and cool for 12 hours, then crumble fine or grind through a meat grinder with a coarse blade.

Toast slowly in low oven until crisp and brown.

Serve with milk and sugar.

For Making Cider Vinegar

Take:

32 gallons soft water	2 quarts molasses
3 lbs. acetic acid	

Mix well together. Let stand from 4 to 6 days; then it is fit for use.

—An old receipe

PASTRY

Pie Safe

E. Foth

Milk Pie
(Very old recipe)

Prepare a regular pie shell.

Put 3/4 c. sugar, pinch of salt, 3 tbsp. flour, and 2 c. milk into pie shell and mix with fingers. (Sounds silly, but only fingers mixes it properly, spoons just don't do it.)

Bake 350° for 1 hour.

Custard Pie

Unbaked pie shell, 9 inch, chilled thoroughly

4 eggs	1 c. light cream, scalded
2/3 c. sugar	1 tsp. vanilla
1/4 tsp. salt	1/2 tsp. nutmeg
1 1/2 c. scalded milk	

Beat eggs slightly. Beat in the remaining ingredients except nutmeg. Pour into pie shell, with high, fluted edges. Sprinkle the nutmeg over top.

Bake in a hot oven 400° until silver knife inserted 1 inch from edge comes clean, about 25 to 35 minutes. (Baking too long makes a watery pie.)

Cool 30 minutes then refrigerate until serving time.

Pecan Pie

1 unbaked pie shell

Cream:

1 c. brown sugar	1 tbsp. butter

Beat:

3 eggs until very light

Combine eggs and sugar with:

1 tsp. vanilla	pinch of salt
1 c. syrup	1/3 c. pecan meats (broken)

Pour into crust and bake in a hot oven for 15 minutes. Then reduce heat to 350° and bake about 30 minutes.

Pumpkin Pie

Mix:

3/4 c. white sugar	1/8 tsp. ginger
1/4 tsp. nutmeg	1/4 tsp. cinnamon

Add:

3 eggs, beaten	1 1/2 c. top milk or
2 c. cooked pumpkin	thin cream

Pour mixture into pie shell.

Bake 10-15 minutes at 450°. Turn oven to 325° and bake till firm 40-50 minutes.

'R faercht sich faer seim egne Schatte.
He is afraid of his own shadow.

Shoo Fly Pie

1 unbaked pie shell
Crumbs for top:
   1 1/2 c. flour   1/2 tsp. baking powder
   1/4 c. butter or margarine   1/2 tsp. salt
   3/4 c. light brown sugar
Mix these ingredients to make crumbs. Set aside.
Syrup:
   1/2 tsp. soda dissolved in   3/4 c. dark syrup
      3/4 c. boiling water

Mix well. Pour syrup mixture into pie shell.
   Immediately sprinkle crumbs on top of liquid.
   Bake 375° for 45 minutes.

Union Pie

2 unbaked pie shells   1 3/4 c. sugar
1 1/2 c. sweet cream   2 level tbsp. flour
1 1/2 c. sweet milk   5 eggs, beaten

Mix sugar and flour. Add cream and milk. Lastly add beaten eggs.
Pour into shells. Sprinkle with cinnamon. Bake at 450° until
brown. Turn oven to 250° until finished. Insert silver knife to test.

Dutch Apple Pie

Plain pastry for one crust. Roll out pastry to about 1/8 inch thickness and line a 9 inch pan. Flute edges.
   Pare and core 6 medium sized apples. Slice into pastry shell.
Mix together:
   3 tbsp. flour   1/4 tsp. cloves
   1 c. sugar
Add 1 c. sour cream, mixing thoroughly. Pour over apples.
Sprinkle over apples a mixture of:
   1/2 tsp. cinnamon   1 1/2 tbsp. sugar

Bake at 450° for 10 minutes; reduce heat to 350° to finish baking,
about 40 minutes. Serve warm or chilled.

Lemon Pie

Prepare syrup by boiling together: 2 c. water and 1 1/2 c. sugar.

Beat 2 egg yolks with 4 level tbsp. cornstarch, adding a little cold water if necessary.

Pour into syrup and bring to a boil. Remove from heat and add the juice and grated rind of 1 lemon. Cool and put into baked pie shell.

Make the meringue: beat the 2 egg whites until stiff. Gradually add 2 tbsp. sugar and 1/2 tsp. baking powder, beating until the meringue holds peaks.

Top the filling and brown in medium oven until the meringue is a golden color.

(This recipe was a favorite of a Pennsylvania Dutch grandmother, greatly enjoyed by her guests.)

Crumb Pie

Have ready 2 unbaked pie shells.
Combine and rub together to make crumbs:

3 c. flour	1 c. lard and butter
2 c. light brown sugar	combined
1 tsp. soda	

Take out 1 c. of crumbs.

Mix remaining crumbs with 1 c. of thick sour milk or buttermilk.
Pour liquid mixture into 2 unbaked pie crusts.
Put the reserved crumbs on top.
Bake in slow oven until slightly brown.
May be served plain or with whipped cream or ice cream.

Raisin Pie
(Funeral Pie)

Soak 1 c. seeded raisins for 2 hours. Drain.
Combine:

1 1/2 c. sugar	4 tbsp. flour

Beat 1 egg and add to the mixture.

Add juice and rind of 1 lemon and 1/4 tsp. salt.

Add 2 c. water and stir well. Cook over hot water, in a double boiler, for 15 minutes. Cool. Put into unbaked pie shell. Cover with strips of pastry in a criss-cross design. Bake at 450° for 10 minutes, then lower heat to 350°. Bake for another 30 minutes.

Butterscotch Pie

1 baked pie shell	2 heaping tbsp. flour
1 c. brown sugar	2 c. water
2 eggs, separated	1 tsp. vanilla
2 tbsp. butter	

Mix sugar and flour in sauce pan. Add water gradually and stir over slow heat until thick. Add butter and the beaten egg yolks. Bring to a boil. Add vanilla. Cool. Fill baked pie shell. Top with meringue. Bake at 350° for 13 minutes or until golden brown.

Meringue: Beat egg whites until stiff. Add 2 tbsp. sugar for each egg white used. Continue to beat until meringue holds peaks.

(Avoid setting meringue pie in a cold place after taking from the oven to prevent tiny drops of moisture collecting on the meringue.)

Fruit Press

Esther Foth

Apple Butter Making

In the fall, just before frost, was the time to pick the tart or sour apples, known as the cooking apples, to make ready for the cooking of apple butter. This event was one enjoyed by all members of the family, and very often involved friends and neighbors. The apples of various kinds had been taken to the cider mill and some of the sweet pungent juice was reserved for the making of apple butter, for cider is the very necessary ingredient of delicious butter. Usually two days were involved in this exciting social event.

The housewife rolled out the huge copper kettle, the 15 to 20 gallon size, from its storage in the shed into the yard. Here the interior was thoroughly shined with salt and vinegar. Then the kettle was placed on a tripod so a fire could be made beneath it. The kettle was filled with fresh apple cider to be boiled down about half. This boiled-down cider was then removed from the kettle to cool.

That evening the family and neighbors gathered to "schnitz" apples; peeling by hand, coring, and removing bad spots. Some families were fortunate to have mechanical apple peelers, which left only coring and quartering to be done by hand. These quartered apples were covered by water in containers. Anywhere from five to ten bushels of apples were "schnitzed". Singing and story telling were favorite pastimes at these parties. Often doughnuts and coffee were served as refreshments.

The next morning the copper kettle was filled with apples and some water, and a fire was set beneath the kettle to cook the apples into a mush. Boiling apple butter required a "know-how", and the stirring process began with a long handled paddle which was made of oak or maple. Constant stirring to avoid scorching was a tiresome job, so frequent changes in persons stirring were made. The boys were usually delegated to keep the fire going. This cooking down required most of the morning. Sometimes kettles of apples were cooked in the house to add to the outside kettle. When the apples looked like applesauce, the boiled-down cider was added, about half as much cider as apples. Then sugar was added, usually four cups of sugar for every gallon of butter for the ordinary taste. Some folks liked to add spices such as cinnamon or allspice.

Cooking continued, with not a moment's hesitation in stirring or else the butter would be scorched. A test of doneness was to place a spoonful on a saucer; if the edges of the mixture appeared watery, more cooking was needed. When the buttery mass appeared to hold shape on the saucer, the butter was ladled into crocks or jars and allowed to cool. Layers of paper were tied over the top of the jar or crock. The attic or a cool place was the usual place for the storing of the delicious apple butter (sometimes under the beds of an upstairs bedroom).

PRESERVING

Strawberry Preserves

1 quart of berries   1 tbsp. vinegar
4 c. sugar

Put vinegar in a granite pan. Add the berries. Cover with the sugar. Bring to a boil and boil ten or fifteen minutes. Stir gently. Cover and set aside for a day or two, until the berries puff up. Can cold. Cover with paraffin.

Dried Corn

8 pints of raw corn   1/4 scant c. salt
    cut from cob   1/2 to 2/3 c. sweet cream
1/2 to 2/3 c. sugar

Simmer the mixture for 20-30 minutes, stirring frequently to completely cook.

Dry in a slow oven (250°), stirring frequently. When completely dry, store in closed containers. (My mother began drying process in oven, then spread corn on cloth-covered screens, to dry in the Kansas sun.)

This corn does not require pre-soaking.

Sauerkraut

Weigh out 5 lbs. cabbage; 2 ounces (3 1/2 tbsp.) salt.

Set slaw cutter over jar, and shred cabbage directly into jar. Add salt evenly.

Press down firmly after 3 or 4 inches of shredded cabbage are added.

If jar is not filled, weigh out more cabbage and salt.

Cover with a cloth and board (any kind except yellow or pitch pine).

Weigh down with a jar filled with water, sufficiently heavy to permit brine to rise and cover the cabbage.

Store at 86° F. for 10-14 days.

Remove scum as it appears. Wash and replace cloth cover and weight often.

If made in the fall, sauerkraut will keep until spring by storing it in a very cool place.

Pickled Beets
"Roat Reeva"

Boil red beets until tender. Slip skins off.
Boil together:

1 quart vinegar	1 tbsp. mustard seed
1 pint sugar	1 tsp. cloves
1 tbsp. cinnamon	1 tsp. salt
1 tsp. allspice	

Place beets in spiced vinegar. Simmer 15 minutes.

Seal in clean hot jars.

"Red Beet" Eggs

Simmer eggs gently for 20 minutes.

Remove eggs from boiling water and plunge into cold water.

Peel eggs and put into a container of red beets and juice. Eggs will turn a rosy red.

At least an hour is required to pickle the eggs; the longer they stand in solution, the redder they become.

Red eggs were a Sunday dinner treat.

Pickled Peaches

3 pounds peeled peaches (free stone variety)
Heat:

1 1/2 pound sugar	5 or 6 sticks of cinnamon
1/2 c. vinegar	1 dozen cloves

Dissolve vinegar and sugar in a heavy kettle. Heat. Put peaches into it and cook until the peaches are soft.

Remove peaches from the liquid. Boil liquid well and pour it over the peaches.

Cool. (Peaches may be canned while boiling hot.)

Bread and Butter Pickles

10 large cucumbers, sliced	1 tbsp. salt
3 large onions (optional)	1 tbsp. celery seed
1 1/2 pints vinegar	1 tbsp. mustard seed
3 c. sugar	1 tbsp. tumeric

Do not peel cucumbers. Mix sugar, vinegar, and spices. Bring to a boil, add cucumbers and onions, let simmer eight minutes, can and seal.

Makes about 3 quarts.

Tomato Juice

14 qts. of tomatoes, cut up without peeling	7 onions
14 stems of celery, cut	1 tsp. paprika
7 cloves	2 green peppers, chopped
4 bay leaves	parsley and carrots, chopped if desired

Boil the ingredients together 1 hour. Put through sieve.
Add:

7/8 c. sugar	1/2 c. salt (or a little less)

Bring to a boil and seal in sterilized jars.

Tomato Sauce

12 large, ripe tomatoes,
   peeled and quartered
2 large onions, chopped
1 green pepper, chopped
3/4 c. brown sugar

1 tsp. cloves
1 tsp. cinnamon
1 tbsp. salt
1/2 c. vinegar

Combine all ingredients and cook until thick.
   Seal in hot sterilized jars.
   Yield: 2 pints.

Corn Cob Syrup

Cut kernels from ears of corn.
   Boil one dozen clean corn cobs (red ones are best) from one to two hours in water. There should be one pint of liquid when done.
   Then strain and add 2 pounds of brown sugar.
   Boil until you get the desired consistency.

Canned Sausage

1 gallon water
1 c. white sugar
3/4 c. salt

1 1/2 tsp. pepper
   less than 1/4 tsp.
   saltpetre

Let mixture come to boil, don't skim. Put pieces of fresh sausage into liquid.
   Boil 15 minutes. Place meat and broth into sterilized cans and seal. (No processing necessary.)

D'r Schaffmann is sei lu waert.
The laborer is worthy of his hire.

Mince Meat

6 lb. beef
6 lb. apples, cut in thin
   slices
4 lb. brown sugar
2 lb. citron
3 lb. raisins
3 lb. currants

1 lb. suet, ground
2 qt. boiled sugar syrup
   (1 qt. water and 8 c.
   sugar
1/2 c. salt
2 tsp. nutmeg
1 tbsp. each of cloves,
   allspice, and cinnamon

Cook in covered granite kettle for 2 hours. Stir frequently.
Fill sterilized jars. Seal. Store in a cool place.

Summer Sausage

(Bologna)

Grind:
   28 pounds beef   7 pounds pork
Mix thoroughly:
   1 1/2 c. salt   1 1/2 c. brown sugar, firmly
   4 tbsp. pepper   packed
   4 tbsp. saltpetre

Combine meat and seasonings. Work with hands for 1 hour or until
real sticky. Make muslin sacks about 3 inches in diameter and stuff
with meat mixture. Hang up to dry several days. Rub outside
with liquid smoke. Let dry again, rub with smoke. Dry for at least
10 days or more before using. The outside may be waxed with
paraffin.

(Good for sandwiches.)

Dried Beef

Mix: 2 parts brown sugar to 1 part non-iodized salt.

Use steak or good roasts to make dried beef. The better the cut,
the better the dried beef. Roll the meat in sugar-salt mixture,
leaving on as much as possible. Pack tightly into large jars and
put a plate on top of meat. Place a heavy weight on top to press the
meat down as much as possible.

Leave for 2 weeks in a cool place. It will produce its own brine
during this time. Drain and spread out on racks. Smoke with liquid
smoke, dipping meat into the smoke. Smoke 2 or 3 times, according
to taste.

To serve, slice very thin.

Sugar Cured Ham

Mix thoroughly:

4 lbs. non-iodized salt	2 tbsp. saltpetre dissolved
1/4 lb. pepper	in 1/2 c. hot water
1 pt. brown sugar	

Rub mixture on hams. Keep in a cool place, for 10 to 14 days. Then smoke. Hang hams in a cool, dry place until ready to use.

Schnitzing Parties

(*"Schnitz"* is the Pennsylvania Dutch word for one-fourth of an apple.)

Winesap or Jonathan apples were favorites for both dried apples and apple butter.

Apple peeling machines were used to remove peelings. Then the apple was quartered and the cores removed by hand.

"Applesnitz" pieces were laid out in hot sun on cloths covered with netting.

Sometimes, to speed drying, the apples were put into a warm oven. Some families had drying racks built with 6 or 8 trays 18 inches by 36 inches. The trays were changed alternately to equalize airing and drying.

A. Brandt

SALADS

Cole Slaw

1 medium head of cabbage cut fine with knife or slaw cutter.
For the dressing, mix:

1/2 c. sour cream   1/3 to 1/2 c. vinegar
3 tbsp. sugar   salt and pepper to taste

Pour dressing over the cabbage and serve.

Corn Salad

Cut kernels from 12 large ears of corn (or use 1 1/2 c. of dried corn).

1 head cabbage, cut fine   1 pint water
5 sweet peppers, cut fine   1 tsp. salt
2 tsp. dry mustard   1 1/2 c. sugar
1 pint vinegar

Mix all ingredients. Cook for 15 minutes.
Serve hot or cold.
Will keep in a cool place for a week or two.

Dandelion Greens

Pick about 2 quarts of tender dandelion leaves. Wash and pat
dry. (Never use dandelions after they begin to flower as they
then may be bitter.)
Fry 4 thick slices of cubed bacon pieces until crisp. Pour over
the dandelion greens.
Slowly heat:

1/4 c. butter   1/2 c. cream

Beat:

2 eggs

Add:

1 tbsp. sugar   1 tsp. salt
1/4 tsp. paprika   1/4 tsp. pepper
4 tbsp. vinegar

Blend the egg mixture into the slightly warmed cream and butter.
Heat the entire amount until it thickens like custard. Pour piping
hot over the greens and bacon. Stir thoroughly.
Serve at once.

SAUCES

Butterscotch Sauce

1 c. brown sugar
1 c. corn syrup
1 c. light cream

2 tbsp. butter
1 tsp. vanilla

Combine sugar, syrup and cream and cook until syrup forms a soft ball when dropped in cold water (238°).
Remove from heat and add butter and vanilla.

Cranberry Sauce

Combine:
1 quart cranberries
1 pint sugar

1/2 pint water

Boil until berries burst. Strain through colander to remove skins. Stir pulp thoroughly and pour into a dish. Set in a cool place until it jellies.

Chocolate Syrup

2 c. cocoa
6 c. sugar
1 c. syrup

4 c. water
1 tsp. vanilla

Mix ingredients, except vanilla, and cook until soft ball stage. Remove from fire and add vanilla.

Egg Butter

2 c. dark syrup or
    sorghum
2 eggs

1/2 c. sugar
1 tsp. butter
nutmeg

Mix syrup, eggs, sugar, butter together and let come to a boil, stirring constantly. Pour into a dish and sprinkle with nutmeg.
    Use as a spread on bread. (A small pinch of soda will cut the strong taste of sorghum.)

SOUPS

Cornmeal Mush with Milk

Gradually add 1 part cornmeal to 4 parts boiling water and 1/2 tsp. salt. (Mixing yellow with white cornmeal makes a better flavor.)

Cook 7-10 minutes, stirring frequently.

Serve hot with cold milk and a dab of butter.

Fried Mush

(Use part milk for the liquid in above recipe.)

Put cooked mush into a pan. When cold, slice and fry in butter or bacon drippings until golden.

Serve with honey, syrup or apple butter.

Potato Soup

Select one potato per serving. Peel and dice. Cook diced potatoes (with one small onion diced if desired) in salt water till potatoes are soft. Try to use a minimum of water.

Add one pint of milk per serving to the potatoes which are not drained. Bring milk to boiling point.

Add 1 tbsp. butter per serving.

Serve with crackers or fresh bread and butter, or toasted bread.

Rivel Soup

Heat 1 qt. milk until a skin forms on the surface.

Put 1 c. flour with 1/4 tsp. salt into a mixing bowl and add 1 whole egg. Mix with either fork or fingers to make rivels or coarse crumbs.

Drop rivels into hot milk and bring to a boil. Cook about 1 minute. Serve in bowls.

If desired, allspice may be sprinkled over the soup.

(A simple dish for a winter night's supper.)

Pea Hull Soup

(Pioneers really knew what "waste not, want not" meant, and so little food was wasted. This pea hull soup is an example of this.)

After the peas were hulled, the pods were tied in a bag made of coarse cotton. The bag was then placed in cold water and slowly heated. The hulls were boiled until the sweetness was extracted and then removed from the water. The bag was squeezed to remove all the liquid, and the liquid was seasoned with salt and pepper to taste. If cream was available, a small amount could be added at serving time.

This was a delicious soup at a very small cost.

A. Brandt

VEGETABLES

Cottage Cheese and Potato Bake

4 large potatoes	2 c. homemade dry
1 egg	cottage cheese
1/2 tsp. salt	1/2 c. cream
2 tbsp. cream	1 egg
1 tbsp. flour	1/2 c. sugar

Thoroughly grease a 9 inch by 12 inch by 2 1/2 inch pan. Peel and grate potatoes. Mix potatoes, egg, cream, flour and salt. Put into baking dish. Mix cottage cheese, egg, cream and sugar. Pour on top of the potatoes.

Bake at 350° for 45 to 60 minutes until potatoes are done and cottage cheese is lightly browned.

Fried Potatoes

Begin with raw potatoes.

Select 2 or 3 potatoes per person to be served. Peel. Drop into water to prevent discoloring.

Slice very thin into a skillet that has 2 or 3 tbsp. of shortening heating. Season with salt and pepper.

Cover and fry over moderate fire, stirring occasionally, until potatoes are done. Some may be browned, but by keeping the cover on the skillet, the potatoes will become soft with a super flavor.

Serve with spring onions and fried eggs.

Apple Cider

From "The Good Old Days", edited by R. J. McGinnis et al in cooperation with Farm Quarterly, Harper Brothers, N. Y. 1960

Just before the first frost, choice apples were picked and stored in cellars. Then the windfalls were gathered into the box-bed of a wagon by the farmer and boys and girls. Winesaps, Pippins, Jonathans, Russetts, and even the lowly Ben Davis were thrown together into the wagon. Each added its delicate flavor to the blend of cider. For extra tanginess several bushels of crab apples would be added. In those early days some farms had a cider press, that neighbors could use to extract that wonderful drink of sweet cider.

The apples were scooped into a grinder which chewed up the apples, skins, cores, seeds and an occasional worm, into a mass of juice and pulp about the consistency of apple sauce. Then the pulp was transferred to a press, a slatted wooden frame over which a cloth had been laid. When the frame was full, the corners of cloth were folded over and the top of the press put into place. By the hand screw process, juice was extracted through the slatted boards and cloth into a trough which led to a barrel or tank. A hand press might turn out 12 gallons of juice from 4 to 5 bushels of apples.

Usually families made two barrels of cider, one for the delightful and healthful beverage and one for vinegar. The cider barrel was rolled into a cool place to maintain the sweetness as long as possible. The vinegar barrel, stored in a warmer place, gradually lost its delicate flavor, some of the sugar changing to starch and bubbles showing fermentation was taking place. As the alcoholic content reached its maximum, another change took place. The hard cider began to sour and a stringy mass formed, composed of vinegar yeast known as "mother". Cider vinegar can be kept for a year or more if tightly stoppered.

The Cook Shack

The cook shack was a frame building, perhaps 9 feet by 24 feet, set upon four wheels. There were doors at each end and hinged drop boards, covering screened openings, on each side. During the day, the shack served as a kitchen and dining room but at night it was used as a bedroom for the women cooks. It was outfitted with a coal or kerosene stove, an ice box, storage space for cooking utensils and other supplies, and a long, oilcloth-covered table. Long benches on each side of the table served as chairs. Granite or tin plates and cups were used for place settings.

Generally two young women from the community were hired for the season by the owner of the threshing outfit. This work usually lasted four to six weeks.

If possible, the cook shack was pulled into place under a large tree, and anchored down at each corner. Tubs, wash pans, and towels were supplied to the helpers. When not in use, these articles would be stored beneath the shack. Hand and tea towels were laundered daily. Milk, butter, and fresh vegetables were obtained from the local farms. Bread and pie were baked daily, and the cooks gained much favor with their baking art.

Breakfast, at early dawn, was quite a large meal and could consist of fried eggs, fried potatoes, cooked cereal, milk and coffee. At noon a hearty meal of fried chicken, mashed potatoes with gravy, cabbage slaw, sliced tomatoes, fresh bread and butter, cookies and fruit, satisfied the weary, hungry men. Supper, at about seven o'clock, might consist of cold sliced meat, potato salad, roasting ears, and pie. For a variety, ice cream with fresh fruits, was served.

Remedy for Short Breath, Weakness, Blood and Cold

3 oz. bitter sweet,
    bark of root
2 oz. black alder,
    bark of bush
2 oz. milk-weed, root.
2 oz. dandelion, root

2 oz. elecampane, root.
1 oz. skunk cabbage, root
1 oz. Indian turnip root
1 oz. prickley ash bark of
    root, or berries.
2 oz. elder bark of root

All to be dried. (Except the dandelion and Indian turnip root.) Put all together into 4 quarts water. Simmer slowly in a tin vessel down to 1 quart. Press out, add 1 pound sugar. Simmer again 10 or 15 minutes. When cold add 1 1/2 gills alcohol.

Dose: 1 tbsp. 3 times a day 1/2 hour before each meal.

South German Pioneers in the Prairie

HISTORY

South German Pioneers in the Prairie

Karl Ludwig, the Reformed elector of the Palatinate, was anxious to repeople his devastated farms and rebuild his ruined cities; so he waived his religious orthodoxy, in order to find farmers and artisans. There was to be freedom of worship, but not in public meetinghouses nor were there to be more than twenty families in one place. They also were asked to pay, as protection money, an annual tribute. Most of the Swiss refugees found a welcome on the estates of noblemen in the fertile Rhine valley. Soon their industry had transformed a ruined land into a garden of plenty.

In 1688 the War of the Palatinate began when Louis XIV commanded his lieutenants to burn up the Palatinate. For the next quarter of a century these Swiss Mennonites in the Palatinate, in spite of wars, cold summers, crop failures, and constant emigration to America, grew and prospered. Ibersheim and Weierhof are examples of two of the rather solid Mennonite communities.

The rich fields of the Palatinate remained, however, an attractive prize for the armies of Germany, France, and other enemies of Central Europe during the eighteenth century. As electors were changed the Mennonites were denied residence in the cities, and could not engage in trade or take up an apprenticeship.

The French Revolution brought about an end to religious intolerance but, because of the rising tide of worldliness among the younger Mennonite people, the church leaders met to consider again the faith and practices of their religious group. They stated that: young men who joined the army should be excommunicated, mixed marriages forbidden, church discipline should be encouraged, ministers must be selected by lot, and serve without pay, sisters must appear at the communion table with covered heads, church membership must be based on conversion (preferably fourteen years or over) and new applicants were to pass through a period of instruction.

When the left bank of the Rhine fell to France in 1801, Mennonites gained full civil rights, but lost their military exemption. If they had the money they could hire substitutes. For a time churches collected money for all young men drafted into service. Families who had no sons objected. Finally each family had to pay the cost itself. The poor and conservative found it necessary to emigrate to America. Between 1830 and 1860 many individuals and groups from Mennonite settlements of South Germany, the Palatinate, Bavaria, and Hesse, migrated to Ohio, Illinois, and Iowa.

About 1802, on the invitation of Max Joseph II, eight Mennonite families left their homes in the Palatinate and moved to Bavaria along the Danube River founding the Mennonite colony of Maxweiler. With great difficulty they turned the marshes into arable and fertile land. In 1855 all of the Mennonites living in Maxweiler sold their property and emigrated to America.

Some common names were Baer, Berger, Dester, Detwiler, Eyman, Haury, Hirschler, Krehbiel, Lehman, Leisy, Ruth, Schowalter and Strohm.

Many of the emigrants left via Worms, Germany, went down the Rhine, to Rotterdam, to LeHavre, France, spending 35 days or more on sailing boats before arriving in New York City. They went by steamer on the Hudson River to Troy or Albany, New York, then by train along Erie Canal to Buffalo. From there they went to Cleveland, Ashland, Hayesville, and Wadsworth, Ohio, Donnellson, Iowa, and Sommerfield and Trenton, Illinois. Mennonite families lived in these above communities, moving from one place to another depending on economic opportunities. Kansas offered homesteads and Mennonite families were encouraged to investigate possibilities of new homelands. Peter Wiebe founded a lumber business in Halstead in 1874, in the fall of the same year John W. Ruth and Daniel Haury of Summerfield went to Halstead, built small houses and began breaking the prairie. Many others followed shortly after this and a large body set out in the spring of 1875. The Halstead Mennonite Church was founded in March 1875. Some of the special considerations were a millsite with dam with water rights extending seven miles upstream along the Little

Arkansas River. Land extending to Moundridge was also purchased and the First Mennonite Church of Christian and the Zion congregations were established.

Christian Krehbiel was pastor of the Summerfield, Illinois and Halstead, Kansas churches for many years and played an important part in assisting the large body of Mennonites to make the shift from the steppes of Russia to the plains of Kansas.

Edward P. Krehbiel quotes the following from his mother's autobiography:

"The fall of 1878 meant much hard work for my sister Katie and me. We were to move to Kansas in March 1879. There was no fruit in the land to which we were going. We had an abundance of it in Summerfield and the art of canning had just become known to us...Every evening after school the children had to pick apples or other fruits...to be put up in some form on Saturday. Some apples went into vinegar, some were dried, others canned in tin,... still others were made into apple butter. We ended up with sixteen barrels of vinegar, three sugar barrels of dried apples, three hundred quarts of canned apples, and one hundred gallons of apple butter. The grape crop was good and we put up seven barrels of wine and also a lot of sweet pickles."*

*Krehbiel, Christian, *Prairie Pioneer*, Faith and Life Press, Newton, Kansas, 1961, p. 85.
Smith, C. Henry, *The Coming of the Mennonites*, Mennonite Book Concern, Berne, Indiana, 1927.

MENU

Breakfast
    Soft boiled eggs
    Cooked oatmeal
    Homemade bread
    or coffee cakes

Dinner
    Meat
    Potatoes
    Sweet-sour cabbage
    Fruit
Supper
    Fried potatoes
    Cheese
    Homemade rye or
    white bread
    Sweet rolls
    Weak coffee with
    lots of milk

BREADS

Bavarian Ring

1 pkg. yeast	1/4 tsp. nutmeg
1/2 c. butter	1 c. flour
1/2 tsp. salt	grated rind of lemon
1 c. warm water	4 eggs
1 c. sugar	2 1/4 c. flour

Put warm water into a large bowl and sprinkle yeast into it. When dissolved stir in 1 c. flour. Beat well. Let rise until light, about 1/2 hour.

In another bowl cream the butter and sugar until light, add lemon rind, salt and nutmeg. Beat in eggs, one at a time.

Stir the egg mixture into the yeast mixture with a wooden spoon and beat well. Beat in 2 1/2 c. flour until smooth. Turn into a 9 inch greased tube pan. Let rise in warm place until about 3/4 inch from top of pan, about 1 hour. Bake in 350° oven, about 45 minutes.

Let cool in pan about 15 minutes and remove from pan.

Coffee Cake
(Grandmother Krehbiel's)

Dissolve 2 pkgs. dry yeast in 1 1/2 c. warm milk to which 3/4 c. sugar and 1 tsp. salt have been added.

Add 1/2 c. melted margarine or butter, 1 beaten egg and 4 c. flour. Beat well while mixing.

Set to rise until double in bulk. Stir down.

Spoon into well greased pans and let rise until very light. Sprinkle 1 c. raisins over the dough or cover with sliced raw apples.

Put the following crumb mixture on top:

1/2 c. flour	1/2 tsp. cinnamon
1/2 c. butter (melted, spread on top)	1 c. sugar

Let rise a little, about 15 minutes and bake in moderate oven, 350°, until browned.

Fastnachts-Kuchen

2 c. warm milk	2 eggs, beaten
1/2 c. warm water	1/2 c. melted butter
5 c. flour, approx.	1/2 tsp salt
3/4 c. sugar	1/2 tsp. nutmeg
2 pkgs. yeast	

Dissolve yeast in 1/4 c. warm water until bubbly, 5 minutes. Add to the milk, eggs, sugar and butter mixture. Gradually add flour, salt and nutmeg, beating well. The dough should be smooth but soft. Knead well and set aside to rise until double, about 30 minutes.

Put small buns of dough on greased cookie sheet, far enough apart so they can spread without touching. Let rise till dough is springy. Pick up one bun at a time with both hands and with thumbs at center of bun, stretch center so this portion gets thin but does not tear a hole. Place raised side in hot fat (365°) and deep fry spooning hot fat on center. When underside is browned, turn. Drain on paper toweling.

Roll in sugar.

Waffeln
(Waffles)

2 eggs	1 scant c. flour
1 c. sour cream	1/2 tsp. salt
1/4 tsp. soda	

Beat egg yolks, add cream in which soda has been dissolved, salt and flour; fold in beaten egg whites last.

Bake in hot waffle iron which has been lightly brushed with fat.

Potato Pancakes

6 raw grated potatoes, medium size	2 tbsp. flour or 4 tbsp. dry bread crumbs
3 eggs, beaten lightly	2 tbsp. milk or cream
1/4 tsp. baking powder	grated small onion,
1 1/2 tsp. salt	if desired

Drain potatoes and mix with rest of ingredients. Preheat skillet and add bacon fat. Drop potato mixture by spoonfuls into hot fat. When browned, turn once.

This mixture may also be made into just one big pancake by baking in a hot oven until crisp and brown. Allow 15 minutes for each side. Serve with applesauce or syrup.

Homemade Yeast

2 quarts water in kettle   4 potatoes
    handful hops tied in bag

Cook potatoes with hops until soft. Remove the bag and press juice from it into the potato water. Discard hop pulp. Mash potatoes. Cool. Add 1 c. sugar, 1/4 c. salt, and 1 c. old yeast (leftover from previous time). Let stand several hours before using.

Store part of this yeast (for the next baking) in a cool, dry place. Use preferably about twice a week.

CAKES AND COOKIES

Anise Cookies

7 eggs   1/2 tsp. baking powder
2 c. sugar   1 tbsp. anise seed or
3 c. flour   1 1/2 tsp. anise extract

Beat eggs and sugar about 30 minutes.

Add flour, baking powder, anise seed or extract and mix well. Drop by spoonful onto a well greased and floured cookie sheet. Let stand overnight or at least 10 hours at room temperature. (This dries the cookie.)

Bake in moderate oven 325° until a delicate yellow.

Brown Almond Cookies

2 lbs. almonds
1/2 c. sugar
5 eggs
2 c. sugar

grated rind of lemon
1 c. flour
1 tsp. baking powder
2 c. flour

Shell almonds and grind. Mix with 1/2 c. sugar and brown over low heat until light yellow.

Beat eggs with 2 c. sugar 30 minutes. Add grated rind of lemon and 1 c. flour sifted with 1 tsp. baking powder. Mix all together and add enough more flour to make a stiff dough (about 2 c. more).

Put spoonfuls on buttered sheet and bake until yellow in 300° oven.

E. Foth

Hazelnut Cookies

4 egg whites
pinch of salt
1 tsp. vanilla

1 c. sugar
1 c. chopped or grated
hazelnuts
1 c. grated almonds

Beat egg whites, vanilla, and salt until soft peaks appear.

Then gradually add sugar and continue beating until stiff peaks appear. Add hazelnuts and almonds.

Drop by teaspoonfuls on a cookie sheet lined with waxed paper.

Bake in a slow oven, 300°, about 25 minutes. Cookies should be dried rather than baked.

Lebkuchen no. 1
Christmas Cookies

2 qt. brown syrup
4 tbsp. lard
1 lb. butter
1 tbsp. allspice and cloves
1 1/2 tbsp. cinnamon
1/2 c. citron, chopped fine
2 lbs. brown sugar
1 c. orange juice
1/2 tsp. ginger

1 1/2 to 2 lbs. each of almonds
   and English walnuts,
   chopped fine
2 tbsp. soda dissolved in
   1/4 c. hot water
20 c. flour, approx.
8 eggs
1 tsp. anise

Boil syrup and cool.
Cream the shortening and sugar. Add syrup. Beat egg yolks and add sifted dry ingredients, alternately with liquid. Add nuts and citron. Beat egg whites until stiff and fold into dough.
Roll out fairly thin and cut into diamond shapes.
Bake at 350° until browned.

Lebkuchen no. 2

Boil for 5 minutes:
   3/4 c. honey   1 c. brown sugar
   2 tbsp. water

Add 1 c. shortening and cool.
Then add:
   1/2 tsp. each of salt,   3 1/2 c. flour
      cardamon and cinnamon   1/2 tsp. soda
   1/4 tsp. nutmeg
Beat 2 eggs and add.
Mix well and let stand 3 days in cool place.
Roll dough out 1/4 inch thick and cut with a cookie cutter. Bake at 325° about 15 minutes, or until nicely browned.
While still warm, glaze with: 1 c. sugar and 1/2 c. water, boiled together. When first indication of a hair appears, remove from heat and stir in 1/4 c. powdered sugar.

Springerle no. 1
(A Special Christmas Cookie)

Sift 3 1/2 c. flour and 1 tsp. baking powder.
Beat 4 eggs until thick and gradually add 2 c. sugar.

Beat well.

Roll dough out 1/8 inch thick. Press floured Springerle board down hard on dough to emboss the designs. Cut out each square and let dry 10 hours or overnight. Sprinkle anise seed lightly over the cookies.

Bake on greased pan in 300-325° oven until very light yellow. Store in airtight container.

Springerle no. 2

4 c. flour	4 eggs
1 tsp. soda	1 tsp. lemon flavoring
1 tsp. baking powder	2 tbsp. milk
butter, size of walnut	anise seed
2 1/4 c. sugar	4 egg yolks

Sift flour, soda and baking powder.

Cream butter and sugar and add eggs, one at a time.

When all are used, beat mixture 15 minutes. Let stand 1 hour. Add extract, milk, and 1 tsp. salt of hartshorn (if desired). Add flour mixture. Roll dough out fairly thin.

Press springerle form on dough quite hard. Cut cookies apart and leave on board overnight. Strew anise seed on top.

Bake 300-325° oven until very light yellow, must not brown. Store in air tight container.

Almond Paste Macaroons

whites of 4 medium eggs	1 lb. almond paste
2 1/3 c. powdered sugar	1/2 tsp. almond extract
	(bitter almond is best)

Beat egg whites until stiff. Then add sugar, a little at a time, beat after each addition; add almond paste and extract.

Grease cookie sheet, cover with a sheet of waxed paper. Drop hazelnut size pieces of dough on this.

Bake at 325° for 15 minutes. Must be very light in color.

"S" Cookies

1 c. butter	4 egg yolks
1/2 c. sugar	grated rind of lemon
3 c. flour	4 tbsp. orange juice

Cream butter and add the sugar and cream well.

Add the flour and mix well. Let dough set in a cool place at least 4 hours. Then take a small amount of dough and make a long roll about 1/2 inch thick. Cut into lengths of about 3 inches. Form into shape of an "S". Put on ungreased pan and bake at 325° for about 12 minutes.

Springerle Designs
Rubbings by E. Foth

CHEESE
Cottage Cheese

Use 1 c. of previously soured milk for each gallon of fresh milk used. (This causes milk to sour quickly and taste fresh.) Put clabbered milk in a stone jar and set in warm place until it separates. Stir several times so it warms evenly. Pour into a 10 pound sugar sack and drain off whey. Pour cold water over cheese and wash well. Drain thoroughly by hanging bag on clothes line. Place cheese in bowl and mix, preferably with potato masher. Season with salt, cream and milk.

This is delicious with potatoes boiled with jackets. Put maple syrup on cottage cheese.

DESSERTS

Bread Pudding
Queen of Puddings

butter size of walnut
3/4 c. granulated sugar
2 eggs, separated
1/2 tsp. lemon extract
1/2 tsp. vanilla extract
1 c. bread crumbs
pint of milk
jelly or preserves

Mix butter, sugar and slightly beaten egg yolks. Add bread crumbs, milk, and extracts.

Bake in greased baking casserole, until thick. Remove from oven and spread jelly or preserves on top. Over this spread the meringue made by beating the egg whites with 1 tbsp. sugar. Place baking dish back into oven until meringue becomes golden brown.

Steamed Pudding

1/2 c. granulated sugar
1/2 c. light syrup
1 egg, slightly beaten
1 tsp. cinnamon
1/2 tsp. ginger
1 tsp. baking soda
dissolved in 1/2 c. water
1 1/2 c. flour with 1/2 tsp.
baking powder added

Put above mixture into a buttered or oiled pan. (Preferably use an aluminum pan.) Tie a clean cloth over the cake pan (an angel food sized pan without the funnel).

Set covered pan into a bucket of warm water to steam for 1 hour. Serve with "Golden Dressing".

DUMPLINGS

Dumplings
Dampfnudeln

Use coffee cake dough or bread dough. Make dough into buns and place on floured metal sheets. Let rise.

Melt 1 tbsp. of shortening in skillet until hot. Sprinkle a little salt over shortening. Carefully place the buns in the skillet. Pour a small amount of water between the buns. Cover with a tight-fitting lid immediately. (No steam should escape.) Do not remove the lid for 10-15 minutes. Use medium low heat. Fragrance will tell you when done. Remove the lid carefully, dropping no water on the damfnudeln. Turn carefully and brown this side. Remove with a pancake turner and serve hot. These may be used with fruit as a dessert.

These *Dampfnudeln* were often made for Saturday supper and eaten with fruit as a dessert.

Noodles

1 egg	1/2 egg shell of milk or
1/2 tsp. salt	water
2/3 c. flour, approx.	

(Dough should be kneadable, soft and very workable.)

Beat eggs until very frothy, add salt, liquid and work in flour. Knead well. Roll out thin on lightly floured board. Dust with flour. Cut into strips about 1/4 inch wide. Scatter noodles on board for drying. Let dry at least an hour before cooking. Cook in water or broth for about 12 minutes.

Spaetzle

2 c. flour	1/4 c. fine dry crumbs
1 tsp. salt	(optional)
2 eggs, beaten	2 tbsp. melted butter
3/4 c. milk	(optional)

Sift flour and salt; add eggs and milk. Beat well. Place in large-holed sieve; hold over large kettle of boiling salted water. Force batter through sieve with wooden spoon. Cook for 5 minutes, stirring constantly, drain. Sprinkle with mixture of bread crumbs and melted butter. Serve meatballs over *Spaetzle*.

Homemade Noodle Kniffles

1 medium egg	2 to 2 1/3 c. flour
2/3 c. water	2 to 3 quarts boiling water
1/2 tsp. salt	1/2 c. butter or margarine
1/8 tsp. pepper	slightly browned

Beat egg, water, salt and pepper with fork until blended; add enough flour to make a stiff batter; from the edge of a tilted bowl cut off strips of batter into the boiling water. Cook for three minutes after last noodle drops into water. Serve with browned butter. Yield: 8 servings.

Use kniffles as meat accompaniment or serve with sauerkraut and pig hocks.

FOWL

Chicken With Dumplings

Cook 3 to 4 lb. chicken until tender. Drain broth. Cool chicken and remove meat from bones. Add chicken to broth, season with salt and pepper. Additional herbs of your preference may be added.
Dumplings:

2 c. flour	2 tbsp. shortening
4 tsp. baking powder	1/2 c. milk
1/2 tsp. salt	1 egg

Sift together the dry ingredients, mix in shortening, add beaten egg and milk. Add more milk if needed to make a soft dough. Drop by spoonfuls in boiling broth. Cook 15 minutes tightly covered. Serve hot.

Kartoffel-Spiess
Potato Dressing for Poultry

1 medium onion, sliced	4 c. mashed potatoes
giblets from poultry	2 tsp. cloves
1 tbsp. butter	1 tsp. salt

Brown diced onion and chopped giblets in butter; add to mashed potatoes. Add cloves and salt. Put into poultry and sew closed. Bake according to type of poultry used.

MEATS

Fleisch-Kraut
Meat and Cabbage

1 pound ground beef	2 c. tomato juice
2 tsp. salt	1 1/4 c. water
1/4 tsp. pepper	1 small onion
1 egg, beaten	1 tsp. minced parsley
1/3 c. uncooked rice	3 tbsp. lemon juice
6 large cabbage leaves	1 tsp. sugar
2 tbsp. butter	

Mix thoroughly the ground beef, 1 tsp. salt, pepper and egg. Add the rice.

Cook the cabbage leaves in boiling salted water until just tender; drain.

For the sauce: melt butter in a skillet; add onion and cook until tender. Blend in tomato juice and water; add parsley, lemon juice, sugar, 1 tsp. salt and pepper. Simmer for 10 minutes.

Place about 1/4 c. of meat mixture on center of each leaf. Roll up each leaf, tucking the ends in toward the center. Use toothpicks to fasten. Place rolls in a large skillet. Pour sauce over rolls; cover pan tightly and cook slowly for 2 hours. Serve immediately. Yield: 6 servings.

Caraway Meatballs With Spaetzle
Kummel und Fleisch mit Spaetzle

1 lb. ground beef	2 c. beef broth
1/4 c. bread crumbs	1/2 c. mushrooms
1 tsp. salt	1/2 c. onion
dash of pepper	1 c. sour cream
1/4 tsp. poultry seasoning	1 tbsp. flour
1/4 c. milk	1/2 tsp. caraway seed
1 egg	

Combine first seven ingredients; shape into balls and brown in a small amount of fat. Add broth, mushrooms, and onion; simmer for 30 minutes. Blend in sour cream, flour, and caraway seed. Cook until thickened. Serve over *Spaetzle*, noodles, or dumplings.

PRESERVING

Peach Butter

1 gallon peach pulp	1 quart apple puree

Use 1/2 as much sugar as pulp.

Flavor as desired with cloves, allspice, stick cinnamon and star anise.

Cook slowly stirring frequently until it thickens.

Remove cinnamon sticks, put into sterilized jars, seal immediately.

Homemade Apple Butter

10 lbs. tart cooking apples
9 c. sugar

4 cinnamon sticks
1 gallon apple cider

In olden days this was cooked in much larger quantities over the open fire in a copper kettle. It was stirred continuously. Today you can follow same recipe but put it on your stove or in a preheated 250° oven.

Wash and core apples, put through medium blade of meat grinder into a large roasting pan. Stir in sugar, cinnamon and 1 quart of the cider. Put into oven. When apples come to boil, stir well. Cook in oven for about 6 hours, adding cider as apples thicken. Remove cinnamon sticks and put into hot sterilized jars; seal immediately.

Grape Jelly

4 lbs. slightly under-
  ripe concord grapes
1 c. water

3/4 c. sugar for each
1 c. of juice

Day before, wash, stem and crush grapes. Put into large pot; add water. Boil for 10 minutes. Remove from heat and pour into a jelly bag. Allow juice to drip over night. Do not press grapes, if possible place in fairly cool place. Next day, measure juice, return to kettle. Add 3/4 c. sugar for every cup of juice, stir and cook slowly while sugar is dissolving. Then boil rapidly to jelly stage, 220°. Pour into hot sterilized jars and seal.

Sauerkraut

Shred cabbage using 3 tbsp. of salt to each 5 pounds of cabbage. Pack into a earthenware crock, pressing down firmly to squeeze out the juice. Cover with a cloth, a plate and a weight. Let stand for 2 or 3 weeks or until sour, washing the cloth daily to keep it it from spoiling. It is now ready to be eaten.

SALADS

Sauerkraut Salad
Sauerkraut Salat

1 1/2 c. sugar
2/3 c. vinegar
1 large can sauerkraut
1/2 c. chopped onion

1 c. diced celery
1 green pepper
chopped fine

Mix sugar and vinegar, bring to a boil. Cool. Wash sauerkraut seven times. Pour vinegar mixture over sauerkraut; add remaining ingredients. Mix, refrigerate. Yield: 8 servings.
This recipe keeps well.

Hot Potato Salad
Kartoffel-Heis Salat

6 medium waxy potatoes
4 strips minced bacon or
2 tbsp. bacon drippings
1/4 c. chopped onion
1 c. chopped dill pickle
1/4 c. chopped celery

1/4 c. boiling water or stock
1/2 c. vinegar
1/2 tsp. sugar
1/2 tsp. salt
1/8 tsp. paprika
1/4 tsp. dry mustard

Cook potatoes in jackets until tender. Peel and slice while hot. Heat bacon in skillet; add chopped onion, celery and pickle. Saute until brown. Heat, to boiling point, the water, vinegar, sugar, salt, paprika and mustard. Pour these ingredients into the skillet containing the bacon etc. Combine them with potatoes and serve at once with chopped parsley and/or chives. Yield: 6 servings.

SAUCES

Vanilla Sauce

1 c. sugar
2 tbsp. flour
1/4 tsp. salt
2 c. boiling water

1 egg yolk, well beaten
2 tbsp. butter
1 tsp. vanilla

Combine sugar, salt and flour. Add water slowly, stirring continuously and cook until thick. Add vanilla and butter. Stir until blended. Serve warm with *dampfnudeln* or with steamed or baked puddings.

Golden Dressing
Served with Steamed Puddings or Gingerbread

1 c. powdered sugar
1 or 2 tbsp. melted butter

1 egg yolk, slightly beaten
1 tsp. vanilla extract

Mix the above ingredients until smooth.
Before serving add the beaten egg white.

Sauce for Bread Pudding

Melt 1 or 2 tbsp. butter, add 1/3 c. granulated sugar, level 1 tbsp. flour; stir in milk to get desired consistency (for pouring). Add 1 tsp. vanilla extract.

SOUPS

Spaetzle Suppen
Spaetzle Soup

2 c. flour	1/3 to 1/2 c. water
1/2 tsp. salt	2 c. diced potatoes
1 egg	4 c. chicken broth

Measure flour; add salt and egg. Stir until well mixed. Gradually add water until a stiff but spongy dough is formed. Boil diced potatoes in a small quantity of water. When cooked, add to chicken broth. Bring broth and potatoes to a boil. Cut dough into broth in very small pieces as for small dumplings. After all dough is added bring mixture to a full boil. Serve. Yield: 4-5 servings.

Vegetable Soup

1 soup bone (with some meat on it)	1 carrot
	2 tomatoes
water to cover soup bone	1 small onion
salt and pepper to taste	spices or herbs (chillies,
3 to 4 medium potatoes	bay leaves, dill)
1/4 head medium cabbage	

Simmer soup bone and water for 3 hours. Remove excess fat and soup bone. Tie spices desired into a cheesecloth bag. Add the spice bag, diced peeled potatoes, carrot and onion. Boil in above liquid until almost done. Add finely chopped cabbage and tomatoes. Cook for 4-5 minutes, until tender. Remove spices. Serve hot.

VEGETABLES

Wilted Lettuce
Salat Speck

4 to 6 strips bacon
1 head lettuce
2 hard cooked eggs

1/4 c. cider vinegar
2 tsp. sugar
1/2 tsp. salt

Cut bacon into 1/2 inch pieces, fry until crisp. Drain and save drippings. Break crisp lettuce into coarse pieces and toss with chopped, hard cooked eggs and crisp bacon. Combine vinegar with 1/4 c. bacon drippings, sugar, and salt; heat to boiling. Pour hot liquid over lettuce mixture to wilt it. Serve at once. Yield: 4 servings.

Berliner Allerlei

An appetizing vegetable plate served on special occasions.

Place a good-sized cooked cauliflower head in center of platter. (Use your biggest and best platter.)

Surround cauliflower with seasoned cooked carrot strips, seasoned and buttered peas, and early small whole buttered, cooked potatoes.

Cover with a hot white sauce and serve.

Sauce: Melt 3 tbsp. butter in pan and add 3 tbsp. flour and blend well. Gradually add 3/4 c. rich milk, stirring constantly. Lastly add 1/4 c. of the liquid the cauliflower was cooked in. Add 1/4 tsp. salt and a dash of pepper.

3

The Coming of
the Swiss

HISTORY

The Coming of the Swiss

In the early eighteenth century after years of religious persecution, the Swiss Anabaptists migrated to other lands. Some went
to Holland, some to the Palatinate, and many settled in the Emmental Valley and Jura Mountains in Switzerland. Driven into the
Hinterlands, they became known as *Die Stillen im Lande*.

Even in these secluded mountainous areas, they were only permitted to rent land. This was usually on the high slopes and
plateaus, away from the villages and markets. The land was stony
but suitable for oats, barley, vetch, potatoes, and flax. The water
supply was uncertain. The only variety of wheat that grew under
these conditions was *Spelt*.

The main occupation of these hardy Swiss forefathers was
farming, cheese making and some cattle raising. In order to earn
a living during the long winter months, everyone had to learn
an extra trade, such as weaving, cabinet making, shoe making
and others. The women spent long hours spinning and weaving,
making use of the flax which had been produced by the farmers.

The bread was make from ground oats, barley and vetch. It
was black and heavy, but contained more food value than the
finest white bread. Foods like potatoes, milk, vegetables and
some meat comprised their daily diet. Butter had to be sold in
order to obtain money to help pay the annual tax, the rent, or to
buy the few necessary articles which could not be made.

The famous Swiss cheese was made by these mountain people

and this art is still continued. Some Swiss cheesemakers have come to the United States and have continued to produce their genuine Swiss cheese.

A new immigrant tide of Mennonites from Switzerland took place between 1820 and 1860. The causes of this immigration movement was militarism, economic distress, political unrest, as well as the fast expansion and economic development of the Middle West in the United States.

Among the first of the immigrants of the new move, were the Swiss from the Jura Mountains and the Emmental Valley. A pioneer of this Swiss movement was Benedikt Schrag from Basel, who located in 1817 in Wayne County, Ohio. Many other pioneers from the Canton of Berne joined these early settlers. In 1833, Michael Neuenschwander began another colony along the banks of Riley Creek in Allen County, Ohio. In 1838, Daniel Baumgartner began a settlement in Adams County, Indiana, to which site large numbers from Switzerland came during the years from 1852-54.

From these pioneer Swiss settlements in Ohio and Indiana, other Swiss communities were established in Fortuna, Missouri; Geary, Oklahoma; and Oregon.

A small group of fourteen families in 1873 under the guidance of Philip Roulet settled at Pulaski, Iowa, later moving to Missouri and Kansas. In 1883, another group of ten families came directly from the Canton of Berne to Whitewater, Kansas.

SOURCES:
James Lehman, *Sonnenberg, A Haven and Heritage*, Chapter 1.
C. Henry Smith, *Story of the Mennonites*, pp. 570-573.

MENU

Swiss Winter Menu

Breakfast
>   Bread, homemade molasses, butter
>   Swiss cheese
>   Fried potatoes
>   Bacon or sausage in patties

Dinner
>   Brown or white bread, apple butter
>   Fried pork chops
>   Boiled potatoes
>   Dried green beans with a cream sauce
>   Fruit pie

Supper
>   Bread, butter, apple butter
>   Vegetable or potato soup
>   Left over cheese and meats
>   Canned fruits, peaches, pears or plums

BREADS

Buttermilk Biscuits

2 c. flour
1/2 tsp. salt
3 tsp. baking powder
1 tsp. soda
3 tbsp. fat
1 c. sour milk or buttermilk

Sift dry ingredients together. Cut in shortening until mixture resembles coarse crumbs. Add sour milk all at once. Stir until dough follows fork or spoon around the bowl. Turn out on floured board and knead 1/2 minute. Roll 3/8 inch thick and cut with cutter. Bake on ungreased sheet at 450° for 12 minutes. Makes 2 dozen biscuits.

Sour Cream Corn Bread

3/4 c. corn meal
1 c. flour
1 tsp. soda
1 tsp. cream of tartar
1 tsp. salt
2 1/2 tbsp. sugar
1 egg, well beaten
2 tbsp. melted butter
1 c. thick sour cream
4 tbsp. milk

Sift flour and corn meal. Measure and add soda, cream of tartar, salt and sugar. Sift again. Add beaten egg, cream, milk and melted shortening. Beat thoroughly. Pour into greased pan 9 inches square. Bake at 425° for 20 minutes.

Rye Bread
Roggenbrot

2 c. rye flour
8 c. flour
1/4 c. sugar
2 tsp. salt
5 tbsp. shortening
1 pkg. yeast dissolved in
1/2 c. water
3 c. lukewarm water

Into 2 c. flour mix the sugar, salt and dissolved yeast. Add 3 c. lukewarm water and beat well. Add shortening and rest of flour gradually. Knead till smooth. Place in greased bowl. Let rise in warm place till double in bulk. Knead down and when double in bulk again, form into loaves and place into pans. Let rise till double. Bake in 400° oven 15 minutes, then reduce heat to 350°. Bake one hour.

Bells!

Bells hung around the animals' necks in the Swiss pastures, add a melodic tone to the pastoral scenery. Listening to the many tinkling sounds, a person soon becomes aware of different tones, coming from different directions. Here is a cow bell! There, that must be a horse in the next field! And faintly in the distance, that must be a sheep bell! On a clear cool morning, a bell choir seems to be in progress and a feeling of well-being is experienced by those listening.

CAKES AND COOKIES

Apfeltorte mit Rahm
Apple Tart with Cream

1 1/4 c. flour	6 c. peeled, cored and
2 egg yolks	sliced apples
1/2 c. and 1 tbsp. sugar	1/2 tsp. nutmeg
grated rind of 1 lemon	1/2 c. heavy cream
1/2 c. butter, softened and	1/2 c. blanched almonds,
cut into small pieces	slivered

Sift flour into a large bowl. Make a well in the middle; put 1 egg yolk, 1 tbsp. sugar, lemon rind and butter into well. Stir together with a fork. Work dough with floured hands until all ingredients are blended together and dough is smooth. Pat dough with fingers into bottom and up on sides of 9 inch pan. Crimp sides with a fork. Chill at least 2 hours. Place apples on top of chilled dough in slightly overlapping circles. Sprinkle with remaining sugar and nutmeg. Bake in 350° oven for 15 minutes. Beat together remaining egg yolk, cream and almonds; drip over fruit; continue baking for 20 minutes or until dough is golden brown and fruit tender. Yield: 6-8 servings.

Was lugst du mi a,
Hadst du mi garn?
Frag der pa
Ob du mi kast ha.

Why do you look at me,
Do you like me?
Ask dad
If you can have me.

Crullers

2 egg yolks, beaten
1 egg white, stiffly
    beaten
2 tbsp. sugar
2 tbsp. cream

2 tbsp. butter
1 2/3 c. flour
1/4 tsp. ground cardamom
    (optional)
2/3 tbsp. fruit juice or
    brandy

Fold the egg yolks into the egg white. Add sugar and blend. Add remaining ingredients in order. Chill overnight. Roll thin; cut into diamond shapes and make a slit in the middle and draw one end through the slit. Fry in deep fat as for doughnuts. Sprinkle with powdered sugar and serve. Yield: 1 dozen.

Molasses Cookies

2 c. sugar
3 eggs
1 1/2 c. lard
1 c. sour milk or
    buttermilk

1 c. molasses
1 tsp. cinnamon and
    ginger (each)
4 tsp. soda
7 c. flour, approx.

Cream lard and sugar. Add eggs, molasses and milk. Beat well. Sift and add the dry ingredients. Dough should be soft yet stiff enough to handle. Chill the dough several hours or overnight. Roll out on floured board and cut with a cookie cutter. Bake until light brown at 375° about 10 minutes.

These cookies were usually made in large round circles.

Lebkuchen

A Christmas Cookie

1/2 gallon molasses
1 c. sour milk
4 eggs
1 quart nuts
2 lbs. raisins

1 lb melted lard
2 tsp. soda
1 c. sugar
2 1/2 tsp. of each: ginger, cinnamon, allspice and nutmeg

Heat molasses until warm. Add the sugar, beaten eggs, chopped nuts, raisins, spices, lard and lastly the milk with the soda dissolved in it. Work in enough flour to make a stiff dough. Let stand overnight.

In morning roll dough thin and cut into diamond or other shapes. Bake in 350° oven about 12 minutes or until done. When cookies are still warm brush on a sugar glaze made by diluting 1 c. powdered sugar with a little water.

Make these cookies soon after Thanksgiving and store for Christmas eating.

Neujahrskuchen

"Swiss Nothings"

Mix together:
3 eggs, well beaten
1 tsp. salt

1 c. light cream

Add about 4 c. flour or enough to make a stiff dough.

Work and knead the dough on a floured board or table top for about 10 minutes. Divide dough into small pieces the size of a large marble and roll out very thin, about the size of a small plate. Fry in deep hot fat at 375°. Keep pushing the cakes down in the fat. This will make little blisters. Drain on paper towels and sprinkle with sugar.

A popular treat for the New Year and special holiday feasts!

"Swiss Nothings" also had several other names: "Elephant Ears" and "Knee Patches".

"Knee Patches" received their name from the fact that the Swiss women used to cover their knees with a tea towel and then stretch the dough over the knee until very thin.

CHEESE

Home Made Cheese

60 pounds or 7 gallons of whole milk. Pour into a copper boiler or an enameled bucket for smaller amount of milk.

Add 20 drops of commercial liquid rennet. Or use rennet tablets, use according to directions on container. Or use 4 inches square of dried lining of calf's stomach, soaked in water.

Heat milk to 86°, add rennet, and let set for ½ hour. When the milk is well curdled, cut the curd into small squares with a long knife. Place on very low heat until 102°—approximately one hour, stirring every 5 minutes. Remove from heat and let stand for another hour, stirring occasionally.

Strain curds through a cheesecloth placed over a cheese mold. Cover with a wooden round lid and a stone for a weight. Turn the cheese in the mold after ten hours and let set another 10-12 hours until well drained.

Place the cheese on a shelf in the basement. Wash cheese in water. Salt it, and turn it daily for two weeks, until the rind is hard. Let cure until well ripened, at least four weeks.

Esther Foth

Fondue Neuchatel Style

1/2 lb Swiss cheese, cut
    into small cubes
2 tbsp. flour
1 clove garlic
    salt and pepper to taste

1 c. dry wine
2 tbsp. Kirschwasser or
    other fruit brandy or
    light rum

Dredge cheese with flour. Rub pan with garlic clove. Add wine. Heat slowly until air bubbles rise to surface, but do not boil. Stir and add cheese cubes by handfuls, waiting until cheese is completely melted before more is added. Keep stirring until all cheese is melted and the fondue is thickened and starts bubbling slightly. Stir in kirschwasser and season. Remove to chafing pan. Keep fondue at boiling point. Serve immediately with white French bread, sliced or in pieces. The guests, one after another, take a piece of bread on the fork and dunk it in the fondue, stirring until bread is well coated. The constant stirring helps maintain the proper consistency of the fondue.

Swiss Puff

6 slices buttered toast,
    cubed
2 c. grated Swiss cheese
3 eggs, slightly beaten

2 c. milk
1 tsp. salt
1/4 tsp. pepper
1/2 tsp. dry mustard

Butter a 2 quart casserole; fill with alternate layers of toast cubes and cheese. Combine eggs, milk and seasonings. Pour over toast-cheese mixture. Bake at 350° for 35 minutes or until a knife, Inserted in center, comes out clean. Serve at once. Yield: 4-5 servings.

Es esh anesh a alta Kela g'zie
Un sie het siw nemma wella
das esh de g'schicht fo de alte Kela.

There was once an old dipper
and she didn't want it anymore.
This is the story of the old dipper.

Cottage Cheese

1 1/2 gallons raw, sour milk   1/2 c. cream
   1 tsp. salt

Heat milk slowly until it is too hot to hold your finger in it, about 115°. Cool. Drain through a cloth bag. Let hang overnight to become quite dry.

When dry, crumble the cheese to make fine curds and add the salt. To serve, add the sweet cream.

Makes about 3 1/2 c.

DESSERTS

Swiss Apple Dessert

Beat 2 eggs and add 3/4 c. granulated sugar.
Sift:
   1/2 c. flour   1 tsp. baking powder
     pinch of salt

Add to the egg mixture and add 1 heaping c. peeled diced apples and 1/2 c. walnuts.

Pour into a greased dish about 7 inches square.
Bake at 350° for 30 minutes.
Yield: 6 servings.

Berry Sturm

1 quart berries (straw-   3/4 c. sugar
  berries, blackberries   12 slices bread, a day old
  or raspberries)   1 pint rich milk

Mash fruit and add sugar. Cut bread into small cubes and add to berries. Let stand 10 minutes. Just before serving add cold milk. (This dish is of Swiss origin.) Makes 6 servings.

Der hot's hinter de Ohre.
He has it behind the ears.

Apple Pudding

1 c. sugar	1 c. flour
1/4 c. butter	1/4 tsp. nutmeg
1 egg	1/2 tsp. vanilla
1/2 tsp. each of soda, salt	2 c. diced apples
and cinnamon	1 c. nut meats

Cream first 3 ingredients well. Add sifted dry ingredients and beat. Add apples and nuts. Put into greased dish. Bake about 40 minutes at 350°.

Old Fashioned Taffy

1 c. molasses	2 tbsp. butter
1 c. sugar	1 tsp. soda
1 c. thin cream	1 c. finely chopped nuts (optional)

Combine molasses, sugar and cream and bring to a boil. Cook until it forms a hard ball when dropped into cold water. Remove from heat and add butter and the soda. If nuts are being used, add them now. Stir well.

Pour into a buttered plate or pan and cool to lukewarm. Butter your hands and pull the mixture until stiff and waxy-looking. Shape as desired and cut into suitable lengths with sharp scissors.

As ish immer so ganga
As wird immer so ga
das die Buba springa
der Maedle so nah.

It has always been that way
and it always will be
that the boys go
courting the girls.

DUMPLINGS

Fried Cornmeal Mush

3 c. yellow cornmeal	2 qts boiling water
1 tsp. salt	1/2 c. white flour

Bring water to a boil. Sift together the cornmeal, flour and salt. Slowly add dry ingredients to boiling water, stirring constantly to prevent lumps. When well blended, cover and cook slowly on low heat for about an hour. Pour into loaf pans to mold. Set in refrigerator to chill. Cut into slices about 1/2 inch thick and fry on both sides on a hot, greased griddle until golden brown.

Delicious with hot maple syrup or apple butter.

Knepp

2 c. flour	1 egg, beaten
2 tsp. baking powder	2 tbsp. butter
1/2 tsp. salt	1/2 c. milk

Sift flour, baking powder and salt into a mixing bowl. Stir in beaten egg and melted butter. Add enough milk to make a moderately stiff batter.

Drop by tablespoonful into boiling, salted water. Cover kettle tightly and cook, without lifting lid, for 20 minutes.

Drain and serve with browned butter.

Spaetzle

2 c. sifted all purpose flour	2 eggs, slightly beaten
1 tsp. salt	1 c. milk

Sift together flour and salt; add eggs and milk and beat well. Place mixture in a coarse sieved colander. Hold over large kettle of rapidly boiling salted water. With wooden spoon, press batter through colander. Cook and stir for 5 minutes, drain.

Serve like noodles or sphagetti to complement meat dish. Yield: 5 servings.

Hinga Hilty Hans' Hecka Hufa
Han i hundert Hasa horen Hushta.

Behind John Hilty's brush pile
I heard a hundred rabbits coughing.

FOWL

Chicken Baked in Cream

1 chicken, cut in serving pieces	1 1/2 tsp. salt
5 tbsp. butter	1/8 tsp. pepper
1/2 c. flour	1 1/2 c. sweet cream or sour cream

Sprinkle chicken with salt and pepper and dredge in flour. Fry in butter until a golden brown. Then place chicken in roasting pan. Pour cream over chicken. Cover and bake at 350° for about 1 1/2 hours. Serve with gravy made with fryings from pan.

Pressed Chicken

Cut up chicken in the usual manner and place in a kettle with a tight fitting lid in order to retain the steam. Cover with 2 c. water and 2 tsp. salt and 1/8 tsp. pepper. Cook slowly until meat easily falls from the bones. Cut or chop the meat and put into a deep pan or dish. Pour the liquid in which the chicken was cooked over the meat. Set in a cool place to gel. When firm, slice and serve.

E. Toth

A Swiss Cave

Near Perceus, in the Jura Mountains in Switzerland, is a cave which served as a secret meeting place for Mennonites many years ago during times of severe persecution. Days for these secret meetings would, of necessity, be arranged well ahead of time, as the people had to walk long distances to reach this spot. Walking was often very difficult. The road was rough and overgrown with shrubs in many places. The worshippers also did not want to be seen as they trudged along.

Arriving near the cave, they had to climb up a long, steep hill and, as they neared the entrance, they had to crawl through brush which hid the cave's opening. The hymnbooks and perhaps a Bible left on narrow ledges along the inside wall after their last meeting, would be opened and the service would commence. At the conclusion of this hour of worship and fellowship, the weary walk back would begin. It must have been with trembling hearts, for who could tell if, on one of these trips, their persecutors might not have seen them!

Today Mennonite visitors to the Jura Mountain area consider a walk up this steep slope one of the highlights of their trip to Switzerland. It is not uncommon to have a brief service at this scene, remembering the hardships suffered by these early Mennonite people, and thanking God for the faith which they held so firm. A faith which they preserved for their children and grandchildren — a living heritage!

MEAT

Liver
(The Swiss Way)

1 1/2 lb. liver
  onion to taste
  top milk

salt and pepper to taste
1 c. bread crumbs

Grind liver; add salt, pepper and onion to taste. Moisten bread crumbs with milk and add to liver. Drop by spoonfuls onto hot greased frying pan and brown well on both sides. Remove to hot platter. Pour about 1 1/2 c. hot water into pan and simmer a little while. Pour over liver patties. Yield: 6 servings.

Three Layer Dinner

1 lb. hamburger, made
  into patties and browned
1 small head cabbage

1 1/2 tsp. salt
1/8 tsp. pepper
1 c. milk
3 c. diced raw potatoes

Shred cabbage and put 1/2 of it in the bottom of greased casserole. Next add 1/2 of the diced potatoes and then 1/2 of the hamburger patties. Sprinkle salt and pepper over each layer. Add remainder in the same order, having hamburger on top. Add milk and bake at 350° for 2 hours. Serves 6-8.

Sauerkraut with Spareribs

1 quart sauerkraut

1 1/2 lbs. spareribs

Cover the spareribs with cold water to which a little salt has been added. Cook until almost tender. Then add the kraut and continue to cook slowly for about 40 minutes. Serve hot with fried or boiled potatoes.

Souse-Gallerig
Jellied Pig's Feet

4 pig's feet   2 tbsp. salt
1/2 tsp. pepper

Cover pig's feet with water. Add salt and pepper. Cook until meat is tender and separates from bones, about 2 hours.

Remove meat from bones and cut into small pieces. Add more seasoning if needed and put into a dish.

Cover meat with 2 c of liquid and chill until perfectly cold and set. Slice and serve.

A Pork Loaf may be made by adding 1 pound lean fresh pork to the above and covering the feet and meat with 3 quarts water. Follow the above instructions.

PASTRY

Strawberry Pie

1 qt. ripe strawberries

Mash half of the berries and cook with 1 c. sugar, 3 tbsp. corn starch and pinch of salt. When thick remove from heat and set aside to cool.

In a cool baked crust set the uncooked berries with point up. Cover with the cooked berry mixture. Cool.

Serve plain or top with whipped cream.

Reis-Rosinen Kuchen
Rice-Raisin Custard Pie

1/2 c. cooked rice   1/2 c. raisins
1/2 c. sugar   1 1/2 c. milk
  2 eggs, beaten   pinch of salt
1/2 tsp. vanilla

Wash and dry the raisins and set aside to be ready for use.

Mix all the ingredients and pour into an unbaked pie shell. Lightly pushing the raisins evenly into the crust distributes them better.

Bake at 450° for 10 minutes then reduce heat to 425° and bake about 10 more minutes.

Pie is done when an inserted knife comes out clean.

Riblie-Kuchen

(Crumb Pie)

Part I

1/2 c. water	1/2 c. molasses
1/4 tsp. soda	1/4 tsp. cream of tartar

Mix and put in unbaked pie crust.

Part II

1/2 c. sugar	1 3/4 c. flour
1/4 tsp. cream of tartar	1/2 c. butter
1/4 tsp. soda	1/4 tsp. salt

Mix like pie crust and put on top of first mixture. Bake at 375° for 45 minutes.

Never Fail Pie Dough

Add 1 tsp. salt to 2 c. flour.

Take out 1/2 c. of the flour and add 1/4 c. water to it.

To the remainder of the flour add 2/3 c. shortening or lard (at room temperature) and blend well.

Combine the two mixtures and mix well.

Enough for top and bottom for 1 pie.

Green Tomato Pie

2 c. chopped apples	1/2 c. cooked raisins
1 1/2 c. green tomatoes, chopped	1 tbsp. vinegar
	1 c. sugar
1/4 tsp. each of cloves, allspice and nutmeg	1 tsp. cinnamon
	little butter

Mix all ingredients well. Pour into unbaked pie crust. Dot with a little butter and cover with a top crust.

Bake at 425-450° for 15 minutes. Then reduce heat to 375° and bake for about 35 minutes.

This pie tastes like a regular mincemeat pie.

A Swiss Heater

The *Kamin* or *Kachel-Ofen* in a Swiss home is a very cosy spot. These heaters, made of tile, are a unique part of the household furnishings. Sometimes these tiles are one colored, but at other times, they are very ornamental and beautiful. The heaters are built so that the opening is either in the central hall or in the kitchen, making it very convenient to restock the firebox. Often a bench forms part of the side structure, making a warm spot on which to sit. The upper part consists of a warming portion and this may keep more than food warm.

In some of the Swiss homes, bags filled with dried cherry or peach pits, were placed in this warming closet in the morning. By evening, when it was time to go to bed, the pits would be thoroughly heated. Each member of the family would take a bag to bed, and, in a short time the sheets and feet would be warm. In the morning the bags would again be put into the warming closet, and the process would be repeated.

E. Foth

Schnitz-Pie

Dried Apple Pie

1 lb. schnitz-dried apple slices	1 orange, juice and grated rind
2 c. sugar	2 tbsp. cinnamon

Prepare pie crust from your favorite recipe.

Cover "*schnitz*" with water and soak overnight. Then add orange rind and juice and boil until soft. Add more water if necessary to prevent apples scorching.

Put through a colander and add the sugar and cinnamon. Pour into unbaked pie crust and cover with a top crust or lattice strips.

Bake in hot oven, 450°, for 10 minutes and then reduce heat to 350°. Bake 30 more minutes or until brown.

Sour Cream Raisin Pie

Wash 1 c. raisins, cover with water and cook until tender.

In the meantime make your favorite pie crust dough and prepare enough for 1 pie.

Drain the raisins, saving 1/2 c. of the liquid in which they have been cooked.

Combine this with:

2/3 c. sugar	1 c. sour cream
1 tsp. vanilla	1 tbsp. flour
1 egg yolk, beaten	1/2 tsp. soda

Mix well and put into unbaked pie shell. Cover with a top crust and bake at 450° for 10 minutes. Then reduce heat to 350° for 15-20 minutes longer.

PRESERVING

Dill Pickles

Make a solution of:
11 c. water	2 c. vinegar
5 tbsp. salt	

Bring to a boil.

fresh dill	1 hot pepper
1 garlic clove	

Wash cucumbers. Place in boiling solution. Simmer until they change color. Drain. Pack into jars with dill, pepper and garlic clove. Reheat solution to boiling point and pour over cucumbers. Seal.

Watermelon Pickles I

Remove all the pink meat and the hard green outer part from the rind of 1 watermelon. Cut the rind into serving sized portions so that there will be about 1 gallon of rind. Using about the same amount of cold water add 1/2 c. pickling salt and pour over the rinds. Let stand overnight. In morning drain and rinse.
Make a syrup of:

3 c. vinegar	6 c. sugar
6 c. hot water	several cinnamon sticks
1 lemon peel, sliced	

Bring syrup to a boil and add the rinds. Cook until rinds are transparent or tender, about 50-60 minutes.

Pour into hot sterilized jars and seal at once.

Watermelon Pickles II

Remove the outer green part from watermelon rinds. Cut into serving lengths. Let stand overnight in salt water, using about 3 quarts water to 1/2 c. pickling salt.

In the morning drain and rinse well. Cook in clear water until tender. Pack into a stone jar or crock. Heat equal amounts of vinegar and sugar with a few pieces of stick cinnamon. Pour over rind. Let stand overnight. Drain and heat syrup again.

Pack in jars and cover with hot vinegar syrup and seal.

Red and Green Pepper Relish

Remove the seeds and centers from 6 large green and 6 large red peppers.

Grind: 6 large onions and the peppers. Cover with boiling water. Let stand 5 minutes. Drain well.

Heat together:

2 c. vinegar	2 c. sugar
3 tsp. salt	1/4 tbsp. celery seed
1 1/2 tbsp. mustard seed	

Add pepper mixture and boil for 5 minutes. Put into hot sterile jars and seal at once.

Makes about 6 pints.

E. Foth.

Sauerkraut

2 heads cabbage   2 tbsp. salt, non-iodized

Wash cabbage heads and take off outer leaves. Save. Slice cabbage very fine into a large bowl. Pound with a potato masher until juicy. Pack into fruit jars pressing down so that juice covers cabbage. Cover kraut with a cabbage leaf. Loosely put the lids on the jars and allow the cabbage to ferment. After the kraut has fermented seal the jars.

Jars with zinc lids are very good for this.

A stone crock with a wooden lid may be used instead of jars. Sauerkraut is ready for serving in 3 to 4 weeks.

Honey in the Jura Mountain area of Switzerland is very dark in color, as it is obtained from the nectar of the pines, so prevalent in the area.

Dried Corn

Use roasting ears of corn. Boil ears for ten minutes. Immerse in cold water. Cut kernels with a sharp knife, close to the cobs. Spread corn on sheets and dry in the sun. Stir occasionally. Dry perfectly before storing in a glass jar.

Strawberry Preserves

Boil 1 pint sugar and 1/4 c. water. Add 1 pint berries. Boil for 4 minutes. Then add another pint of sugar and another pint of berries. Boil 4 or 5 minutes.

Let stand in earthenware container until cool. Put in jars and seal.

Hot mers net im Kop,
do hot mers in de Fees.

If you don't have it in the head,
you have to have it in the feet.

Apricot and Rhubarb Conserve

1 1/2 c. pitted and chopped apricots	3 c. diced rhubarb 2 1/2 c. sugar

Mix all ingredients and cook until thick, stirring often to prevent settling at the bottom of the kettle. When thick put into hot jars and seal at once.

SOUPS

Potato Soup

6 medium potatoes	2 tbsp. butter
3 c. water	1/2 tsp. salt
1 onion grated	pepper to taste
1 quart rich milk	

Cook potatoes in 3 c. of water until tender; drain and mash. Save the water. Add scalded milk and potato water to mashed potatoes. Add other ingredients. Cook a few minutes. Serve with crackers or toasted bread.

Chicken Noodle Soup

3 to 4 lb. chicken	1 small onion
3 quart water	1 bay leaf
2 tsp. salt	1 sprig parsley
1 tsp. pepper kernel	

Cut chicken in serving pieces and cover with water. Bring to a boil. Take off scum as it forms. Allow to simmer 3 hours, adding more water if necessary. One-half hour before serving skim off fat. Add pepper, onion, bay leaf, and parsley and cook till done.

Cook about 3 c. noodles in boiling, salted water until tender. When done, drain well and add to the chicken soup.

Chicken pieces may be removed and served on a platter or left in the soup.

VEGETABLES

Swiss Green Beans

2 pint green beans
3 tbsp. flour
2 tbsp. butter
2 c. sour cream
1/2 c. slivered almonds

1 medium onion, finely
  chopped
1/4 tsp. salt
1 8 oz. pkg. Swiss cheese,
  grated

Place beans in buttered casserole. Blend flour into melted butter. Gradually add sour cream, stirring constantly. Stir in onion and salt. Cook until thickened, stirring constantly. Add cheese; stir until melted. Pour cheese mixture over beans. Bake at 350° for 20 minutes or until completely heated. Top with slivered almonds. Yield: 6-8 servings.

Spinat
Spinach

Combine 2 slices of bacon, chopped, and 1 small miced onion in a skillet. Cook until bacon is brown. Add 1 tbsp. flour and blend well. Add enough water to make a gravy. Lastly add 1 c. of cooked spinach, stirring constantly. Let boil for a few minutes.

To serve arrange slices of hard cooked eggs on top.

Hot der arme Mann was,
dann hot er ke Fass;
hot er a Fass,
dan hot er not was.
Has the man something,
then he has no barrel;
If he has a barrel,
he has nothing to put into it.

E. Foth

Gummere-Salat
Cucumber Salad

3 or 4 large slicing
  cucumbers
1 medium onion
  sliced

1 c. sour cream
1 tbsp. vinegar
  salt and pepper to
  taste

Peel and slice the cucumbers very thin and add the chopped onion. Lightly sprinkle with salt and let stand while preparing the cream mixture.

Combine the cream, vinegar and pepper and mix well or beat the mixture. Add additional salt if needed.

Drain the cucumber mixture and add to the cream. Mix well and serve.

4

Swiss Galician Mennonites

HISTORY

The Galician Mennonites

Galician family records date back to 1671 in Bern, Switzerland, where Anabaptist were persecuted and banished from their homeland for their religious convictions. Forty-three years later, we find families in the Rheinpfalz area in Germany.

In Austria, Jospeh II had become the Emperor of the newly acquired province of Galicia. He was looking for hardy farmers; and, hearing that the Mennonites were thrifty and hardworking, he invited them to come to this province. He promised them religious freedom and also some land and buildings. The picture appeared promising, and so a delegation went to Galicia to investigate the situation. Between 1780 and 1789, our people migrated from Germany to Galicia, Austria. They started a settlement in a small colony called "Einsiedel" near the Dorf of Blyszvody. Later as more families came, villages, or *Doerfer* as they were called, came into being. Some of these were: Ehrenfeld, Falkenstein, Kernitzi, Dornfeld, and Pudusilna. By 1857, there were four or five congregations in these villages. The farmers also lived in the villages, having their homes and other buildings along the village street. The farm land was further away. Most of the land given our people was in timber and so had to be cleared before crops could be seeded or harvested. It might be interesting to note that the Galicia Mennonites speak about the same dialect as the Swiss Mennonites who migrated to Russia do.

In the years between 1881 and 1885, seventy-five Galician

families migrated to America. Some settled in Minnesota and a smaller group came to Kansas, settling in the Harvey, McPherson, Kingman, Reno, and Hodgeman counties.

A trip across the ocean also meant much preparation for the women, as meals were not served on board as they are at the present time. So the Grandmother had to bake all sorts of breads for this trip; and, as something special to put on this bread, she made *Koch-Kaese* which would keep well on the trip.

Remember When

Back in the long ago, women spent much of their time in their kitchens. There were no fancy gadgets to get out of whack, no water from faucets, no fancy clocks that ran automatically, no beautiful shiny refrigerators that kept the perishable food in tip top condition.

The sturdy black iron cook stove, which had no thermostat or controls of any kind, played an important role every day all year long. It kept an even heat if it was fed regularly with fuel, such as coal, corn cobs, or cut wood. Then, too, the ashes had to be removed from the space below the fuel box with regularity if you wanted to get the best results.

A large door adorned the front of the cook stove; this was the gateway to the oven which baked the best bread and the most delicious pies and coffee cakes. It served as a roaster for all kinds of meat. On damp and wet days, it dried out the wet mittens, caps, and socks. It was also a perfect place to warm cold toes and feet.

The warming closet, which was attached to the back of the stove, served as an ideal place to keep left-over food warm on cold days. This was a special treat for the men who usually spent most of the daylight hours doing outdoor chores. School children always peeked to see what delicacies it held after their walk home from school. How they loved to find some of their favorite goodies! Sometimes, however, it was almost as bare as Mother Hubbard's cupboard.

At the far end of the cook stove, there was an attached, rather large, tank which was kept filled with water. This warm water was used for the few "quickie" baths that were taken in a portable tub.

During the very cold weather the heavy sad irons were kept on top of the stove near the back edge. When the weather was the coldest, these hot irons were wrapped in papers or flannel cloths and tucked in the beds at the foot end. These helped to take off the chill to some degree.

Occasionally new born baby pigs and sickly baby calves were brought into the kitchen for the night. They were put into wooden boxes which were then partly covered and put near the faithful cook stove. Often by morning these creatures were in better condition and roamed around in the kitchen. Later they could be taken to their regular quarters.

Sometimes when we had an early supper, a large heavy black skillet was greased heavily with bacon drippings, then a layer of popcorn was put into this skillet and covered with a heavy iron lid. With careful movements and constant watching there soon was a big bowl of fluffy white popped corn. By adding salt, we had a zesty tasting treat for the entire family. Apples were brought up from the outdoor cave, and all enjoyed a real snack before going to bed.

The sturdy wooden kitchen table was surrounded on three sides with chairs of various sizes and vintages. A home made bench was placed on the side next to the wall. This was where the smaller children sat; they could not fall off so easily. Here the family gathered three times daily for prayer, physical food, and conversation.

We always had delicious homemade breads, coffee cakes, and cookies; cakes and pies were baked for special occasions. Then there was home churned butter. After it was churned and washed, the butter was packed into a wooden mold. Then it appeared on the table with a beautiful design on the top of the lump. Meats and sausages made from home raised and butchered animals, newly laid eggs, fresh or canned vegetables and fruits from the garden or orchard, and jellies and jams made from various berries that grew in the garden or wild along the creeks in the pastures; all these gave variety to our tasty meals.

There were no garbage disposals; the scraps were fed to the cats, dog, or pigs. There were no electric dish washers, but there were willing and toilworn hands ready to wash and wipe the dishes immediately after the meals.

Electric alarm clocks were non-existent, but the roosters never failed to crow at the right time. Usually the entire family was up at the crack of dawn. Every member had assigned chores to do before breakfast. Much planning was done daily, and usually everything was completed on schedule. Children were prompt in coming home from school and doing their nightly chores. By evening all were ready for a restful night's sleep. No tranquilizers were needed. Sleep and rest came naturally.

There is something nostalgic about the olden days,
And the hard work we all did in so many, many ways.
But we all managed to get along quite well somehow,
And lived just as well, if not better, than now.

MENU

Breakfast
    Bacon and eggs
    Whole wheat bread
    Butter and preserves
    Coffee

Dinner
    Sauerkraut cooked with bay leaf and seasoned with
        cured bacon grease
    Boiled back bone
    Mashed potatoes
    Bread and butter
    Coffee

Supper
    Raw fried potatoes
    Scrambled eggs
    Cottage cheese
    Bread
    Butter and preserves
    Coffee

BREADS

Bread

Be gentle
    When you touch bread.
Let it not lie
    Uncared for — unwanted.
So often bread
    Is taken for granted.

There is so much beauty
    In bread —
Beauty of sun and soil,
    Beauty of patient toil.
Winds and rains have caressed it,
    Christ often blessed it.
Be gentle
    When you touch bread.

                        Author Unknown

One Loaf of Bread

1 c. water	1/4 c. shortening
1 pkg. dry yeast	1 tsp. salt
1 tsp. sugar	3 c. sifted flour

Dissolve yeast and sugar in 1 c. lukewarm water in mixing bowl. Let stand until foamy, about 5-10 minutes. Add remaining ingredients, mix and knead well, and cover with towel. Let rise in warm place until double in bulk, 30-40 minutes. Shape loaf and place in buttered bread pan. Cover and let rise again until double in bulk, 30-40 minutes. Preheat oven to 350° and bake 45 minutes or until done. Remove from tin. Butter the crust, and let cool.

    For whole wheat loaf, use 2 c. white and 1 c. whole wheat flour. A little more white flour might have to be added for stiffness.

Kaese-Kuchen
Cheese Cake

2 eggs	1/2 c. sugar
2 c. dry cottage cheese	1/4 c. raisins
1/2 c. sweet cream	1/4 tsp. cinnamon
salt	

Beat eggs. Add all other ingredients, mixing well. Line a 9 inch pan with coffee cake dough (recipe below), bringing sides up well. Let dough rise about 20 minutes. Pour cheese mixture into dough cavity and bake at 350° for 30-40 minutes.

Coffee Cake Dough

Dissolve: 1 1/2 packages yeast in 1 c. warm water. Add 1/2 c. sugar. Put into mixing bowl and let sit until it begins to bubble. Add:

2 eggs, beaten	1/2 c. butter, melted
1 tsp. salt	1/2 c. sugar
5 c. flour	1 c. lukewarm milk

Beat batter well. When too stiff to beat, put on baking board and knead. Cover and set in a warm place until double in bulk.
Divide into 4 portions and press each into a greased baking pan.

Kaffee-Kuchen
Coffee Cake

1 1/2 pkgs. dry yeast	1/2 c. butter or margarine
1 c. lukewarm water	1 tsp. salt
1 c. lukewarm milk	1/2 c. sugar
2 eggs, beaten	5 c. flour

Dissolve yeast in 1 c. warm water. Add 1/4 c. sugar. Put in mixing bowl and let sit until it begins to bubble. Add rest of ingredients. Knead well. Cover and set in warm place. Let rise until doubled in bulk. Divide into four portions and press into greased baking pans (9 inch size). Let rise for 20-30 minutes. Glaze with sweet cream. Sprinkle generously with sugar and cinnamon mixture. Bake at 350° for 20 minutes.

Cottage Cheese-Filled Pancakes

2 c. flour
3 eggs
1 tsp. salt

1 tsp. baking powder
1/2 c. milk

Filling:
1 c. cottage cheese
2 tbsp. sugar

1 egg, well beaten

Beat eggs. Add dry ingredients and milk alternately. Beat until smooth. Pour about 1/2 c. of dough into greased skillet and let it "flow" over whole pan, and brown. When upper side is set, place on waxed paper with brown side up. Spread with cottage cheese filling and roll. Repeat until all batter is used.

Place rolls in baking pan. Sprinkle with sugar and brown in moderate oven (350°) 10-15 minutes.

Potato Pancakes

6 medium-sized potatoes,
   peeled and grated or
   ground coarsely
3 eggs

1 1/2 tsp. salt
1 tsp. baking powder
   shortening
3/4 c. all-purpose flour

Beat eggs. Add flour, salt, and baking powder to make thick batter. Add grated potatoes and mix well. Spoon onto hot, well greased griddle. When bottom is brown, turn and cook other side. Makes 12 4-inch pancakes.

Corn Bread

1 c. flour
1 tsp. salt
3 tbsp. sugar
3/4 c. yellow cornmeal

2 eggs, well beaten
1 c. milk
1/4 c. melted butter or fat
3 tsp. baking powder

Sift flour, salt, baking powder, and sugar. Mix with cornmeal. Combine eggs, milk, and shortening and add to dry ingredients. Stir only until well moistened. Bake in a 9 inch square pan about 20 minutes in hot oven.

Serve with butter and syrup or with milk and sugar.

Making Doughnuts

In the kitchen with its well scrubbed floor,
Hollyhocks outside the open door, the curtains moving
in the breeze blowing in from Mother's cherry tree;
the patch of lettuce in the back.
The plum trees!
Oh! There is no lack of memories while here I
stand and labor with a practised hand . . . making
DOUGHNUTS.

Anne Campbell

Fastnachts-Kuchen
Doughnuts

2 c. warm milk	1/2 c. melted butter or oleo
1/4 c. warm water	2 eggs, well beaten
3/4 c. sugar	1/2 tsp. salt
2 pkgs. dry yeast	1/2 tsp. nutmeg
5 c. flour (approx.)	1/2 c. raisins or apples
	(optional)

Dissolve yeast in warm water in large mixing bowl. When bubbles form (about 5 minutes) add all other ingredients and knead well. Cover and let rise about 30 minutes. Shape doughnuts the size of a tablespoon or roll out and cut into squares. Place on well greased cookie sheet. Cut a slit in each square. Let rise again for about 30 minutes in a warm place. Fry in hot fat, about 350°.

Roll-Kuchen
Crullers

2 eggs	1 c. milk
1 tsp. baking powder	1/4 tsp. salt
2 c. flour	

Beat eggs and add the liquid. Sift dry ingredients and add. Mix together to form a soft dough. Roll out thin. Cut in strips 2 inches by 4 inches. Make a slit in the center. Fry in deep fat until brown. Roll in granulated or powdered sugar.

Roll-Kuchen

1/2 c. sweet milk
1/2 c. sweet or sour cream
2 eggs

1 tsp. salt
1 tsp. baking powder
flour, about 2 c.

Add beaten eggs to the liquid and sifted dry ingredients. Add enough flour to make a dough which can be rolled out. Cut into oblong strips, making a slit down the center. Pull the one end through this opening to form a bow. Deep fry until brown.

CAKES AND COOKIES

Lebkuchen
Old-fashioned Ginger Cookies

2 c. shortening, melted
3 c. sorghum molasses
1 c. sugar
8 to 10 c. flour
1 1/2 c. buttermilk or sour milk

2 tbsp. soda
1 tbsp. ginger
1 tbsp. cinnamon
1 tsp. salt

Heat sugar and molasses together. When sugar is dissolved, add the shortening, stirring until it is melted. Remove from heat and cool to lukewarm.

Add sifted, dry ingredients alternately with the milk. Stir until a medium soft dough is formed, then knead on a board for about 5 minutes. Chill dough for several hours or overnight.

Turn dough on a lightly floured board and roll out 1/4 inch thick. Cut with a large round cookie cutter.

Glaze with a beaten egg. (Dip a small piece of cheesecloth in beaten egg and rub lightly over cookies.) Place 1 1/2 inches apart on greased cookie sheet. Bake at 350° for about 20 minutes.

This is a soft chewy cookie that was a favorite in grandmother's day. It is still very popular among Mennonite families.

Makes 8 dozen cookies.

Sugar Cookies

Cream thoroughly:

1 c. white sugar
1 tsp. vanilla
2 eggs

3/4 c. soft butter or
    margarine

Sift:

2 1/2 c. flour
1 tsp. salt

1 tsp. baking powder

Add flour mixture to creamed portion and mix well. Dough should be soft yet stiff enough to roll out.

Roll out on floured board about 1/4 inch thick. Cut into desired shapes. Place on ungreased baking sheet and bake at 350° for 8-10 minutes. Cookies should be almost white in color.

Sugar may be sprinkled on top of cookies before baking.

Makes 3 dozen cookies.

Weisse (White) Cookies

1 c. sugar
1 c. sour cream
1 egg
    flour for stiff dough

1 tsp. soda
2 tsp. baking powder
1 tsp. lemon or
    vanilla flavoring

Mix in usual way, roll on floured board, cut with cookie cutter in any shape desired.

Peppernuts
Pfeffernuesse

1 c. shortening
1 c. sugar
6 c. flour (approx.)
3 tsp. baking powder

1 c. sweet cream
1 c. milk
1 tsp. peppermint extract
1/2 tsp. salt

Cream shortening and sugar. Add flavoring and sweet cream, and beat until fluffy.

Sift flour, measure and add baking powder and salt. Sift again. Add sifted ingredients to creamed mixture, alternately with milk. Beat until a medium soft dough is formed. Chill for several hours or overnight. When dough is thoroughly chilled, divide into 6 parts. Take one portion at a time, leaving rest of dough in a cool place, and form into finger-like sticks, rolling with the flat part of the hands. Place these rolls in parallel rows on baking board and cut across several rows at a time, making pieces the size of a small marble.

Place on greased baking sheet.

Bake at 425° until a light golden brown.

Especially popular at Christmas time.

Weisse Pfeffernuesse

1 lb. flour (4 c.)
1 lb. sugar (2 c.)
4 eggs
    grated rind of 1 lemon

1 tsp. each of: nutmeg,
    cinnamon, cloves and
    baking powder

Sift dry ingredients. Add lemon rind. Beat the eggs well and add to the dry ingredients. Mix thoroughly to make a pliable dough which can be rolled into long rolls, about 1/2 inch thick. Cut off into small, fairly thin pieces and put on a greased cookie sheet.

Bake at moderate hot oven, 375°, until done.

Macaroons

3 c. sugar
5 c. flour
1 tsp. soda, dissolved in
    1/2 c. hot water
1 c. ground almonds

1 tsp. each of: nutmeg,
    cinnamon, cloves, salt
    and almond flavoring
5 eggs

Beat eggs, add sugar and beat thoroughly to a creamy consistency. Add sifted dry ingredients and soda water. Make a soft dough which can be rolled out. Roll into long strips about 1/2 inch in diameter. Cut off pieces 1 inch long and put on greased cookie sheet. Flatten cookies. Bake at 350° about 12 minutes.

Holiday Customs

In grandparent's family, it was the custom to have a meatless Good Friday. On this day the noon meal always consisted of noodles, some kind of fruit, and scrambled eggs. For supper there might be fried potatoes and cottage cheese. Cereal and hot drinks were used for breakfast.

For Christmas our parents always trimmed the tree on the afternoon of Christmas Eve. Father took a branch from our orchard and went to the neighbors for cedar branches, which he tied onto the bare branch from our orchard. For decorations, we children made popcorn strings or colored paper chains, which we hung on our tree. There were always candles to add to the Christmas glitter.

Our parents would place plates on the table after putting up the tree. There was one plate for each child. In these plates a few pieces of candies, a few nuts, and occasionally an orange and a small gift, were put. When our parents were ready to have us enter the parlor, the door would be opened and the candles lit. Each child would then receive his or her plate of goodies.

Father would read the Christmas story and we would all join in singing, *Stille Nacht, Heilige Nacht.* By then it was time to do chores and get ready to go to the Christmas Eve services in our little church.

Baptismal Day was also another important event in the life of our church community. Children of the ages of 14 to 16 years, were instructed by the pastor for about a year. The *Katechismus* was studied, and for each question and answer, there was a Bible reference that each child memorized. Upon confession of faith and belief in Jesus Christ as personal Savior, the candidates were baptized. For this service, the girls wore black instead of the usual Sunday white. Black was worn as a sign of the Lord's suffering.

In those early days, all members of the church wore head coverings of some kind. No baptized woman or girl entered the church with an uncovered head.

DESSERTS

Apple Dumplings

1 c. flour	1/3 c. water or milk
2 tsp. baking soda	4 apples
1/4 tsp. salt	1/2 c. sugar
2 tbsp. shortening	little cinnamon

Mix and sift flour, baking powder, and salt. Cut in shortening to make crumbs. Add the liquid, mixing to a soft dough. Roll out on well-floured board to 1/4 inch thickness. Divide dough into 4 or 5 inch squares.

Wash, pare, and cut apples in half. Place halves into center of each square and add 1 tbsp. sugar-cinnamon mixture. Bring the four corners of dough up around the apple pieces. Pinch to seal. Pierce with fork to allow steam to escape.

Bake on greased tin in moderate oven for about 25 minutes.

Serve with hot, sweetened milk, or with whipped cream, or a pudding sauce.

Soft Custard
Brei

1 c. milk, scalded	2 eggs
1/2 tsp. vanilla	1/4 c. sugar
1/4 tsp. salt	1/4 tsp. nutmeg

Beat eggs slightly with a fork and add sugar and salt. Add luke-warm milk gradually, stirring constantly. Cook over hot water continuing to stir until the mixture coats a spoon.

Add the vanilla and remove from heat.

Apple Fritters

1 c. flour	1 egg, beaten
1 1/2 tsp. baking powder	1/2 c. plus 1 tbsp. milk
1/2 tsp. salt	1 1/2 c. chopped apples
2 tbsp. sugar	

Sift dry ingredients. Beat egg and add milk. Pour into dry ingredients and stir until the batter is smooth.

Pare apples and dice very thin. Add to batter and mix well. Drop by spoonfuls into deep, hot fat, 370 to 375°.

Fry until a golden brown on all sides.

Makes about 15 fritters.

Rhubarb Pie

Pie Crust: Mix together 3 c. flour and 1 c. lard and 1 tsp. salt until crumbly. Add ice water by spoonful until dough clings together when pressed into a ball. Divide dough in half. Roll out half of dough and line bottom and sides of pie plate. Save other half for top crust.

Wash rhubarb and remove strings. Cut into cubes and fill pie crust. Mix 1 1/2 c. sugar and 2 tbsp. flour and pour over rhubarb. Put top crust on and seal edges tightly. Sprinkle sugar over crust. Bake at 450° for 15 minutes and reduce heat to 375° and continue baking for about 25 more minutes, or until crust is nicely browned.

DUMPLINGS

Zweimal Gekochte Knoedel
Cheese Dumplings

2 c. jacket potatoes
1 c. dry cottage cheese
2 eggs
2 tbsp. flour

1/4 c. cream
1 tbsp. butter or oleo
1/4 c. bread crumbs

Boil jacket potatoes till done. Peel and mash to make 2 c. Beat eggs. Add cottage cheese, eggs, and flour and mix well. Form into balls the size of small eggs. Roll in flour. Drop into boiling salted water. Dumplings will rise to top. Cook for about 10 minutes. Remove into sieve and drain. Put in serving bowl. Melt butter in skillet. Add cream and bread crumbs. Cook until crumbs are brown. Pour over dumplings.

Knepp

3 c. flour
pinch of salt
2 tbsp. baking powder
1 tsp. sugar

1 egg
milk
2 qts. ham broth

Sift the dry ingredients into a bowl.

Add 1 egg and enough milk to make a smooth batter.

Drop by spoonfuls into boiling ham broth. Cook about 20 minutes.

Dip knepp out of ham broth and serve with ham.

Damp Nudeln
Fried Bread

Make buns the size of an egg from bread dough that has risen to double its bulk. Grease skillet and add extra shortening, perhaps 2 or 3 tbsp. as for frying. Put buns into the skillet. Let rise. Add 2 c. water and cover tightly with lid. Let fry over medium heat until buns have browned. Turn over with fork or spatula and brown top side. Sprinkle with salt and serve while hot.

Pirogi (Berrogi)

Peel and boil 4 medium potatoes with 1 medium diced onion. Add salt to taste. When done, drain off the water and mash the potatoes. Blend in 2 c. dry cottage cheese and add enough cream to make the mixture sticky.

Mix 3 c. flour, 2 eggs, 4 tbsp. cream, and 1/2 tsp. salt. Mix well to form a soft dough, stiff enough to roll out. Roll out the dough and cut out as many pieces as you can with a large round cookie cutter.

Put small amount of potato mixture on each round of dough and fold over. Seal securely. Drop several sealed pieces into a large kettle of boiling water. When "dumplings" come to the top of the boiling water, they are ready to be taken out.

Melt margarine or butter in a skillet and add a little cream. Heat and pour over the hot *berrogis.* Serve at once.

Evening Prayer

Ich bin klein
Mein Herz is rein,
Niemand kann drin wohnen
Als Jesu allein. Amen.

I am small,
My heart is pure,
None can live therein
But Jesus alone.

MEATS

Hollaptse
Holleburgers

3 c. grated potatoes
1 medium onion, thinly
sliced
3/4 c. oatmeal
2 tbsp. oleo or fat

1 tsp. salt
1 c. sauerkraut
4 slices bacon cut into
bits and fried
1 1/2 c. diced smoked ham

Mix ingredients. Put in greased casserole. Cover and bake 45 minutes 350°.

Huliptica

1/2 lb. fresh bacon, diced
2 c. grated potatoes
2 c. sauerkraut (with juice)

1 c. oatmeal
salt and pepper to taste
water, as needed

Fry bacon in large skillet. Drain off excessive grease. Add grated potatoes and continue cooking. You may add chopped onions, if you wish, at this time. Add sauerkraut and juice. Stir well and continue to simmer all ingredients, adding water as needed. Add 1 c. oatmeal, salt and pepper. Add water as needed and stir often. If you have sour cabbage leaves, put some of mixture in each leaf and place in a roaster and finish cooking in the oven at medium heat.

This recipe comes from Galicia, brought to Kansas in 1884.

Jellied Pig's Feet

Cook pig's feet in enough water to cover. Add salt to taste and 1 medium bay leaf. Cook until meat is tender. Cool.

Remove the meat from the bones and put into a pan.

Reheat the broth, add 2 tbsp. vinegar, or to taste, and pour over the meat. Set in a cool place and let jell.

Slice to serve.

Good with fried potatoes.

Spare Ribs With Sauerkraut

2 lbs. spare ribs   4 cans sauerkraut

Boil spare ribs until tender in salt water. Have plenty of broth. Add kraut and boil for 10 minutes. Sometimes our mother added cubed potatoes and made a one-dish meal.

Butter Making

On our Oklahoma farm, we had a milk house with a trough near the windmill, which pumped the water into the trough and then out into the stock tank. In that trough, our mother kept the cream. On churning days, the cream was put into a three-gallon crock churn that had a stomper that we stomped up and down until we had butter. The butter was then rinsed with cold water, after which it was salted. Mother would then press it into a wooden mold and when the butter was pressed out of this mold, it had an oak leaf pattern on top. The one-pound molds of butter were taken to town and exchanged for staple groceries or for cash to buy needed articles. Only necessary items were bought in the early pioneer days in Oklahoma.

MISCELLANEOUS

Poultry Dressing

Take the neck, liver, gizzard and heart of a fowl and boil until tender. Bone neck and cut meat. Toast bread cut into croutons. Add the giblets, a minced onion and 1/2 c. celery. Mix with a little broth to moisten. Add salt and pepper to taste. Stuff into fowl and roast.

Put 2 c. water into bottom of roaster and your product will be a nice moist roast and the juice in bottom of roaster will help make a tastier gravy.

Horseradish

Clean the crown and larger roots. Save the short and thinner roots for replanting.

3 1/2 c. ground horseradish	1/2 c. boiling water
1/4 c. sugar	1 tbsp. vinegar (optional)
1 tbsp. salt	

Mix first three ingredients. Pour boiling water over mixture. It will turn white. Add vinegar if desired. Pour into jars and seal. Keeps well in refrigerator but should be kept covered.

Kaiserschmarren
A Bachelor's Dish

1 c. flour	1 tsp. soda
1 egg	1/3 stick margarine
1 tsp. salt	1 c. buttermilk

Blend entire mixture in a mixing bowl and pour into a medium heated, well greased frying pan. Stir constantly until mixture has turned a golden brown.

Recipe in dialect:

Nemm a Kopchia Mehl und lerr es in a Schuessel. Mach a Viertie-fung in dem Mehl in der Mittle, und dann memm a grosses Ei, odder zwee klena, und brech des Ei in die Viertiefung im Mehl... Dann add a teaspoon Saltz, un a teaspoon soda. A drittle stick oleo mit a drittel cup Buttermilch. Of course des Mehl muss mann sifta und des oleo muss gemellt sei. Das ganze mixutre muss zusamma gebeat werde. Nemm a frying pan und Fett oder vege-table oil, und grease die pan und heat zu medium. Dann giess das mixture un die pan un ruehr constantly biss das mixture a goldness braun iss.

Cottage Cheese

1 1/2 gal. sour, raw milk   1 tbsp. salt
1/2 c. sweet cream

Heat milk, stir slowly until too hot to hold finger in it. Drain thoroughly in cloth bag or strainer. Hang bag to drain or put in a strainer. When dry, crumble cheese curds fine. Add the salt.
When serving, add sweet cream.
Makes 3 1/2 c. cheese curds.

PRESERVING

Sauerkraut

Cut cabbage and place small amount in crock. Sprinkle with salt. To each quart of cabbage, add 2 tbsp. pickling salt.
Stomp down with potato masher until juice forms. When crock is tightly packed, add enough hot water to fill completely. Cover with a cloth. Put plate over this and weigh down; a filled fruit jar is good for this. Wash cloth, plate and weight, several times each week. The kraut will be ready to be used after several weeks.
If a jar is used instead of a crock, use the handle of a heavy knife to stomp the cabbage down. Place lid on jar but do not tighten. Let stand on a tray and allow to ferment for several days. When no longer fermenting, remove lid and add enough water to fill jar. Close tightly.

Storing Vegetables

An outdoor cellar was used to store the canned fruits and vegetables. These were placed on shelves and beneath these shelves, compartments for the storing of the potatoes were built. The potatoes had to be sorted and then sprinkled with lime before being stored. The lime helped to preserve them.

Toward spring the potatoes had to be gone through and the sprouts pulled off. The good potatoes were also used for the farmer's seed potatoes in the spring, and so needed to be well stored.

A hole was dug below the frost level in which the root vegetables, such as carrots, beets etc. were stored. Cabbage was wrapped in paper, to keep it clean, and also stored in a hole or trench. As late as March, cabbage stored this way, would be as crisp as it was when stored.

Lattwaerich
Apple Butter

Wash and slice apples. Cover with water and boil until soft. Press through sieve to remove skins and seeds. Bring apple juice to boil. Add apple pulp and 1 c. sugar for each c. of pulp. Add 1 tsp. cinnamon, 1/4 tsp. cloves, 1/4 tsp. allspice. Cook until it thickens, stirring constantly. Cook until thick enough to spread. Pour into jars and seal. Use same recipe for peach or apricot. Use cinnamon sticks for peach and no spices for apricot.

Drying Vegetables

Green beans were cleaned and washed, then blanched for perhaps 5-7 minutes. Corn was cleaned, washed and put to boil about 5 minutes. When cool, cut kernels off the cob. Then the vegetables were spread out on a clean cloth and covered with another cloth or screen and put on the roof of our lean-to kitchen to dry. They were taken in every evening and put out the next day, or perhaps finished drying in the oven. When perfectly dry, they were put into flour sacks and hung in a dry place. In the winter, my mother took as much of the vegetable as was needed for a meal and soaked them over night and cooked them the next day. Mother always used a cream sauce with the corn, and my! how good it smelled and tasted when four or five hungry school children came home from school and found the corn warming on the back of the old black cook stove!

SALADS

Heisser Grumberre-Salat
Hot Potato Salad

Cook amount of potatoes needed in their jackets until done. When cool, peel and slice, allowing about 2 1/2 to 3 c. for the recipe.

Saute: 1/2 c. diced smoked bacon with 1 medium diced onion. When bacon is crisp, add 1 tbsp. flour and stir until slightly browned.

Add diced potatoes and enough water to make a gravy. Before serving add 1 tbsp. vinegar and salt and pepper to taste.

Gurken-Salat
Cucumber Slaw

1 medium cucumber, peeled and thinly sliced
1 small onion, minced
Mix together:

1/2 tsp. salt	1 tsp. vinegar
pepper to taste	3 tbsp. sour cream

Add cream mixture to cucumber and onion and serve.

SOUPS

Chicken Noodle Soup

2 to 3 lb. chicken, cut
   into pieces
1 onion

parsley
1/2 tsp. whole peppercorns
1 bay leaf

Cook in enough water to cover until meat is done. Add noodles. Cook until noodles are tender. Salt as needed.

Noodles

6 eggs, lightly beaten
2 tsp. salt

6 tbsp. water
flour to make a stiff
   dough

Mix all ingredients. Roll out thin on floured board and let dry. Roll up and cut in thin slices. Separate and dry some more. Use as needed.

Red Beet Borscht

4 medium sized beets
1 medium onion, diced
parsley
salt

2 tbsp. flour
1 tbsp. vinegar
1/4 c. cream

Cut beets into cross section strips. Cover with water. Add onion, parsley and salt to taste and cook until beets are tender. Make thickening with flour and water. Add to beet mixture, and cook until slightly thickened. Add vinegar. Remove from heat and slowly add sweet cream. Serve at once.

Sauerkraut-Mashed Potato Soup

3 slices bacon
1 small onion
2 tbsp. flour
salt

6 c. water
2 c. mashed potatoes
2 c. sauerkraut

Cut bacon in small pieces and fry.
   Saute onion, add flour and stir until well mixed.
   Add water, potatoes and kraut, bring to boil.
   Add salt to taste.

Bread Soup

2 slices bread   2 tbsp. butter
2 c. milk   1 tsp. salt
   pepper to taste

Cube bread and brown in melted butter.
Heat the milk, adding salt and pepper.
Add the browned bread, and heat to boiling point.
Serve at once.
This soup was often served to a sick family member.

Plume-Moos

2 quarts water   1/2 c. sugar
1 c. seedless grapes   6 tbsp. flour
1 c. dried prunes   1/2 tsp. salt
1/4 c. dried peaches   1 tsp. cinnamon
1/4 c. dried apricots   1 c. sweet or sour cream

Wash fruit and add warm water. Cook until almost tender, then add
sugar. While fruit is cooking, prepare flour paste by combining
flour, salt, cinnamon and cream. When fruit is done, slowly add
paste, stirring constantly. Cook until slightly thickened. Serve
warm.

   This dish is served traditionally as a dessert or side dish in some
Mennonite communities for Easter, Pentecost, or Christmas
dinners.

   It makes 8 servings.

Potato Soup

4 medium potatoes, diced   1 tsp. salt
1 medium onion, diced   1/8 tsp. pepper
   sprig of parsley   1 tbsp. vinegar
1/4 c. sour cream

Put potatoes, onion and parsley in kettle. Cover with water and
cook until potatoes and onion are tender. Add salt and pepper
to taste. Add vinegar and sour cream slowly.
   Serve at once.

Rivel Soup

1 1/2 c. flour   pinch of salt
        1 egg   1 quart milk
Work flour, egg and salt until crumbly with pieces not larger than a bean. Heat milk to boiling. Drop rivels in milk and simmer for 10 minutes. Ham or beef broth may be used instead of milk.
    A good supper dish!

Beef Soup

1 lb. stew meat   1 onion, chopped
5 potatoes   sprig of parsley
4 carrots   2 c. canned tomatoes
1 c. diced celery   1 bay leaf

Cook beef in 2 quarts salted water until tender.
    Peel and dice the potatoes and carrots. Cut the onion and celery and add vegetables to soup. Add parsley. Cook until vegetables are done, about 12 minutes. Add the canned tomatoes and heat. Serve hot.
    If preferred cooked rice or noodles may be used instead of the potatoes. These may be cooked previously or added to the soup about 15 minutes before it is ready.

Hog Killing Days

On the day designated to prepare our year's supply of pork, our father was up before the rooster thought or arousing his sleeping harem to get into the production line.
    I remember this day in particular because it was filled with chills and thrills. Our uncle had come from his farm three miles away and was ready to shoot and stab the first victim... here is where the chills came in. Our father had the scalding water boiling in the large black kettle. The thrills came when we youngsters came home from school and found the house and, yes, the yard filled with fragrant aromas which can only be associated with butchering days.
    After the first pig had been killed, it was strung up on a three legged trestle with a pulley and rope fastened to the apex of the triangle. A singletree was fastened to the already slit tendons above the hind feet of the hog. The animal was dunked into the scalding water until its hair came off easily.

While several of the men, and sometimes my grandmother, scraped the hair off the carcass, father prepared another kettle of water for the next pig. The head was removed and the entrails taken out. The men then went to work scraping the intestines into a tissue thin casing. The women had to remove all the fatty substances from the intestines by taking them apart. Both sets of intestines were used . . . the small for the stuffing of the *Bratwurst* and the large for the *Liverwurst* and *Blutwurst*.

When the Blutwurst was made, my grandmother would be ready, with a warm gallon crock and a large wooden spoon to catch the warm blood as it gushed from the open wound. Luckily the animal never knew what was happening! The shooting had taken care of that... Grandmother seemed to be the official blood stirrer, perhaps she was the only one in the family who had the nerve to this unpleasant job. Her European background had influenced her life far differently from what her third, fourth and fifth generation descendants, born in Kansas and Oklahoma, believe in.

As the now snowy-white carcass hung on the trestle, two men would cut it down along the spine. In this way the carcass was divided and the halves were laid upon a work-table where the shoulders and hams were cut off. During this process of cutting the meat with knives honed to a sharp edge, the meat for the different sausages was also cut.

The entire morning, from sunrise until noon, was usually spent in the killing, scalding, scraping and separating of the different

sections of the meat. The side meat was set aside to be cured and smoked into a tasty bacon later on. This procedure has become a lost art on our farms today. The afternoon was spent in grinding meat for the different sausages, and stuffing the ground meat into the casings, which had been carefully cleaned, scraped, washed and salted. This part of the butchering day was part of our young lives. It was usually at this time when we youngsters came home from school...hungry and ready to sample little patties of fresh fried Bratwurst, served with homemade bread, which our mother had ready for her hungry school children.

It was not all work on these days, really. The men would take time off at ten and then again at four, for a lunch. Usually Father had a bottle of homemade wine. (This was a no-no for us children, but we often managed to get a sip while no one was watching.)

And so, the chills and thrills of butchering day return to us as pleasant memories, for we realize that this event, so important in former years, is no longer part of our modern, twentieth century farm life.

E.E.H.

VEGETABLES

Ham and String Beans

2 lb. cured ham, diced	1 quart water
4 c. string beans	1 c. potatoes, diced

Cook ham in water 1/2 hour. Add beans and potatoes and cook until tender.

Peas and Carrots Fresh from Garden

1 tbsp. sugar	2 c. peas
1 tsp. salt	2 c. diced carrots
sprig of parsley	2 tbsp. flour
3 tbsp. sweet cream	cold water

Add the sugar, salt, and parsley sprig to the peas and carrots. Cook in sufficient water to have approximately 1 c. of liquid when the vegetables are tender.

Make a paste by mixing a little cold water to 2 tbsp. of flour. Gradually stir the paste into the cooked vegetables and bring to a boil. Let cook several minutes.

Add 3 tbsp. sweet cream.

Heisses Kraut
Smothered Cabbage

6 c. cabbage, finely
shredded
5 tbsp. fat
1/2 tsp. salt

1 1/2 tbsp. sugar
1/2 c. cream
2 or 3 tbsp. vinegar

Melt fat in heavy skillet. Add cabbage and fry slowly 15 minutes. Stir often. Mix other ingredients and add to cabbage. Bring to a boil. Cover skillet with heavy lid, reduce heat, and steam for 15 minutes. Serves 6.

Lambs-quarters
(Mock Spinach)

In early spring gather lambs-quarters. Wash well and cook in boiling, salted water for about 5 minutes. Drain well.

3 slices bacon, chopped
1 small onion, chopped
1 tbsp. flour

1 tbsp. vinegar
salt and pepper to taste
milk

Saute bacon and onion until bacon is browned. Add flour and brown. Add enough milk to make a smooth mixture. Add drained greens, vinegar, salt, and pepper.

Cornmeal Mush

1/2 c. cornmeal
3/4 tsp. salt

2 3/4 c. boiling water

Sprinkle cornmeal into rapidly boiling, salted water, stirring constantly. Cook about 30 minutes over direct heat, or 60 minutes in a double boiler.

Serve with milk and sugar as a cereal.

The cooked mush may also be substituted for potatoes.

To fry this mush, put the cooked cornmeal into a bread pan which has been rinsed in cold water. Smooth the top surface. Cool until very firm. Cut in 3/4 inch slices and fry in hot fat, similar to pancakes.

Boiled Rice

1 c. rice   8 c. boiling water
1 tsp. salt

Wash rice and drain. Sprinkle into boiling, salted water. Continue cooking until rice grains are plump and tender, but not "mushy".
Serve with milk and sugar.
Rice may also be used as a substitute for potatoes and served with meat and gravy.

Illness and Funerals

In the early years many people, young children especially, died due to epidemics and general hardships. When sickness entered a home, relatives and friends offered their help. This service was often a difficult decision to make during times of serious contagious diseases. Multiple deaths in a family were not uncommon. At one time a couple lost three grown children within a week. The minister went willingly to this home to help the bereft parents. Upon his return home, he took off his clothes and burned them on the spot. He then took a bath, from head to foot, in hot sudsy water. How glad he was later on that his family did not contact this terrible disease because of his contact with this disease.

Funerals, therefore, were often very sad affairs but, here again, friends and relatives lent a hand. Families would conduct the funerals and because the bodies were not embalmed, the burial would be made as soon after death as possible. The caskets were homemade and would be placed in the back of a spring buggy or farm wagon to be taken to the cemetery. No elaborate funeral hearse or cars!

Mourners were always dressed in black as a sign of their sorrow. Besides a black dress, the women would also wear a black veil. The men would wear a black band around their coat sleeve and, if possible, a mourning hat. These signs of mourning would often be worn for several months.

5

Swiss Volhynian Mennonites

HISTORY

The Swiss Volhynian Mennonites

After two centuries of persecution, many Swiss Anabaptist families finally decided to leave their homeland. In 1671, two groups left by different routes, both finally arriving in Volhynia, Russia. One group left Canton Bern for the Palatinate, Germany. Among these were Krehbiels, Millers, Schrags, Zergers, and others. In the Palatinate, their original Swiss language gradually gave way to a more South German dialect. In 1874, some of these families moved to Galicia, Austria. Others joined the Hutterite *Bruderhof* in Raditchev, Russia, but left again in a few years for Michalin, and in 1818 moved to Eduardsdorf, Volhynia, where some of their group had already settled earlier.

The second group, leaving Canton Bern in 1671, crossed the border into France and settled near Montbeliard. These were Amish families: Goering, Graber, Kaufman, Stucky, Flickinger, and others. In 1791 due to Napoleonic wars, they migrated to Poland and by 1837 also arrived in Volhynia, Russia. After about 75 years in Volhynia, they had grown to four congregations: Sahorets, Waldheim, Horoditch and Kotozuvka, when they migrated to America in 1874. Here they settled around Freeman and Marion in South Dakota, and around Moundridge and Pretty Prairie in Kansas. Other families having joined these groups in time are: Albrecht, Dirks, Muendelheim, Ortman, Preheim, Ries, Schwartz, Sutter, Senner, Unruh, Voran, Voth, Waltner, Wedel, and others. Although some were originally Amish, by the time they came to America, they joined the General Conference Mennonite Church.

As farming was the main occupation, the food was almost entirely produced on the farms. About the only food staples purchased in a store were salt, sugar and flour. Even flour was obtained by taking their wheat to the mill and having it ground, or exchanged for flour. The menus were simple, but nourishing, including breads, soups, meat, potatoes, cheese (especially cottage cheese), poultry, eggs, vegetables and fruit in season. There was a variety of soups of which the Russian Beet Borsht was the traditional one. There were others, too, like sour cream potato soup, beef soup, noodle soup and others.

Every housewife made her own bread, both white and rye. These were large crusty loaves which were baked several times a week, depending on the size of the family. There were also coffee cakes, *Sonntags-Kuchen,* made from sweet dough with cream brushed over the top and then sprinkled with sugar and cinnamon. There were Apple *Pirogi, Kaese-Kuchen* made from cottage cheese used as the filling with a sweet dough crust. Also *Russischen-Kuchen* and, most traditionally, the *Mack-Kuchen* or Poppy Seed Rolls, which were almost always baked for Christmas and Easter and other special occasions. Many years ago the wedding "cake" was *Gorovei,* a very rich type coffee cake. Many people also served this at Christmas and Eastertime.

Maehl Speis or dishes made from flour were often served. Among these were: *Kaese-Knep, Kaese* or *Kraut Pirogi, Balabuski, Nalles-Nicki, Loeffel-Knep,* and others.

SOURCES: Martin H. Schrag, *European History of the Swiss Mennonites from Volhynia,* 1973; *Mennonite Life,* Oct. 1954 and July 1958; *Mennonite Encyclopedia,* Vol. IV, pp. 844-847; Emil J. Waltner, *Banished for Faith,* 1968; Peter P. Wedel, *Swiss Mennonites,* 1929.

MENU

Menu for a Typical Day

Breakfast
    Bacon
    Scrambled eggs
    Fried potatoes
    Oatmeal with sugar, milk, or cream
    Rye bread
    Jam
    Coffee

Dinner
    Chicken noodle soup
    Sauerkraut Berogi
    Boiled potatoes
    Rye bread
    Jam
    Bread pudding
    Coffee

Supper
    Cottage cheese
    Fried potatoes
    Rye bread
    Jam
    Apple sauce
    Milk

BREADS

Light White Bread

1 cake Red Star or   1 tsp. sugar
   Fleishman's yeast

Dissolve in 1 c. lukewarm water. Let set 10 minutes.

Take 3 c. lukewarm water, 6 c. flour, add yeast mixture and beat well. Set in warm place. Let rise for 1 1/2 hours or until bubbles break.

When making up dough take 1 tsp. bread "pep" or "bread step", dissolve in water. Add 2 tbsp. salt, 3 tbsp. sugar, 2 tbsp. melted lard. Work in 7 or 8 c. flour to make a stiff dough. Knead well. Let set in warm place 1/2 hour. Work down. Let set again and work down. Let set 1 hour. Make loaves and place in greased pans. Let rise 1 1/2 hours. Bake in a 375° oven for 1 hour.

Use Stucky's Best Family Flour for best results.

Alta Milling Company, 6 miles south and 4 miles west of Moundridge, Kansas. (Recipe from Alta Milling Co.)

White Bread

2 pkgs. dry yeast   1 c. warm milk
1/2 c. warm water   3/4 c. warm water
1/4 c. sugar   6 to 7 c. white flour
1/4 c. shortening   1 tbsp. salt

Soften yeast in 1/2 c. warm water. In large mixing bowl, blend sugar, shortening, salt, milk, 3/4 c. water and 2 c. flour. Beat with wooden spoon till smooth. Add softened yeast mixture.

Gradually add remaining flour to form stiff dough. Knead on floured surface until smooth and satiny, adding flour as necessary (7 to 10 minutes). Place in greased bowl, cover with towel. Let rise in warm place (85 to 90°) until light and double, about 1 1/2 hours. Punch down dough, cover, let rise 30 minutes more. Place on lightly floured surface, knead for 1 minute to remove air bubbles. Divide into 2 portions, cover, let rest 10 minutes.

Place in well greased 9 by 5 by 3 inch loaf pans, seamside down, cover with towel. Let rise in warm place until tops of loaves are well over pan edges, about 1 hour. (Do not over-rise.) Bake at 375° for 35 to 40 minutes or until brown. Remove from pans immediately, cool on wire racks.

Note: Recipe may be doubled for 4 loaves, using 3 pkgs. yeast.

THE ALTA MILLING CO.

STUCKY BROS., Mgrs.

MOUNDRIDGE. KANSAS

DO YOU KNOW?

That you are always paying more for Flour than you should compared with the wheat price?

There is only one place where you can get flour at the right price. Take your wheat to the Alta Mills and exchange it for flour, at the rate of 7 sacks for 10 bu. of wheat testing 57 pounds or more. This would mean if your wheat is worth 80c per bushel your flour will not cost you over $1.15 for a 48 lb sack of the best flour.

All we ask is that you bring us good sound wheat. We don't want smutty wheat or wheat that heated in the bin.

There is no mill that can make any better flour than this mill is making, and none can make it for as low a price. We exchange any amount from 1 to 50 bushels.

We want all the farmers to bring us Old wheat after harvest up to Nov. 1, this will insure you to get old wheat flour until the new wheat will be alright.

We make OUR BEST WHITE FLOUR — WHOLE WHEAT FLOUR — WHOLE RYE FLOUR — CORN MEAL — CREAM OF WHEAT or GRITZ — BRAN — SHORTS.

Yours truly,

THE ALTA MILLING CO.

Rogge-Brot
Rye Bread

2 c. rye flour	1 pkg. yeast dissolved in
8 c. white flour	1/2 c. warm water
1/4 c. sugar	3 c. lukewarm water
2 to 3 tsp. salt	5 tbsp. shortening

Use about 2 c. flour to start. Mix in sugar, salt and yeast. Add 3 c. luke warm water and beat well. Add shortening, rye flour, gradually adding white flour, kneading it into a medium-stiff dough. Knead until dough is smooth, about 10 minutes. Place in greased bowl, let rise in warm place until double.

Punch down and when double in bulk, punch down again. Turn out on lightly floured board. Divide into 3 or 4 balls and allow to rest about 10 minutes. Shape into loaves. Place in well greased pans, allow to rise until loaves are double in size. Bake at 400° for 15 minutes, reduce heat to 350°, allow to bake about 1 hour longer. Remove immediately from pans, brush with shortening.

Note: 2 c. whole wheat flour (graham) may be used instead of rye flour.

Basic Sweet Dough
Sonntags-Kuchen

1/3 c. warm water	1/2 c. dried skim milk
1 tsp. sugar	1/2 c. oleo or butter
1/4 tsp. ginger	2 tsp. salt
1 pkg. dry yeast	2 eggs, well beaten
1 c. warm water	3 c. flour
8 tbsp. sugar	2 c. flour

Combine first 4 ingredients, let stand in warm place until bubbly. In large bowl, stir together 1 c. water, 8 tbsp. sugar, 2 c. flour, and 1/2 c. dried milk. Add yeast mixture, beat well. Add soft shortening, salt, eggs and 2 c. flour. Stir until dough clears bowl. Spread remainder of flour (1 c.) on board. Turn out dough, allow to rest 10 minutes. Knead about 8 to 10 minutes using only enough flour to make a soft smooth dough. (Just so it can be handled.)

Return to greased bowl, brush with a little butter, cover, allow to rise until double. Punch down, let rise again. Dough must be in warm place (85 to 90°) to rise. Punch down. Turn out on board, divide into 4 balls. Let rest about 10 minutes. Shape into rolls or

coffee cake. Let rise until light. Bake coffee cakes at 375 to 400°
from 15 to 20 minutes, depending on size. Bake *mack-kuchen*
and cinnamon rolls at 350 to 375° from 25 to 30 minutes.

Note: When making coffee cake or rolls, 1/2 to 2/3 c. raisins
may be added to dough before kneading.

Topping for coffee cake: before baking, brush with cream.
Sprinkle with mixture of following:

2/3 c. brown sugar   1 1/2 tsp. cinnamon
1 1/3 c. white sugar

Balabuski

Using your favorite rye or graham bread recipe, shape into small
rolls, the size of a walnut. Place on greased pan about 1 inch apart.
Let rise about 30 minutes. Make dents across top with thumb or
knife. (This is where you break the roll after it is baked.) Brush
with white of an egg beaten with 1 tbsp. water. Let rise until it
doubles in size and bake in a moderately hot oven (375°) until
light brown. Brush with water and finish baking. Remove from
oven and brush each roll with cut side of a clove of garlic. Break
rolls where indented and place in bowl. Have the following sauce
ready:

Heat 1 or two tbsp. fat and slowly add 1 1/2 c. cream. Simmer
a minute or so. Add a little salt. Pour over the crusty rolls. Serve
at once. 1 or 2 tbsp. flour may be added to the fat to thicken the
sauce a little. It should be thin. A crushed clove of garlic or garlic
salt may be added to sauce while it is being heated.

Weddings

In the early days, weddings were celebrated in Church on a
Tuesday or a Thursday, but seldom on a Sunday. The time of day
was at 2:00 in the afternoon or sometimes at 10:00 in the morning.
There were very few or perhaps no decorations, such as flowers
in the church. Two chairs were placed in front of the pulpit, which
were fastened together with a white ribbon tied into a big bow.
The bridal couple walked in together, followed by their attendants.
The bride and groom were seated on the two chairs and the rest
of the party sat on benches just to the back, the girls on the side for
women and the boys on the side for the men. The music consisted of

some songs from the "*Gesangbuch mit Noten*" sung by the congregation. There was a rather long sermon by the regular pastor. If one of the guests happened to be a minister, he was also invited to say a "few words". Then the vows were exchanged, a song sung, and the benediction given and the wedding party filed out followed by the congregation.

The reception was held in the home of the bride's parents. Usually a hearty meal was served; a menu consisting of meat, potatoes, sauerkraut or other cooked vegetables, pickles, white and rye bread, and butter. For dessert there was a mixture of dried fruits, such as apricots, prunes and raisins cooked together and sweetened. Cakes and cookies and at many weddings in the early years "*Gorovei*", which is a very rich bread. Coffee and tea were the beverages. In later years, a large elaborate wedding cake was used to grace the bride's table.

Tables were set up everywhere possible to accommodate the guests. Furniture was moved out of the bedrooms, except one room left intact so that the bed could be used for the wedding gifts.

The relatives helped with the wedding preparations. Silverware and dishes had to be borrowed. The breads, cakes and cookies were baked by various people in their own homes. About two women, who were noted for their culinary talents, were delegated to take over the duties in the kitchen. Young people, who were friends of the bridal pair, were asked to act as waiters and waitresses.

The day after the wedding the nearest relatives came back to help "straighten up" and take home their belongings that had been borrowed. Food being left over resulted in another "celebration of sorts", which was almost as important as the wedding itself. As for the young couple, they spent their honeymoon getting settled in their own home and going back to work, he to work in the field and she to her household tasks.

Gorovei
(Rich Coffee Cake)

2 c. flour

2 cakes yeast dissolved
in lukewarm water

Add enough water to make a thick batter. Let stand about 1 hour or until spongy.

Heat:

1/2 c. lard or shortening
2 c. sweet cream
1 tsp. salt

1/2 c. butter
2 c. sugar

Cool. Add 6 eggs, beaten thoroughly. Add to the first batter. Add enough flour (about 5 or 6 c.) to make a smooth dough, and knead. Let rise, punch down. Let rise again and form into 4 large buns about the size of a soft ball, each in a greased pie pan and let rise until double in size. Bake in a 350° oven for 30 minutes. This makes 4 cakes. Frost with a cream and sugar frosting or powdered sugar frosting. Decorate with corn candy.

This cake was baked and served at weddings or holidays in the Swiss Mennonite communities in the early days.

Poppy Seed

Mack-Kuchen
(Poppy Seed Rolls)

#1   2 c. poppy seed   2 c. sugar
      1/2 c. cream or evaporated   2 tbsp. honey
         milk, approx.   1 tsp. cinnamon

Pour boiling water over poppy seed and drain, using a fine sieve. Grind very fine. Add sugar, honey, cinnamon and enough cream to make a stiff paste. Cool.

Use your favorite sweet roll dough recipe and roll out as for cinnamon rolls, about 1/4 inch thick. Spread a thin layer of the poppy seed mixture and roll up. Place on a greased pan. Let rise until double in bulk. Brush rolls with 1 egg yolk diluted with 2 tsp. water. Bake in moderate oven, 350°, 30-45 minutes. Serve cold.

#2   2 c. poppy seed (whole)   2 tbsp. white syrup
      2 c. sugar   1 egg
      2 tbsp. cornstarch   1/3 - 1/2 c. cream

Grind poppy seed like #1. Mix all ingredients together. Cook until mixture thickens, stirring constantly. Cool.

Knee-Pletz

Use your regular bread dough for this or make these when baking bread.

Pinch off balls of raised bread dough about 3 inches in diameter. Stretch over the hand making it as thin as possible. Fry one at a time in deep fat at 365 to 400° until golden brown.

Drain on paper towels and sprinkle with sugar.

Grumbere-Pfankuche
(German Potato Pancakes)

3 c. raw grated potatoes   pinch of baking powder
2 eggs, beaten   1 3/4 tsp. salt
1/2 c. onion, grated   2 level tbsp. flour

Peel potatoes several hours before using and keep in cold water. Then grate. Add eggs and onion.

Sift: flour, salt and baking powder and add.

Bake like ordinary flat pancakes in a hot greased skillet.

Nalles-Nicki
(Filled Pancakes)

2 eggs   1 1/3 c. milk
1/2 tsp. salt

Flour enough to make a thin batter resembling the consistency of heavy cream (about 1 c.). Mix together. Pour a small amount of batter in a hot greased skillet. Lift slightly so batter runs over the whole skillet. It should be a very thin pancake. Brown slightly. Flip over onto a flat surface. After all have been fried fill with following:

2 c. cottage cheese   1 tbsp. sugar
1 egg   salt and pepper

Mix and spread on pancake. Fold over once and then again forming a triangle. Return to skillet and lightly brown on both sides. Serve with sugar and cream. They may also be filled with cooked, mashed apples to which a little sugar and cream are added.

Apfel-Pirogi (Berogi)

Prepare a basic sweet dough.

Filling:

1 tbsp. flour   1 tsp. cinnamon
2/3 c. sugar   1 large or 2 small eggs

Combine and beat well. Add 3 c. peeled, shredded or sliced apples and 1/2 c. to 2/3 c. cream or rich milk.

Roll out raised sweet roll dough into 12 by 9 by 1/4 inch rectangle. Place filling on center third of dough, making about a 6 inch slash down the center of the outside sections. Fold edges toward center, pulling slashes through each other, to form a steam vent. Pinch remainder of sides and ends together. Place on greased pan. Let rise 30 minutes. Bake at 350° for about 45 minutes. This filling is enough for about 3 rolls. Cooked dried apples or cooked prunes and raisins were also used.

Christmas and Other Holiday Celebrations

Christmas was observed with church on the morning of the 25th and the 26th of December. For the children the important part of the festivities was the Christmas Eve Sunday school program. On the Sunday after Thanksgiving slips of paper were handed out to each child by the Sunday School teachers, telling the songs and Bible verses to be learned for the program. After several rehearsals and much anticipation, the important day finally came. The tree decorated on the 24th, was standing there in all its splendor complete with many lighted candles. Since this was a fire hazard, it took the constant watching of four to six people. The program consisted of the poems, Bible verses, dialogues, and songs which the children had learned, a prayer, a small sermonette by the pastor, the benediction, plus a song by the choir, and also some carols by the congregation. But the highlight of the evening for which each child had been anxiously waiting for weeks, was a mound of brown paper sacks piled up in a corner behind the tree. These contained candy, nuts, an apple and orange, which were distributed to each child by their Sunday school teacher at the end of the program.

In the homes the customs were different with the different families. Some observed Christmas at home with an exchange of gifts right after the Christmas Eve services at church. Others had theirs on the morning of the 25th when they came into a room with a decorated and lighted Christmas tree. Instead of hanging up stockings, the children placed soup bowls on the dining table before retiring, for the "*Christkindchen*" to fill. In the morning they would find nuts and candy and perhaps an orange or apple. Other gifts were placed around the tree. Toys could only be examined and admired briefly, for everyone had to scurry around to get ready to go to church. Guests were often invited to dinner at noon or in the afternoon and asked to stay for supper and the evening. It was family get-together time with much visiting back and forth.

Easter time was another very important church holiday. Much preparation was made. The house had to be thoroughly cleaned. There was the baking of *Mack-Kuchen*, *Sonntags-Kuchen*, cookies and cakes and later pies. In some homes the very rich sweet bread or *Gorovei* was baked. Eggs were also boiled and dyed, usually on Saturday afternoon. They were hidden in nests out of doors for the children to find on Easter morning.

On Good Friday there was always church in the morning at which time Holy Communion and Foot Washing were celebrated. Easter Morning was church and Sunday School. Easter Monday was also observed with a church service in the morning.

Pentecost, seven weeks after Easter, called for a two day holiday. Regular church service and Sunday school on Sunday and another service on Monday.

On Ascension Day, which is on a Thursday about ten days before Pentecost, there was also a church service in the forenoon.

E. Toth

CAKES AND COOKIES

Cream Cake

1 c. sugar	1 1/2 c. flour, sifted with
2 eggs, beaten	2 tsp. baking powder
1 c. heavy cream	1 tsp. vanilla

Cream sugar, add beaten eggs. Sift dry ingredients and add alternately with cream.

Bake at 350° until done.

Sweet Cream Icing

1 c. sugar	1/3 c. cream
1 tsp. vanilla	

Boil sugar and cream to soft ball stage. Remove from heat, add vanilla and beat until it is right consistency to spread.

CHEESE AND MEATS

Stuffed Pork Stomach

Clean the stomach by peeling out the inner lining. After it is clean put into a quart jar and fill with water, add 2 tbsp. salt. Let stand about 2 days in a cold place (or refrigerator). Change the water after the first day.

Stuffing:

6 medium potatoes, peeled and diced	1 medium onion
	1 1/2 tsp. salt
2 c. cubed tenderloin	pepper to taste

Mix ingredients and stuff into stomach, stitch. Cover and bake in moderate oven for 3 hours.

A one dish meal can be made by adding carrots, celery, and peas to the stuffing.

N.B. — This may also be cooked in a pressure cooker at 10 pounds pressure for 1 hour.

Cottage Cheese

E. Foth

Cottage Cheese

One gallon whole raw milk. (Instantly chilled or homogenized milk won't do.) Let stand in a stone crock in a warm place until clabbered. Skim off the cream and pour clabbered milk into a stainless steel or granite kettle. Using low heat, let stand on the fire until the curds separate from the whey and the curds are medium firm. Pour into a small muslin flour or sugar bag and allow to drain for 6 or 8 hours or until cheese is dry.

To serve:
Crumble cheese into a bowl and add enough sweet cream (or half and half) to blend nicely. The mixture should be a medium consistency. Add salt to taste.

This was almost always served with fried potatoes.

DESSERTS

Cottage Cheese Kuchen

3/4 c. sugar	1/4 tsp. salt
1 1/2 c. cottage cheese	2 eggs
(uncreamed)	1/2 c. cream

Mix in order given.

Pour into a 9 inch pie pan lined with bread dough. Sprinkle with cinnamon. Bake at 400° for 10 minutes. Reduce heat to 350° and bake until custard is set or knife inserted will come out clean. (See recipe for bread dough.)

Russische (Russian) Kuchen

3/4 c. sugar	1 c. cream
3 eggs	1 c. milk
1 level tbsp. flour	

Mix together in order given. Pour into a 9 inch pie pan, lined with bread dough. Sprinkle with cinnamon. Bake in a hot oven, 400°, for 10 minutes. Reduce heat to 350° and bake until custard is set or knife inserted will come out clean.
(See recipe for bread dough.)

Dutch Apple Pie

Mix together:

2/3 c. sugar
1 level tbsp. flour
1/8 tsp. salt
1 tsp. cinnamon
1 large or 2 small eggs

1 c. rich milk or
evaporated milk
3 apples (about 2 c.),
finely sliced

Line a 9 inch pie plate with sweet dough. Add the sliced apples. Pour custard over the top of the apples. Bake for 10 or 15 minutes. at 425°. Reduce heat to 350°. Bake for another 30 minutes or until a knife inserted in pie comes out clean.

DUMPLINGS

Kaese-Knepp
(Cottage Cheese Squares)

1 1/2 c. dry cottage cheese
1 tsp. salt
1/3 c. flour

1/4 tsp. soda
1 egg
1/8 tsp. pepper

Mix all ingredients together and pat out on a floured board about 3/4 inch thick. Cut into squares or 2 by 1 inch oblong pieces. Drop into boiling, salted water and boil for 5 to 8 minutes. Carefully lift out of kettle into a colander. Drain and place into serving dish. Season with hot bacon fat or lard in which 1/3 c. small cubes of bread have been browned. The cheese squares can also be baked in a greased pan and baked for 20 minutes at 375°, or another method is to deep fat fry them in a skillet.

In either method, they may be served with the following sauce: Melt 5 tbsp. bacon grease in pan. Stir in 5 tbsp. flour. Gradually add 2 c. liquid, milk and cream mixed, 1/2 tsp. salt and 1/8 tsp. pepper. Bring to a boil and boil 1 minute. Pour over *Knepp*.

Loeffel-Knepp
(Dumplings)

1 c. flour
1 small egg

salt to taste

Mix together and add enough milk to make a dough stiff enough to drop from a spoon. Drop by teaspoonful into rapidly boiling salted water. Cook approximately 15 minutes. Drain. In the meantime cook 1 large potato (which has been cut as for french fries) until tender. Mix with the *knepp*. Brown 1/3 c. small cubes of bread in about 1 1/2 tbsp. of hot bacon fat or lard. Pour over *knepp* and potatoes. Serve hot.

Dampf-Nudeln

Use your favorite bread dough recipe. Let dough rise until double in bulk. Knead down and let rise again. Pinch off little buns about the size of an egg. Place on a greased tin and let rise until double in size.

Put 1 c. water, 1/4 c. shortening, and 1/2 tbsp. salt in a heavy, deep skillet (or Dutch oven) with a tight fitting lid. Bring to a boil and carefully add the buns. Cover and simmer for about 30-40 minutes. Do not uncover while cooking.

Serve with cream.

These may also be served with stewed, dried fruit.

Kaese or Kraut-Pirogi (Berogi)

Make a stiff dough of:

2 c. flour	1/2 tsp. salt
water to make a stiff dough	2 egg whites

Roll dough out thin (not quite as thin as for noodles). Cut into 3 or 4 inch squares. Place a small amount of the following cheese filling on each square:

Filling:

2 c. cottage cheese (dry)	pepper and salt to taste
2 egg yolks	

Moisten 2 edges of squares. Fold over into a triangle and pinch the 2 moistened sides tightly together. Drop into boiling water and boil 7 to 8 minutes. Carefully lift out with slotted spoon and place onto a platter. Heat 2 tbsp. lard in a skillet and brown 1/2 c. of bread cubes until very light brown. Pour over *pirogi* and serve.

For variety (1) fry *pirogi* in fat till lightly brown, (2) use sauerkraut instead of cheese.

Bohnen-Pirogi (Berogi)
(Bean Dumplings)

Cook 2 c. of pinto beans until well done. Mash and add 2/3 c. sugar and 1/2 tsp. salt. Stir well. Set aside.

For the dough: Dissolve 1 cake yeast in 2 c. warm water with 6 tbsp. sugar and 1 tsp. salt. Let rise a little.

Add enough flour to make a sponge and beat well, adding 6 tbsp. melted shortening. Add flour enough to make a medium stiff dough, approximately 6 c. Let rise 20 minutes.

Work down and let rise till double in bulk. Take a small amount of dough, flatten it in the palm of the hand into a circle 3 inches in diameter and 1/4 inch thick. Place 1 tsp. of the prepared bean mixture in the center. Bring edges together to form an envelope and press tightly together. Place on a baking sheet with sealed edges down. Let rise about 20 minutes and bake in a moderate oven. Serve with a dip made of the following sauce:

Simmer 1 1/2 c. cream or rich milk with 1/2 c. sugar for about 10 minutes. Serve hot.

Grumbere Knepp
(Potatoes and Dumplings)

Peel 2 or 3 medium potatoes. Cut into strips as for french fries. Boil in 2 quarts of salted water until nearly tender. Add *knepp* (recipe follows), and boil for about 3 minutes. Drain in colander. Pour into serving bowl. Add cream dressing and serve hot.

Knepp
(Dumplings)

1 1/2 c. flour	1 tsp. salt
1 egg	

Mix and add enough extra flour for a stiff dough. Knead until smooth. Roll out as for pie dough. Cut into strips 1 1/2 inches wide. Stack 2 strips on each other, dusting enough flour on the dough to keep from sticking together. Cut crosswise into 1/4 inch strips. Repeat until all the dough is cut up. Add the *knepp* to the boiling potatoes. Proceed as indicated above.

Dressing

3 tbsp. lard or margarine   3/4 c. sweet cream or
                                half and half

Bring to a full boil and pour over the potatoes and dumplings in the serving bowl.

PRESERVING

Drying Beans
(Snap Beans)

Dried green beans were a specialty for the Swiss immigrants at Christmas time and Easter.

TO DRY: Pick the green beans when they are not fully mature. String, wash, and drain on a towel. Spread out on paper. Place in a sunny, open area or on a screened porch, until thoroughly dry. Put into muslin flour or sugar sacks and store in a dry place.

TO USE: Measure out about 2 c. of the dried beans. Wash in several waters. Soak overnight. Drain. Add fresh water and boil for about 30 minutes. Drain again. Add fresh water again and boil. When beans have cooked another 20 minutes or so add a ham hock and salt, if needed, and cook for another 1 1/2 hours or until thoroughly done.

Saure Gurken
(open jar dill pickles)

Pack into a 3 gallon stone jar, thoroughly washed cucumbers 3 to 6 inches in length. Add 1 or 2 cloves of garlic cut up. Cover with a layer of dill, heads and stalks.

Boil together:

13 c. water   1/2 c. pickling salt
1/2 c. vinegar

Pour hot over the cucumbers.

Cover with a large plate and place a weight on top of it (a jar filled with water will do), so the pickles are covered at all times with the brine. Tie a clean tea towel or cloth over the top of the jar.

The pickles will be ready to eat when the green color of the cucumbers turns slightly yellowish.

E. Foth

Pickled Pig's Feet

2 fresh pig's feet	1 clove garlic
1 fresh ham hock	few whole allspice
2 tsp. salt	1/2 c. vinegar

Cut away any surplus fat from feet and hock. Cover with water, adding salt. Cook until meat falls from bones. Remove meat and cool.

Add garlic, vinegar, and allspice to broth and cook 15 minutes longer. There should be about 3 c. broth. Add water to make this amount if necessary.

Remove meat and skins from bones and cut into smaller pieces. Place into a square or oblong glass dish. Pour the strained broth over the meat and cover. Cool overnight. Remove excess fat from the top. Cut into serving pieces about 1/2 inch thick.

Good served with fried potatoes.

SOUPS

Navy Bean Soup

Soak 2 c. Northern or navy beans overnight. In morning put into a large kettle with 2 c. diced ham, a ham bone, 2 whole cloves, 1 1/2 tsp. salt, 1 large slice onion and cover whole with 2 quarts water.

Cover kettle and simmer for about 2 hours.

Add 1 medium potato, diced, and cook for 1 more hour.

If desired the onion may be sauted in a scant tbsp. bacon fat and added just before soup is removed from stove. Then the ham and ham bone are omitted.

Borscht

2 c. navy beans	3 small beets, diced
piece of ham hock or	3 medium potatoes, diced
fresh pork hock	water to cover well
1 tsp. salt	1 c. sour cream
4 whole cloves	1 small onion

Put beans, ham, onion, and cloves into a kettle. Cover with water and boil. Add water as needed to keep level up. When beans are partly done, approximately after 2 hours, add the finely cut beets and cook until vegetables are done.

Add the cut up potatoes and cook. 1/4 tsp. dill seed may be added here.

Lastly add 1 c. sour cream slowly. Heat only to the boiling point. Serve hot.

If sweet cream is used, add a little vinegar to give it a sour taste.

Sour Cream Potato Soup

3 or 4 medium potatoes	1 1/2 tsp. salt (or to taste)
3/4 tbsp. fat (bacon or lard)	1/4 tsp. pepper
1 small onion	1/2 c. sour cream
6 c. water	1 scant tbsp. flour
2 whole cloves	

Melt fat in a kettle. Add finely cut onion and saute 'till very lightly browned. Add potatoes (which have been cut as for french fries), cloves, salt, and water. Cover and cook until potatoes are done. Take from heat. Blend sour cream with flour until smooth. Carefully combine with soup stirring well. Return to fire and leave only long enough to heat thoroughly. Do not boil. Add pepper and serve.

VEGETABLES

Gedaemftes Kraut
(Sweet Sour Cabbage)

8 c. shredded cabbage	1 large onion, chopped
1/3 c. sugar	1 to 2 tsp. salt
1/3 c. water	3 tbsp. shortening
1/3 c. vinegar	

Saute onion in the shortening until slightly golden. Add sugar, vinegar, salt, and water. Blend well. Slowly add cabbage. Cover and cook over medium heat until cabbage is tender, about 20-25 minutes.

New Potatoes With Green Beans

Wash and scrape about 1 1/2 to 2 pounds new potatoes. In a kettle melt 1 tbsp. lard or bacon fat. Add potatoes. Let them brown slightly. Add 2 or 3 c. fresh green beans. Salt to taste. Add enough water to prevent sticking, about 3/4 c. Cover tightly and cook until potatoes and beans are tender.

Gummere Salat
(Cucumber Salad)

3 or 4 slicing cucumbers
1 c. sour cream
1 medium onion, sliced

1 tbsp. vinegar
salt and pepper to taste

Peel and slice cucumbers very thin. Slice onion. Sprinkle with salt and set aside while preparing cream dressing. Drain cucumber mixture when ready to be served.

Cream Dressing: Beat the cream, vinegar, and seasoning. Pour over the drained cucumbers and onions.

E. Foth

6

The Hutterites

HISTORY

The Hutterites

The Hutterites originated in Moravia in 1528. As an offshoot of the Swiss Brethren, they are one of the many Anabaptist groups that arose directly out of the Protestant reformation struggles of 16th century Europe.

The founders of the Hutterian Brotherhood subscribed to the Anabaptist beliefs of adult baptism and separation of church and state. They were strongly opposed to war. They interpreted the New Testament literally, insisting on complete sharing of worldly possessions. The Hutterites, as well as other Anabaptist groups, were often the object of severe persecution.

In 1533, Jacob Hutter came up from Tyrol, visited the colony, and joined it. He was a hatmaker by trade; therefore the name Hutterite, meaning "hatmaker". Through the efforts of Hutter and his assistants, a well-defined communal pattern was established, which has continued to the present. Hutter was burned at the stake in 1536 for his convictions.

Almost 100 years were spent in Moravia where the nobles considered the Hutterites as good tenants and protected them from attacks by the Catholic Church and the Emperor as long as possible. However, the power of the nobles was broken in 1620, and the Hutterites were forced to flee Moravia. For more than 150 years, they wandered through Hungary and neighboring countries. Although often close to extinction, a small group always managed to survive and carry on the faith.

Finally, upon the invitation of Catherine the Great, the surviving Hutterites moved to Russia in 1770 to settle the Ukraine frontier. There they were given refuge and allowed to practice pacifism. An edict nullifying their grant of exemption from military service was issued in 1871. After an appeal to the crown failed, their non-resistance policy demanded they emigrate.

A delegation was sent to America by the Mennonites, and thus the Hutterites decided to send two delegates along. They were Lorenz and Paul Tschetter. When they returned to Russia, they told of favorable conditions here, and it was decided to sell out and move to America. Upon arriving in Dakota, the Hutterites had a good chance to decide on private farms or communal living. Therefore, those favoring colony life joined the colony, and those prefering private farming settled on individual farms. From 1874 to 1879, approximately 100 families of Hutterites arrived from Russia. Many of those settled near Freeman, South Dakota, affiliated with the General Conference Mennonite Church.

It took years for those on the farms to separate from some of the colony customs. They had the colony style of dress at first, but later they changed. Cooking was on the same order, and they talk the same dialect to this day. It took many years for some of the church customs to change.

Hutterite Colony Life

As a child, I had the opportunity to visit the Tschetter Colony, which was about 12 miles west of my home at Freeman, South Dakota, with my grandparents on Sunday afternoons. We would leave after dinner in order to spend the rest of the day with my grandpa and grandma's relatives in the colony.

This colony is one of the largest in the country with about 25 families and about 175 people. The colony owns approximately 3500 acres of land. They usually keep about 150 stock cows, 60-70 dairy cows, 1,000 hogs, and, sometimes, sheep. They also have chickens, turkeys, geese, and ducks. They also make and sell brooms. They also sell honey and garden goods for extra income.

The Hutterites are easily told apart from their neighbors by their clothing and life style. All married men wear full beards and black clothes. The women wear floor-length dresses, usually dark colored, and dark polk-dotted headscarves with bright patterned half aprons. They make almost all of their own clothing and shoes. Women do not cut their hair but comb it Hutterite style (parted in the middle, braided, and pulled to the back in a bun).

German is the native tongue and is used by all. They do use English in school because of state ruling, of course. All children go to school until the eighth grade. A few go on in order to become schoolteachers for their own schools. Some take high school through correspondence courses.

Each family has his own home, which consists of about three or four rooms. Members of the colony have a common kitchen, dining hall, and laundry. A few dishes and minor utensils are kept in individual homes in order to serve the sick members of the family or special guests.

All persons must eat in the colony dining halls. There are usually two—one for the children, five to fifteen years, and the other for adults. Men and women sit on opposite sides of the room. They do not pass the food. Instead it is set at each end of a table set for eight so that everyone is close enough to reach the food. A short prayer in German precedes the meal; prayer also is given after the meal is finished and before all leave.

The younger children (two to five years) go to the kindergarten building from 8 a.m. to 4 p.m. They eat breakfast, dinner, and supper there under the supervision of several mothers and older girls. From age six to fifteen years, all children attend the German school held daily before the public school begins and after the public school is dismissed.

The daily menu is planned by the "Boss's" wife who is usually the head cook. Women take turns weekly in making meals. That way every woman shares in all the different jobs—cooking, baking, preparing the food, and cleaning. The head cook, who does not rotate, arranges the details of the women's work. Meals are very large. Most of the dishes are German and come from the old country.

They attend the church daily. About 6 p.m., men don their black jackets, and everyone goes to the school building for the service. Men sit on one side and women on the other. They are seated by age with children in the front and older ones in the back. There is a song, sermon, and a prayer (members kneel). The sermons, which are read, have been used for generations. They are copied by hand from traditional handwritten books by the minister. No musical instruments are used. The singing is done by the preacher chanting a line at a time and then sung by the congregation. After church, the oldest men file out first followed by the women.

The leaders of the colony make up the Board of Elders, which make all basic decisions. Usually this board consists of seven members which are elected by voting members (baptized and married male members of the congregation). The minister is the head of the colony. He is chosen by lot on a trial period and is then ordained for life if he does a satisfactory job. He is responsible for the religious services, which are held every weekday evening and twice on Sunday. He has an assistant, or second minister, who usually teaches in the German school. The other members of the board are the steward or householder, farm manager or field boss. The householder is the business manager. Therefore he takes care of all monies, sale and purchase of goods, etc. The field boss takes care of all the work details. Under him is the cattle man, chicken man, hog man, shoemaker, blacksmith, cabinetmaker, and head cook. Important jobs in a colony are often taken care of by both husband and wife. For instance the preacher's wife, or sometimes the manager's wife, is usually the head cook. She also is the midwife. The German teacher and his wife both supervise the children during mealtime. The dairyman's wife tends the milk house; while he supervises the milking. The manager's wife often is the seamstress and purchaser of bolts of yard goods for the colony.

There are few jobs which are not shared by all members. Every boy or girl works not only in a group but also as an apprentice. At fifteen years, every person is given a work assignment by the colony. Young men do field work, bulldozing, etc. A married man is often the head of a department of work such as field boss, pig man, welder, carpenter, German teacher, or gardener. They do use modern equipment such as tractors, trucks, combines, bulldozers, etc., in order to do a more efficient job of farming. Almost every tool or implement that is needed but can't be bought is homemade from scrap iron. This includes even machine operated noodle cutters for the dining hall to supply the many noodles for the favorite Sunday dinner, "Noodle Soup", that is common to all Hutters.

There are very few luxuries. There is one laundry and one bathhouse. Since cars are used mostly for pleasure, they are forbidden. There are no radios, TV's, magazines, books, cameras, etc. If they would allow these things, influence and temptation from the outside world would be too great.

Families sleep in household units, but they don't eat or work as family units. Families are large. When a boy is ready to think of marriage, he can either find a bride in his own colony (no first cousin marriages are allowed) or in another colony. He may choose his own mate, but he must have the approval of both parents and the minister. If he has the approval of the girl, both sets of parents, and the minister, then a meeting of the congregation is called, and final approval is usually granted. Only baptized members marry. No dating is allowed. Weddings are relatively simple. The ceremony is performed at the end of the worship service while the couple sit in their usual places. After the sermon, they come forward to the preacher who performs the usual question and answer ceremony. The wedding dinner is served in the dining hall. After that, the young people gather at one of the homes and have their "sings". After the evening meal, the couple is shown their apartment. Here they receive small gifts from friends who get a special allowance for this purpose.

The bride gets from the colony organization a large chest, a sewing machine, bedding, and an allowance of goose feathers. The groom gets a table, chairs, bed, and other limited furniture.

In the colonies, everyone is well taken care of. The old are given special care. Respect for the elderly is a "must". They make every effort to get good medical care. There are no rules against surgery and modern health measures.

Funeral services are much like other Protestant funerals. The dead are not embalmed. The wooden coffins are homemade. Very small tombstones mark the graves.

Colony people are very content. There is a feeling of peace and security in the colony. The Hutterites are always willing to show visitors their large colony and will answer any questions. They allow pictures to be taken of the buildings, etc. but not of themselves. The official motto of the colonies is to "Provide from the cradle to the grave".

The family names and originating country of the first colonies members are now found among all Hutterites in America, living either in the colonies or on private farms: Decker—Prussia, Glanzer—Austria, Gross—Germany, Hofer—Austria, Kleinsasser —Switzerland, Knels—Holland, Mendel—Bohemia, Waldner—Coronthia, Walter—Switzerland, Wipf—Switzerland, Wollman—Austria, Wurz—Bohemia.

Background material: *Hutterite Life*, John A. Hostetler, Herald Press, and an article written by Tarrel Miller entitled "The Hutterites and Colony Life" published in the *Freeman Courier*.

MENU

Menu for Probably a Winter Day

Breakfast
  Homemade Bacon *(speck)*, either cold or fried
  Cooked Oatmeal *(Hoaber Gritz)*
  Rye Bread
  Coffee

Dinner
  Dampfleisch (Stewing Beef)
  Sauerkraut
  Fried Potatoes (these were halved potatoes and not sliced
    as usual)
  Rye Bread
  Plain White Cake for dessert

Supper
  Smoked Sausage, fried
  Fried Potatoes (perhaps sliced)
  Dill Pickles or Pickled Beets
  Rye Bread with Plum Jelly
  Fruit for sauce

BREADS

Stritzel

Filling mixture:
Mix:

1 c. sour cream	1 tsp. soda
1 egg, beaten	2 tbsp. tart jam
1/2 c. sugar	1 1/4 c. flour
1/3 c. chopped nuts	1/4 tsp. salt

Bottom: Take a regular sweet bun dough and roll out 1/4 inch thick. Spread the filling mixture evenly on dough with a knife. Roll up gently like for a jelly roll and seal with toothpicks.

Place on a greased cookie sheet. Let rise about 45 minutes. Bake in 350° oven, about 1 hour. Do not overbrown.

Dochelen

Mix:

2 eggs, beaten	6 crackers, crushed or
salt	dried bread crumbs
2 tbsp. flour	1 c. milk or more
1 tbsp. shortening	

Pour on greased frying pan and fry as pancakes. Were often served with watermelon.

Everlasting Yeast

Boil 4 or 5 potatoes. Then mash the potatoes and put them in a kettle with 2 quarts of warm water (some potato water). Add: 1 cake yeast and 1 c. sugar. Let it stand overnight in a warm place. In the morning take 1 quart out and use it for bread. Set the quart that is left over in the refrigerator until the next baking. Then again boil potatoes and add them to a quart of water and a cup of sugar. Put the fresh mixture in with the leftover mixture. Always put in as much as you take out. If you take good care of it, it will last for weeks. Keep in the refrigerator.

Ringwurm

Wenn du a ringwurm host tua tabak brea draf.
(If you have a ringworm put on tobacco juice.)

Rosinen Hankelich
(Raisin Coffeecake)

Cream:
>   1/2 c. shortening   1 1/2 c. sugar

Add:
>   1/2 c. tart preserves or   1/2 c. sour milk
>   1 c. ground poppyseed   or buttermilk
>   1/2 tsp. salt   1 1/2 c. raisins
>   1 tbsp. cocoa   (plumped in hot water)
>   1 tsp. soda, dissolved   2 c. flour, approx.,
>   in the sour milk   enough to make a
>   rather thick batter

Line a well-greased pan with a thin layer of bun dough, bringing it up well on the sides of the pan. Let rise until light.

Spread the above cake batter over the top of the dough.

Sprinkle a mixture of sugar and cinnamon or nutmeg over the top.

Bake in slow oven for about 30 minutes.

Hankelich
Coffee Cake

Line a greased cake pan with a bun dough and bring up on the sides. Let rise. When light add the filling.

Filling:
>   2 c. tart preserves   1/2 c. cream
>   1/2 c. sugar   1 c. raisins
>   4 tbsp. flour

Spread crumb mixture over top of this.
>   1 c. flour   1/3 c. shortening
>   1 tsp. salt   1/2 c. sugar

Sprinkle with cinnamon or nutmeg. Let rise a little.

Bake in moderately slow oven for about 30 minutes.

Shuten Hankelich

Take bun dough and spread about 1/4 inch thick on greased cookie sheet. Mix 2 c. dry cottage cheese with an egg, a little cream, syrup to sweeten and pour over dough. Let rise 20 minutes. Bake at 350° until brown, about 30 minutes.

Buns

1 package yeast	4 tbsp. sugar
1/2 c. warm water	1 tsp. salt
1 c. scalded milk, cooled	1 egg, beaten
2 tbsp. butter, melted	3 1/2 c. flour, approx., to make soft dough

Dissolve yeast in warm water.

Add to milk, butter, sugar, salt and egg.

Gradually beat in enough flour to make a soft dough, approx. 3 1/2 c.

Let rise until light. Knead down. Let rise again until double. Shape into buns. Put on greased pan, and let rise until double. Bake at 350° for 15-20 minutes.

Schnits-Krupfen

Use your favorite bun recipe and roll circles of dough into 3 inch diameter size and about 1/4 inch thick. On each circle place a heaping tbsp. of the following dried fruit filling. Fold dough over filling to form a semicircle and pinch dough to enclose filling. Prick each *krupf* with a fork at several places. Let rise until doubled in size at room temperature or between 30-45 minutes. Bake at 350° for 20-25 minutes or until nicely brown. (When placing *krupf* on cookie sheet, set each one on the pinched side.)

Filling:

2 c. dried fruit	1 c. prunes pitted
1/4 c. raisins	

Cover with water in a saucepan and cook until fruit is real soft. Mash.

Add:

2 tbsp. cream	2 eggs
1 c. sugar	2 tbsp. flour
2 c. fine bread crumbs	

Mix well and add to fruit mixture. Cool. These freeze well. Makes about 30.

Roll-Kuchen

Dissolve 1 cake yeast in 1/4 c. warm water.

Beat:

3/4 c. sweet cream	1/4 c. milk
3 tbsp. sugar	1 egg
1/2 tsp. salt	

Add yeast to the creamed mixture. Add 1/2 c. raisins and enough flour to make a soft dough. Let rise. When light, roll out and cut into oblong strips.

Fry in hot lard.

A geschenkten Gaul schaut mer nit in maul.
You don't look into the mouth of a gift horse.

Alla Hankelich
Egg Custard Coffee Cake

Line a 9 inch by 13 inch cake pan with your regular bun dough and
bring up on the sides of the pan. Let rise well.
Make a custard of:

3 eggs, beaten	1 c. cream
1/4 c. flour	1/3 c. sugar
vanilla or almond	
flavoring	

Pour into dough crust. Sprinkle with cinnamon or fine crumbs.
Bake in 375° oven about 30 minutes or until done.

Variety: Fresh fruit cut into pieces, such as apricots, peaches
etc. may be added to the custard mixture. Sugar fruit well before
adding.

E. Foth.

Kuchen
(Old-Fashioned Bismarcks)

Dissolve 1 cake yeast in 1/2 c. lukewarm water to which 2 tsp. sugar has been added.

When spongy add to:

1/2 c. sugar	2 c. lukewarm milk
few tbsp. cream	5 1/2 c. flour, approx.,
1/2 c. raisins	enough for soft dough

Mix well and let rise until double in bulk. Roll out quite thin and cut into oblong pieces. Let rise again.

Deep fry in hot fat.

DESSERTS

Crackling Cookies

1 1/2 c. brown sugar	1/2 tsp. nutmeg
1 1/2 c. crushed cracklings	1 c. raisins
3 eggs, beaten	1 c. nuts
3/4 tsp. soda	dash of salt
1/2 tsp. cinnamon	1 tsp. vanilla

Combine all ingredients and add enough flour to make the dough so it may be rolled into small balls. Flatten the balls with a fork and bake in a 400° oven for 10-15 minutes.

Apfelkuchen

Sift:

1 c. flour	1 tbsp. sugar
1/8 tsp. salt	1 tsp. baking powder

Add:

1 egg, beaten	1/2 c. cream

Mix and roll out fairly thin to fit pan.

Peel and slice 2 apples very thin. Arrange slices on dough.

Sprinkle with 2 tbsp. sugar and a little cinnamon. Bake 20-25 minutes at 375°.

Halves of blue plums may be substituted for the apple slices. Increase sugar, using about 1/4 c.

Kroffeln
(Fruit Pockets)

Cook till soft in enough water to cover well:
1/2 lb. dried apricots	1/2 c. prunes
1/2 lb. dried peaches	1/2 c. raisins

Drain and remove prune pits and add:
1/2 c. sugar	3 eggs
1/2 c. cream	1/2 c. cracker crumbs

Mix well and cool. Roll out a basic sweet dough and cut into individual 3-4 inch circles. Put filling on and fold over and pinch ends shut. Place on greased cookie sheet and let rise until double, about 1 1/2 hours. Bake 350° for 25-30 minutes.

Wenn du Kupfweh host leag Katufla-schlizen drauf.
(For severe headache put wet potato slices on the forehead.)

Wenn du in a Nolgel trates tua den Fuss in haas wasser.
(If you step onto a nail, soak your foot in hot water.)

Rhubarb Mus

4 c. diced rhubarb	1 c. raisins, if desired
4 c. water	

Cook until rhubarb is tender. Add a thickening made of:
1 c. sugar	1 c. cream
2 tbsp. flour	

Cook until thick. Serve warm or cold.

Cherry Mus

Cook: 1 quart sour cherries in 1 quart water.
Add paste made of:
2/3 c. sugar	5 tbsp. flour
1 c. sweet cream	

Cook until thick.
  2 c. of bing cherries, canned, may be added for variety.

Gooseberry Mus

Bring 1 quart water and 1 c. sugar to a boil.
Add:

1/2 c. raisins   2 c. gooseberries

Cook to soften.
Make a thickening of:

1/2 c. sweet cream   1 heaping tbsp. flour

Gradually stir into the boiling soup and cook a few minutes.
Serve either hot or cold.

Poppy Seed Pie

Mix well:

1 1/2 c. milk   1/2 c. cream
1/2 c. poppy seed   2 eggs, beaten
3/4 c. sugar   2 tbsp. cornstarch

Cook until thick, stirring constantly.
Put into baked pie shell and let cool.

Swiss Cheese

DUMPLINGS

Cottage Cheese Dumplings

Mix well:

2 c. dry cottage cheese

1/2 c. onions, fried in a
little lard

3/4 c. bread crumbs

3 eggs

salt

Dough:

2 c. flour

1/2 c. milk

2 eggs

1 tsp. salt

Mix well and knead till smooth.

Roll out with rolling pin, 1/8 inch thick, then cut out with large round cookie cutter. Put a rounding tbsp. cottage cheese mixture in each, fold in half and pinch together. Boil in salted water for about 15 minutes. Fry light brown on both sides and serve with melted butter or sour cream. They freeze well.

Multochen

Filling: Crumble fine 8-10 sweet rolls (bread crumbs may be used).

Add and mix well:

1 tsp. salt

2 eggs

enough cream to
dampen (not wet)

Mince and fry until lightly browned 2 medium sized onions in 5 spoons of lard. Add and stir well: 5 eggs. Combine the two mixtures.

Dough: Make a dough of 3/4 c. water, pinch of salt, and enough flour to make a soft dough. Roll out quite thin, in oblong shape (roll dough into long narrow roll and then roll with rolling pin). Spread filling. Roll up as for jelly roll. Close ends. Cut crosswise into 1-1 1/2 inch pieces. Close up both ends of each piece. When all are made, put into boiling water and cook from 5-10 minutes. Dip out of water and serve. Leftovers may be fried for later meal or you may lightly brown in fat and serve. May also be served with a cream gravy.

Wootie

When kneading down bread dough, take out as much as you want and make large buns. Let rise.

When light, drop into boiling water and boil 15-20 minutes without covering.

Serve with gravy: 1 c. milk, 1 tbsp. flour, sugar to taste (3 tbsp.) Add a little milk to the flour and sugar, enough to make a paste. Stir into hot milk, and bring to a boil. Serve hot.

Der Hoerer on her Wand hat uft sei agana Schand.
The one who is an eavesdropper often gets to hear his own shame.

Potato Dumplings
Kattufal-Knadel

Mix and shape into balls:

2 c. grated potatoes, pressed
1 c. flour
1 egg

1/4 tsp. soda dissolved in
2 tbsp. heavy cream
salt to taste

Drop into salted boiling water and boil 15 minutes.
Serve with white sauce.
A favorite Hutterish dish.

Knadel

1 large c. warm water
pinch of salt

flour to make stiff dough
and yet sticky

Dip knife in boiling, salted water and cut off small pieces and drop into water. Cook about 10-15 minutes. Drain and serve with cream which has been heated.

Noodles

3 whole eggs   3 egg yolks

Beat eggs and egg yolks together and add about 2 3/4 c. flour or as much as can be worked into the eggs to make a stiff dough. Knead well and roll very thin on lightly floured board. Dry partially. Roll up and cut in fine strips with knife or noodle cutter. Spread out loosely and dry thoroughly. Note: They will mold when stored if not thoroughly dried.

MEATS

Gripen Flake
"Crackling Cake"

Mix:

1 c. milk   2 eggs, beaten
1 tsp. salt   1 1/2 c. ground gripen
                                   (cracklings)

Sift and add:

2 to 3 tsp. baking powder   2 1/2 to 3 c. flour

Mix well.

Dough should be so soft you can stir by hand. Put in greased 9 by 13 inch pan and bake at 375° till done.

This was usually served Saturday afternoon for lunch. The "cake" was topped with jam or jelly and cut into squares to serve.

Dampffleisch
Stewed Beef

Bring to boil and simmer slowly:

1/2 c. lard   3 lbs. stewing beef, cut
1 c. water   into serving pieces
1 onion cut into quarters   salt and pepper to taste

Simmer slowly for 2 hours or until tender. Serves about 6.

Fleisch-Kuechle
Meat Pockets

Mix 3 c. flour and 1/2 tsp. salt with equal amounts of water and cream to make a soft dough.

Roll out. Cut into 3-4 inch circles.

Spread 1/2 of circle with meat mixture. Fold over and press edges together. Fry in deep hot fat.

Filling:
Melt 2 tbsp. drippings in frying pan.
Add:

1 c. hamburger	1 small onion, minced
1 c. pork sausage	salt and pepper to taste

Brown. Add 1/2 c. water and simmer 10 minutes. Spread on circles of above dough.

Gritz-Wurst
Buckwheat Sausage

Clean the head of a pig, split in half and cover with water. Cook until the meat is done and falls from the bones. Remove the meat and grind it. (Cut excess fat off.) Let cool.

Pour stock in which meat was cooked, over 6-8 c. of *gritz*. Mix well and bake in oven till soft, about 45 minutes. Cool.

Mix the *gritz* with the ground meat, adding salt and pepper to taste. Put in sausage maker and form into rings. Put into a moderate hot oven and bake till brown . . . Best if cut into 3 inch serving pieces while baking so it does not crack open.

MISCELLANEOUS

Fried Sauerkraut

1 quart sauerkraut	2 tbsp. lard
1 c. water	2 tbsp. flour
1/4 c. sugar	

If kraut is very sour rinse it with hot water and drain well. Put into saucepan and add the water and sugar. Boil until soft.

Melt the lard in a pan. Add the flour and brown.

Add to the kraut and mix well.

Serve hot.

Dicke Gritz

To 1 c. *gritz* add:
1/4 tsp. salt   2 1/4 c. boiling water

Mix well.
Put into a greased pan and bake in 350° oven, 40 minutes.
Serve with sweet white sauce.

PRESERVING

Canned Sausage

Place prefried red or country sausage pieces (about 3 inch serving pieces) into jar.
    Heat:

1 gallon water	pepper
1 c. brown sugar	little salt peter
1 tsp. salt	

Pour over sausages, enough to fill jar. Seal. Process 1 hour.

Sauerkraut

Shred cabbage fine, pack loosely into glass jars. Add 1 tsp. salt to a quart jar. Fill jar with boiling water. Seal tightly. Place jars in a pan while fermenting since some juice will run out.

Making Sauerkraut

Dill Pickles

Combine:

17 c. water	1 c. coarse salt
2/3 c. vinegar	

Put in kettle and bring to boil.

Pack 4-6 inch cukes in jar with dill, cover with hot brine, garlic, and 1 small red pepper. Seal.

Set in boiling water 20 minutes until they turn color.

Was Haenschen nit glernt hat,
das lernt dar Hans auch nit.

If young Johnny didn't learn,
older John won't learn either.

Man is olt wie kuha und lernt much allba der zura.
One is as old as a cow but is still learning.

SOUPS

Nukla Supp
Dumpling Soup

Mix: 4 eggs and 4 tbsp. butter, melted.

Add: Salt and pepper to taste and 1 c. flour or enough to make sticky dough.

Spoon into chicken or beef broth and cook 15-20 minutes.

Gashla Supp
(Riblet Soup)

Beat well 1 egg and add 3/4 c. flour.

Knead and rub with grater immediately. Drop into chicken broth and cook until done. These rivels may be dropped into milk and cooked.

Green Bean Soup

Cook either beef or chicken for soup. Take broth and add:

2 c. canned beans and some juice	3 to 4 medium potatoes diced
salt and pepper	butter, size of an egg

When vegetables are tender, add 1/2 c. cream in which 1 tbsp. flour has been dissolved to thicken soup.

When meat wasn't available, more potatoes were added.

Corn Soup

Cook 3 potatoes in water. Mash them a little. Let water on and add 1 quart corn, a piece of butter, season with salt, pepper, 2 slices onions. Stir 2 tbsp. flour with a little milk and add to water. Boil till thickened. Add milk as much as you need for your family.

Noodle Soup

1 cut up stewing hen. Simmer slowly about 3 hours or until tender in 3 quarts water to which 2 tsp. salt has been added. Add a few whole peppercorns and a few whole allspice about 6-10 each. Strain broth and bring to boil again. Add noodles (about 1 pound, or as made from the noodle recipe) and cook about 5 minutes or until noodles are tender. Serve. Chicken may be served with the soup if desired. Other traditions leave the chicken pieces in the soup and skim off the fat.

Die Jungen sein sut klug sey hoeren das Grass wachsen.
The young are so wise, they can hear the grass grow.

7

The Netherlands Mennonites

HISTORY

Mennonites in the Netherlands

Few Mennonite tourists from America visiting the Netherlands fail to go to Witmarsum to see the monument erected to Menno Simons, or go a little farther to the little hidden church in Pingjum, which Menno had served at one time. Although he was not the first Anabaptist in the Netherlands, it was his name that was given to his followers . . . the Mennonites.

Menno was a Frisian from the northern part of the Netherlands, born in Witmarsum. He studied for the priesthood and was ordained in 1524. He soon became concerned about some of the church doctrines and began to study the Scriptures more diligently. His new perspective made him leave his position and also make a public committment to Christ in 1536. After this he went into hiding with the help of some Anabaptist friends. He finally was baptized and ordained to serve this new group.

Persecution followed Menno and other Anabaptists and many became martyrs. Menno's wife, son, and daughter died due to hardships suffered during this period. Menno traveled throughout the northern country, establishing church groups, writing devotional books and later settled near Hamburg where he established his own printing press. Here the *Menno Linde* is still a landmark of this period of his life. Mennonites found refuge in many areas especially in northern Europe. Such settlements as Koenigsberg, Danzig, Elbing, Marienburg became familiar names in Mennonite history. However, not all Mennonites left Holland.

Those that remained suffered great persecution for some time.

The Dutch Mennonites took active part in whale and herring fishing trade, especially with Greenland, and so soon made a place for themselves in the life of the country. They became ship builders and built textile mills. In the 17th century a large percentage of the doctors in the Netherlands were Mennonites. Many were engineers and helped with the draining of the swamps. Others became farmers and leaders in the food industry. Writers, poets, and artists were also found among them. The mid-nineteenth century saw a renewed growth in the church and the *Algemeene Doopsgezinde Societeit* was formed as a general conference of all congregations. Foreign missions were started and missionaries were sent out to Java, Sumatra, and other places. They worked for improvements of the school systems, welfare institutions, and became interested in caring for the aged and the sick. Active youth groups founded Youth Centers which gave a peace witness. Services became avenues for youth activities.

The 20th century saw the Dutch Mennonite or *Doopsgezinde* Church, develop as the largest organization outside of North America. The peace principle gained strength and conscientious objectors established a camp on the Island of Texel. Youth have regular conferences and Sunday School attendance has greatly increased.

The women have not been left behind, they also have well organized groups. They have been very active in the *Algemeene Doopsgezinde Societeit* and Dutch women were the first to be ordained as ministers or pastors in the church.

Although the Dutch Mennonites are actually not part of the group celebrating this centennial, they have been included in the *Cookbook*. They have made many contributions to the world in the field of art, pottery, farming, etc.

The Low German Mennonites came originally from the Netherlands. That includes most of the Mennonites of Kansas and Manitoba and the states between. (See the write-up in this book entitled, "From Dutch to German".)

Sinterklaas and Christmas in Holland

The Feast of *Sinterklaas* has been celebrated for centuries in Holland. This is the day in which St. Nicholas, the patron saint of merchants and sailors, is honored. The children observe the coming of St. Nicholas and *Piet* into Holland by watching a grand parade sponsored by the local business people and other prominent citizens. During the night *Piet* distributes the gifts and the candy. In exchange he receives some hay or a carrot for his horses, which the children have put into their shoes placed before the fireplace.

In the morning the gifts and sweets, often hidden in many different places, and accompanied by poems and jingles, are found. The sweets consist of candies made exquisitely of chocolate and marzipan, gingerbread doll cookies; and for each child at least one candy initial. The poems are read and each child exclaims, "Thank you, *Sinterklaas*," and the day of fun continues.

Christmas in Holland is a religious festival when the family attends church services and enjoys an evening of singing Christmas songs. On the 26th the *Zondagsschool* program is held. This is often between 2:00 and 5:00 in the afternoon or between 5:00 and 9:00 in the evening. This is a special day for the young children and their parents.

Preparations for this program, however, starts in the beginning of the month. Then the Sunday School teachers or officers go out to collect money with which to buy gifts for the children. These gifts usually include a good book, candy, an orange, and nuts. Each child receives a bag filled with the sweets. The children also bring a cup to the service and during the evening a cup of hot chocolate is served.

In some churches the ladies society sew articles of wearing apparel for the children and one garment is given to each boy and girl. This is especially appreciated by the mothers!

MENU

Prayer

Ach, blijf met Uw genade,
Almachtig! ons nabij,
En dek ons voor de schade
Van ijd'le hoovaardij.

Abide with us, our Savior,
nor let Thy mercy cease;
From Satan's might defend us,
And grant our souls release.

Introduction

It is a Dutch custom to serve one hot meal per day. Time for this may vary in different homes—noon or evening. The other two meals are based on bread, spread with butter or meats, cheese, liver sausage, herring, or jam.

Coffee for the morning coffee hour may be made in the regular way or served with milk. The latter is made by pouring hot milk and strong coffee into the cup at the same time, so that there are equal amounts of both.

Afternoon teas may be served with a plain cookie. Usually fancy cakes and cookies are kept for company or special occasions. When soup is served, as at dinner time, no drink is used. Should there be company a cup of coffee may be served somewhat later, away from the table.

The Dutch housewife, as a whole, does not bake her rolls or bread. Bakeries are very handy and very good, and offer a wide selection for every occasion. For the main meals, however, tasty nourishing foods are served which are enjoyed by family and any visiting friends.

Menu for a Day

Breakfast
>   Toast or bread with cheese
>   Boiled egg, once or twice per week
>   Tea, sweetened

Coffee break, 10:00 a.m.
>   Coffee with milk
>   Coffee cake

Dinner
>   Bouillon soup
>   Cooked potatoes
>   Cauliflower with white sauce
>   Pork chops with gravy
>   Pudding, vanilla or chocolate, or Yogurt

Supper
>   "Open-faced sandwiches" made with dark bread, buttered,
>   and spread with cold cuts, cheese, "raw" bacon, or
>   "raw" herring
>   Milk

BREADS

Flensjes
A Thin Pancake

For serving one person use:

1 c. milk	1/2 c. flour
1 tbsp. sugar	1 tbsp. shortening, melted
1 egg	

Beat all ingredients together. Pour a very thin layer of the batter over bottom of large pan. Turn *Flensjes* carefully so as not to tear them. Brown both sides and remove to a warm platter. Spread with butter and a sugar-cinnamon mixture, or some of your favorite preserves. Roll up on a fork and serve hot.

Oliebollen
Dutch Doughnuts

1 cake yeast	1 1/2 c. currants and raisins
1 egg	1 tsp. salt
1 c. milk	1 tart apple
2 1/4 c. flour	fat for deep frying

Dissolve the yeast in a little milk. Sift the flour and salt. Add the milk, mix to a batter with the yeast and egg. Add the currants, raisins, and peeled, minced apple. Leave the batter in a warm place to rise until double.

Heat the fat to 375°. Put two metal spoons into the batter and shape balls with them. Drop into the hot fat. Fry them for 8 minutes or until brown.

The doughnuts should be soft and not greasy inside. If fried too slowly they become greasy. Drain on absorbent paper. Serve them piled on a dish and cover thickly with sifted confectionery sugar. Eat hot, if possible.

Oliebollen are a traditional treat for New Year's Eve.

Gewone Pannekoeken
Ordinary Pancakes

4 c. flour
salt

1 cake yeast
4 c. lukewarm milk
butter or margarine

Put the flour and salt into a bowl and make a well in the center. Add the yeast dissolved in a little milk. Add 2 c. milk and mix to a smooth batter. Then add the rest of the milk and let rise for 3/4 an hour.

Put a little butter or margarine into a frying pan and heat. Pour a little batter into pan, forming cakes, and fry on both sides. You may toss the pancake into the air for turning if you like or use a spatula. Serve with sugar or syrup.

CAKES AND COOKIES

Jan Hagel Cookies

1/2 pound butter
1 c. sugar
2 c. flour

1/2 tsp. cinnamon
1 egg, separated
nuts

Cream butter and sugar. Add the flour, cinnamon, egg yolk, and 1/2 c. ground nuts. Spread thinly on cooky sheet. Brush the top with the unbeaten egg white and sprinkle with sugar.

Bake at 325° for 20 minutes or until light brown.

Cut into squares while warm.

Kletskoppen
Lace Cookies

2 c. brown sugar
2 eggs, beaten
1 tsp. soda

1 c. butter
1 c. flour
1 tsp. cream of tartar

Melt butter, add the sugar and mix well. Add the egg. Sift and add the dry ingredients and mix. Drop by tsp. on heavily greased and floured pan quite far apart—only about 8 to a cookie sheet as these cookies spread. Bake in hot oven, 400°. When done allow to stand 2 minutes to cool and then remove carefully with a spatula.

Suiker Koekjes
Sugar Cookies

1 c. butter	1 c. sugar
2 c. flour, sifted	1/2 c. cold water
1/4 tsp. soda	1 tsp. vanilla

Cream butter and sugar. Add vanilla. Sift in the dry ingredients alternately with the water. Roll dough out very thin and cut with fancy cookie cutter. Bake in a slow oven until done, they should be almost white.

A hand made card, received in a Dutch home, is cherished far above a bought one.   H.K.

The Dutch love for beauty is carried over into the realm of food; and the pastry shops reveal astonishingly beautiful cakes and candies.   H.K.

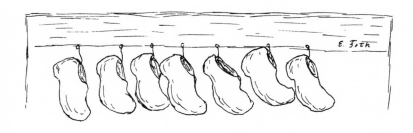

Friesche Koeke
Frisian Honey Cake

1 c. honey	1 egg
1 c. syrup	1 tsp. cloves
1 1/2 c. sugar	1 tsp. cinnamon
2 tsp. baking soda	1/2 c. cooking oil
2 tsp. baking powder	2 packages yeast
2 tbsp. shortening	6 c. flour

Preheat oven to 350°.

Soak yeast in 1/2 c. warm water.

Mix syrup, honey, sugar, soda, baking powder, spices, and oil. Add yeast to mixture. Add the flour at four different times and mix well. (The yeast does not need to rise.) Put into 2 or 3 greased loaf pans and bake at 350° about 50-55 minutes.

Snipper Koek

1 c. syrup	1 egg
1 c. sugar	1 c. cold coffee
5 c. flour	1 tsp. baking powder
1 c. candied orange peel	1 tsp. soda, dissolved in the coffee

Mix the sugar, syrup, and the egg. Beat well. Add the sifted flour and baking powder alternately with the coffee and soda. Add the orange peel. Put into greased and floured loaf pans and bake in a moderate oven, 350°, for 30 minutes, or until done.

To make candied orange peel: Cut rind of oranges very thin. Add 1 c. water and cook a few minutes. Drain. Add 1/2 c. syrup, 1/2 c. sugar, and 1/2 c. water. Cook until liquid has boiled down.

Sinterklaasje
Dutch Santa Claus Cookies

1 c. butter	1/2 c. sour cream with 1/2
1 c. shortening	tsp. soda dissolved in it
2 c. sugar	4 tsp. cinnamon
4 c. flour	1/2 tsp. nutmeg
1/2 c. nutmeats	1/2 tsp. cloves

Cream the butter, shortening, and sugar. Sift the dry ingredients and add to the creamed mixture, alternately with the cream.
Knead the dough and form into a roll 3 inches in diameter. Set aside over night in a cool place.
Cut into thin slices and spread with a fork.
Bake in moderate oven until browned.
A good treat for December 5th on St. Nicholas Day.

Gevulde Boterkoek
Butter Cake

For the dough:

2 c. flour	1 egg
1 c. butter	pinch of salt
1 c. sugar	

Knead the above ingredients into a firm ball. Divide in half. Press one part into a buttered pie pan, 8 inches in diameter. Make the filling:

2 c. blanched almonds	1 small egg
1/4 c. sugar	grated rind of 1/2 lemon

Grind the blanched almonds and mix with other ingredients and grind once more. Place this almond paste on top of the layer of dough and press the other half on top of both. Bake in a moderate, 350°, oven until golden brown, about 1 hour.

Remove from pan and cool on rack.

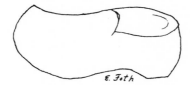

E. Joth

Pepernoten
Peppernuts

2 1/2 c. flour	pinch of salt
1 tsp. soda	1/4 tsp. each of cinnamon,
1/2 c. brown sugar	nutmeg, and cloves
3 tbsp. water	some anise seeds
1 egg yolk	2 T. butter

Knead all ingredients into a soft ball. Butter two baking sheets. Form dough into about 90 marble-sized balls. Place on pans. Flatten each ball slightly. Bake in moderate oven, 350°, for 15-20 minutes or until done.

These cookies are a special treat for December 5th, St. Nicholas Day. On this day "Black Peter", St. Nicholas' helper, gives these and many other goodies to the children who come around singing songs for the Christmas season.

Speculaas
Dutch Spice Cookies

Cream:

1/2 c. butter	1 tbsp. rum
1/2 c. sugar	

Add 2 egg yolks or 1 whole egg and beat.
Sift:

2 c. flour	1/2 tsp. cardamon
1 tsp. cinnamon	1/2 tsp. salt
1/2 tsp. soda	

Gradually add dry ingredients to creamed mixture. If dough is too stiff to roll out, add 1 or 2 tbsp. milk.

Add 1/4 pound slivered almonds.

Cool 1 hour. Roll out thin and cut in fancy shapes.

This cookie is usually shaped in windmills in Holland. Due to different type flour, these cookies taste somewhat different when made with our flour. But they are still good eating!

DESSERTS

Griesmeelpap met Rozijnen
Farina Cream with Raisins

4 c. milk	2/3 c. sultana raisins
3 oz. farina	4 tbsp. sugar
pinch of salt	1/2 tbsp. butter

Bring the milk to a boil with the washed raisins and salt. Mix the sugar and farina well and stir into the boiling milk. Boil gently about 15-20 minutes (the coarser the cereal, the longer the cooking time). Add the butter. Serve in a deep plate.

Griesmeelpudding met Bessensap
(Farina Pudding with Red Currant Sauce)

4 c. milk	2/3 c. farina
2 tbsp. corn starch	1/4 c. sugar
pinch of salt	1 1/2 tbsp. butter
1 egg yolk, beaten	1 tsp. vanilla
1 egg white, beaten stiff	

Add vanilla to milk and bring to a boil. Mix the farina, starch, sugar, and salt and add to milk, stirring vigorously. Turn the heat to low and add the butter. Carefully add the egg yolk and bring to a boil. Fold in the beaten egg white.

Pour pudding into a mold rinsed with cold water. Chill.

Sauce:

small jar red currant jelly	juice of 2 lemons
1/2 c. boiling water	

Put jelly in saucepan, add lemon juice and water. Bring to a boil Stir until smooth. Chill.

Turn the chilled pudding onto a platter and surround it with part of the sauce. Serve the remainder of the sauce in a pitcher and let each person help himself.

The Lord Is My Shepherd

De Heer is mijn Herder!
'K heb al wat mij lust:
Hij zal my geleiden
Naar grazige weiden;
Hij voert mij al zachtkens
Aan wat'ren der rust.

Citroen Pudding
Lemon Pudding

1 1/2 c. sugar	3 lemons
6 eggs, separated	1 tbsp. gelatin
1/4 c. cold water	

Beat egg yolks. Add juice of 3 lemons and the grated rind of one. Cook in double boiler for a short time. Then add the gelatin which has been dissolved in the water. Continue cooking until the pudding has become thick. Remove from heat. Fold in the stiffly beaten egg whites. Chill.

Room Hoorns
Cream Horns

Make a rich pastry by using:

1 c. butter	1 1/2 c. flour
cold water	

Cut butter into flour and add enough water to make a dough which can be rolled out. Cut into strips about 4 by 5 inches. Roll dough around finger-shaped molds. Bake until lightly brown in a hot-moderate oven, 375°.

When cool, fill with whipped cream or a cream filling.

Zand Taart
Sand Tarts

1 c. butter	2 c. sugar
2 1/2 c. flour	3 eggs, less 1 egg white
	pinch of salt

Cream butter and sugar. Add the lightly beaten eggs. Sift in the flour and salt. Roll dough very thin on a well floured board. Mix equal parts of sugar and cinnamon and sprinkle over dough which has been brushed with the white of 1 egg. Cut in squares and place a blanched almond in the center of each square. Bake quickly in a hot oven. Must be a delicate golden color.

Schoenlappers Taart
Brown Betty

6 large apples	3 eggs
5 slices dry bread or rusks	3/4 tsp. cinnamon
1/2 c. butter	1/2 c. sugar

Pare, core, and cook the apples to a sauce. Add the sugar, butter, cinnamon, and broken bread or rusks. Beat eggs separately and fold into the above mixture, adding the whites last. Bake in a buttered dish in a 350° oven until brown.

Yoghurtsla met Vruchten
Yoghurt Cream with Fruit

4 c. yoghurt, in Holland
   this is rather thin, like
   custard
1 package instant vanilla
   pudding

4 c. milk
1/2 lb. fruit in season
   sugar to taste

Wash the fruit and put into a glass bowl. Cover with sugar to taste and allow sugar to permeate fruit for a few hours.

Take enough pudding powder to mix with 4 c. milk and prepare according to directions. Chill. Mix well with chilled yoghurt and pour over fruit just before serving. Decorate with a little fruit and serve with wafers or lady fingers.

Appel Pudding met Geklopte Room
Apple Pudding with Whipped Cream

1 lb. sour apples
3/4 c. sugar
1 tbsp. gelatin

3 c. water
1/2 grated lemon rind
1 c. whipping cream

Peel and core the apples. Cook in water to which rind has been added. Strain the liquid and add sugar and dissolved gelatin. Add whipped cream. Pour into a mold and chill.

"De Morgenstond heeft Goud in de Mond."
(The morning hour has gold in its mouth.)

Hollandshe Appel Koek
Dutch Apple Cake

Combine:

2 c. flour

2 tsp. baking powder

1/2 tsp. salt

Add:

1 egg, beaten

3/4 c. milk

1/4 c. shortening

Mix till blended. Pour over apples.

Fill a deep pan with 6 to 8 cored, sliced apples. Sprinkle 1 1/2 c. sugar mixed with 1 tsp. cinnamon over apples. Cover with batter and bake in moderate oven for about 25 minutes.

To serve make the following sauce:

Combine:

1 c. brown sugar

1 tbsp. flour

1 tbsp. butter

Add 2 c. hot water and boil 2 minutes.

FOWL AND FISH

Gebraden Kip
Roast Chicken Dutch Style

Place 1 c. butter in a kettle (iron preferably) and melt. Put in a whole chicken which has been thoroughly dried. Brown on all sides.

Add 1/2 c. water and cover tightly. Cook slowly, adding not more than another 1/2 c. water, to keep chicken from burning.

Cook 1 hour and salt the chicken to taste. Allow 3 hours for a 1 year old chicken to become tender.

Make a gravy with the liquid remaining by making a paste of flour and water and bring liquid to boil. Serve on chicken.

Gestoofde Paling
Stewed Eel

1 1/2 lb. eel	1/4 c. butter or margarine
lemon	bread crumbs
salt	water

Cut the skinned eel in slices and wash. Salt the slices and put them into a casserole dish. Add a little water, lemon juice, and butter. Sprinkle bread crumbs over the fish and bake in a hot oven, covered, for 15-20 minutes. Lower the temperature, remove the lid, and cook for another 10 minutes.

Serve with boiled potatoes and a green salad.

Gebakken Vis
Fried Fish

Use any fillet—whiting, haddock, etc.

Clean and wash the fish, season with salt and pepper. Dip into flour or milk. Fry in a skillet with cooking oil, 1/8 inch deep. When one side is browned, turn and fry the other side. Sprinkle with lemon juice.

Serve with home fried potatoes and a green salad.

Haddock is also good served with stewed beetroots.

It is interesting to note that Mennonites own and operate a large pottery factory at Makkum and a small one at Workum.

MEATS

Hutspot
A Main Dish

1/2 lb. pot roast　　　　　1 onion, sliced
4 diced carrots　　　　　　salt and pepper
4 diced potatoes

Cover the meat with water and add 1 1/2 tsp. salt. Cook until half done and add the carrots. Cover and cook half an hour longer. Add the potatoes and onion and cook until done.

Remove the meat to a platter. Slightly mash the vegetables and arrange around the meat. There should only be a very little liquid left by this time.

Saucysebroodjes
"Pigs-in-blanket"

Crust:

4 c. flour　　　　　　　　1 tsp. salt
3 tsp. baking powder　　　1/2 to 1 c. milk
1 c. butter

Meat:

2 lbs. pork　　　　　　　　1/2 c. bread or rusk crumbs
1/2 lb. beef　　　　　　　　1/2 tsp. nutmeg
salt and pepper

Crust: Sift dry ingredients. Cut butter into the flour mixture. Add milk enough so dough can be easily handled. Divide into four parts and roll out fairly thin. Cut into strips 3 by 4 inches. Fill.

Meat: Grind the meat and add the remainder of the ingredients. Roll mixture into sausage-like rolls 3 inches long. Wrap each meat roll into a strip of dough. Seal well. Brush tops with a lightly beaten egg or cream. Put on a greased pan about 2 inches apart and bake in 350° for about 30 minutes.

Uitsmijter
"Chucker Out"

A quick meal to make when in a hurry. It also is very substantial. Top 2 slices of white bread, buttered, with a liberal portion of cold, cooked, thinly sliced roastbeef, ham, or veal. Top this with 2 fried eggs. Salt and pepper to taste. Serve.

When only 1 egg is used, it is called a *"halve" uitsmijter.*

Gehakt
Large Meat Balls

1/2 lb. ground beef	bread crumbs
1/2 lb. ground pork	pinch of pepper
1/2 c. milk	1/2 onion
4 slices stale bread	1/4 c. fat
1 tbsp. salt	1 tsp. tomato-paste or
1/2 tsp. nutmeg	1 tbsp. tomato juice

Mix the meat in a large basin. Soak bread in the milk. Fry the onion in a little fat. Add to meat mixture. Add the seasoning and mix well. Shape into 4 to 8 balls. Roll in flour and fry until brown in the fat. Add a little water and simmer for 15 minutes. Add the tomato paste to the gravy and serve with boiled potatoes and boiled vegetables.

Kalfslapjes
Veal Slices

4 thin slices of lean veal	bread crumbs or Dutch
salt	rusks
1/2 c. butter or margarine	1 lemon

Wash the meat and season it with salt. Coat it in bread crumbs or finely ground rusks. Melt the butter or margarine in pan until browned and fry the veal slices in the butter, browning them on both sides. Cook slowly, without a lid, for 20 minutes. Turn slices occasionally. Remove from pan but keep hot.

Make the Dutch gravy "jus" by adding water. Good gravy should be 1/3 fat and 2/3 brown stock.

Serve the veal slices with a slice of lemon on top and serve the gravy with boiled potatoes.

E. Toth

SALADS

Aardappelsla
Potato Salad

1 tbsp. dry mustard	3 tbsp. chopped parsley
1/2 small onion	1 c. French dressing
2 tbsp. vinegar	3 c. cold boiled potatoes
mayonnaise	salt and pepper

Mix the mustard, chopped onion, vinegar, mayonnaise, parsley, and dressing in a rather large bowl. Slice the potatoes and carefully stir through the sauce, adding salt and pepper to taste.

Haringsla
Herring Salad

1 small cooked beetroot	2 tbsp. vinegar
2 cooking apples	salt
few pickled onions and	mayonnaise
gherkins	3 fresh salted herrings
8 cold cooked potatoes	some lettuce or curly
2 hard boiled eggs	endive
2 tbsp. salad oil	

Soak the salted herring in milk or water for 24 hours before serving, renewing the liquid at intervals. Remove the bones and cut the herring into small pieces. Keep a few pieces for decorating. Cut the peeled beetroot and apples into pieces. Chop the onions, gherkins, potatoes, and 1 egg. Wash the lettuce or endive and shred it very finely. Put all these ingredients into a large bowl. Mix well with the salad oil, vinegar, and salt. Put the salad on a flat dish and smooth the top with a wet spoon. Coat the salad with mayonnaise and decorate with 1 quartered egg, pieces of herring, and surround with small pieces of lettuce.

Serve with toast and butter.

Commemorative pieces of pottery are often sold by the church or youth groups in order to raise money. A popular design bears the Dutch Mennonite motto:

> *Dopen wat mondig is;*
> *Spreken, dat bondig is.*
> *Vrij in 't Christelijk geloven;*
> *Daden gaan woorden te boven.*

Freely translated:

> Baptize those who are of age;
> Speak that which is true.
> Free in Christian belief;
> deeds are above words.

SOUPS

Fruit-Barley Soup

Add 3/4 c. pearl barley and 1 piece cinnamon stick to 6 c. water.
Cook until barley is done.

Add 1 1/2 c. washed raisins and cook about 15 minutes longer.
Add 2 c. currant juice, grape juice, or boysenberry juice. Sweeten
to taste. If too much water has boiled away, add a little more.
Serve cold.

Erwtensoep
Dutch Pea Soup

2 c. split green peas	1 lb. potatoes
3 quart cold water	4 tsp. salt or to taste
1 pig's ear	2 leeks
1 pig's trotter	1 bunch celery greens
1 c. bacon squares	and stalk
4 frankfurters	2 onions

Wash and soak the peas overnight (unless quick cooking peas
are used). Boil gently in the water they were soaked in for at
least 2 hours. Then cook the trotter and the ear and the bacon in
the same liquid for 1 hour. Add the sliced potatoes, salt, diced
celery, leeks, and onions and cook until everything is done and the
soup is smooth and thick. Add the frankfurters for the last 10
minutes.

The longer the soup simmers the better the taste. In Holland
this usually is about 3 hours. The soup becomes quite thick when
cool. Even tastes better the next day. That is why such a large
quantity is made.

(A trotter is a pig's foot.)

Vegetable Soup

2 large potatoes
3 large carrots
1/2 c. celery

salt and pepper
10 kernels of whole
allspice

Add the diced vegetables to 2 quarts water. Add the spices. Cook about 5 minutes. Add small meat balls make according to your favorite recipe. Add 1 1/2 c. fine vermicelli and continue cooking until the meat and vermicelli are done, about 20 minutes.

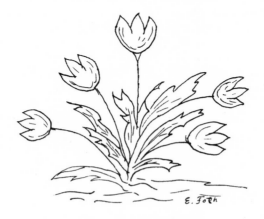

E. Foth

VEGETABLES

Aardappelpuree
Dutch Mashed Potatoes

"Always make nice and white mashed potatoes from freshly boiled potatoes. If made from cold boiled potatoes they are not white."

2 lbs. potatoes
1 1/2 c. milk
grated nutmeg

salt
1/4 c. butter or margarine

Boil the peeled potatoes and mash when still hot with a fork or put them through a mincer or a sieve. No lumps. Bring the nutmeg, butter, salt, and milk to a boil. Add the mashed potatoes at once and stir well. With a wooden spoon whip the mixture well until it is white and creamy. Serve. These potatoes may also be put into a casserole, dotted with a little butter and lightly browned under the grill or broiler.

Rode Kool
Red Cabbage, spiced

1 small red cabbage	2 cooking apples
1/4 c. butter or margarine	1 tbsp. sugar
3 cloves	salt and some vinegar

Remove the outer leaves from the cabbage and cut into halves. Remove the core. Shred cabbage very thinly. Put a little butter or margarine in a saucepan and add 1 c. water. Add the cabbage, cloves, the peeled, cored, and sliced apples. Simmer with a tight fitting lid for about 3/4 hour. Then add the rest of the butter, sugar, some vinegar and simmer for another 5 minutes.

Spinazie met Harde Eieren
Spinach with Hard Boiled Eggs

4 lb. spinach	8 fingers of bread
salt	2 eggs
2 tbsp. flour	butter to fry bread in
2 tbsp. butter	

Wash the spinach, add salt, and cook without water. Toss spinach after it has boiled a few minutes. Continue cooking about 10 minutes. Drain, cut, or chop up the spinach, stir in the flour and add the butter. Bring to a boil so it thickens.

Fry fingers of bread in butter. Hardboil the eggs.

Decorate spinach with fried bread, standing upright and the eggs cut into eights.

Gekookte Aardappelen
Boiled Potatoes

The Dutch are very particular about the texture of their boiled potatoes; which often are the main staple for the evening meal. Potatoes must be flaky when dished up!

2 lb. potatoes	salt
1 c. water	

Peel the potatoes and put at once into cold water. Put 1/2 inch water in a saucepan with a tight fitting lid. Add the potatoes and the salt. Bring quickly to a boil and lower the heat so as to just keep the steam "under" the lid of the pan. Cook for 20 minutes, drain, and shake well until dry and flaky.

8

The West Prussian Mennonites

HISTORY

From Dutch to German

Plattdeutsch (Plautdietsch), a Low German language spoken by Mennonites who originally came largely from the Netherlands, and settled in Danzig and along the Vistula River, whence they spread into Russia and North and South America. All Mennonites are primarily of two ethnic and linguistic backgrounds, the Swiss-German, Pennsylvania German, and the Dutch-German or Low German.

The Dutch Background

When the Mennonites from the Netherlands settled along the Vistula, they adhered to their Dutch language until the second half of the 18th century. The native language of the country was a form of Low German or *Plattdeutsch* with peculiar local characteristics, spoken in some form in all of North Germany. It is linguistically related to Dutch and English. That the similarities between Low German, Dutch, and English are in some respects greater than those between Low German and High German, the official language of German-speaking countries, can be seen in the word for *water:* Dutch *water*, Low German *woata*, and High German *Wasser*. Whereas Dutch has remained a literary language, most of the Low German dialects are now colloquial languages, although there is a large body of Low German literature.

In 1762 the first German sermon was preached in the Mennonite church of Danzig, for which the minister received special permission, but no appreciation was expressed. The Danzig church record was henceforth kept in German. The first German Mennonite hymnal, replacing the Dutch, was printed in 1761. In 1788, when the first Mennonites migrated to Russia, some were still using Dutch. Dutch Bibles and other books were taken along to Russia, some of which even reached the United States and Canada during the migration of 1874. However, the first migrants to Russia, coming from the poorer classes of the Danzig and Elbing area and settling at Chortitza, primarily spoke Low German. Dutch was no longer in use and High German was still a foreign tongue. It is particularly this form of Low German which has been perpetuated among the more conservative Mennonites of Manitoba and Mexico.

C. K.

From the Netherland to West Prussia

The first Mennonites came to West Prussia in the 1530's. At this time Protestants in the Netherlands were being persecuted due to the Spanish Inquisition. As West Prussia was one of the countries favoring Protestantism, many religious refugees found their way to this country, often by means of trading vessels. As these people had the reputation of being very industrious, their help in rebuilding the war torn Prussian countryside was in their favor.

They seemed to prefer the lowlands to the hilly wooded areas in which they found themselves; therefore many moved to the Danzig Werder region. This was a difficult life. But in less than a century they had converted this swampy country into one of the most productive farm areas. Settlements were founded at Ellerwald near Elbing, at Tiegenhof and at Danzig.

As these Mennonites were not permitted to win new converts, family names remained the same through the years. Even as late as World War I, surnames were no different from what they had been in the Netherlands. Some of these were: Penner, Wiens, Wiebe, Claassen, Dyck, Janzen, Enns, Janz, Ewert, Regier, Pauls, Neufeld, Friesen, Reimer, Fieguth, and so on. Often there would be several ways to spell the same name as is still common today: eg. Enns and Entz; Regehr and Regier.

In 1728, the Mennonites were permitted to build churches which had not been possible previously. Also a few of the larger groups now began using organs in their services. By 1750 the West Prussian Mennonites gradually accepted the German language and by this act they at last actually became "Germans". Soon many moved to Russia.

During the 19th century, Mennonites were again faced with the loss of their freedom due to strong militarism. Thus some groups left for Russia—between 1853-1860. Others fearing that this question would also be a problem in Russia, decided to look to America for religious freedom. So Kansas and Nebraska became the new challenge to these Prussian Mennonites, especially those from the Heubuden area. Later several groups from here also went to Canada.

World War II meant much suffering for the Prussian Mennonites. When in 1945 the Russian army entered Prussia, these Mennonites were forced to flee. As no plans for escape had been made in advance, many families became separated. Many perished. In the battle for Danzig, many Mennonites were able to get passage to Denmark. Often these refugee ships were bombed and all aboard perished. With the fall of Danzig, four hundred years of Mennonite history in Prussia seemed to have come to an end.

It was following the difficult years after World War II that many of the Prussian Mennonites, as well as others, regained some new hope. The Mennonite Central Committee sent food, clothing, and workers to help their brethren in distress. M.C.C. workers visited the Danish refugee camps, and opened the way to have hundreds sent to South America, Canada, and U.S.A. Some were resettled in Germany.

MEMORIES OF GRANDMOTHER

She often wore an apron starched and white,
Her hair was brushed back neat and braided tight;
She worked around the kitchen every day
And all she did was in an ordered way.
When she cooked food, none ever went to waste,
Her gravy was like nectar to the taste.
And how she loved to supervise the bread!
The rules for baking it were in her head.
Her Zwieback and her apple coffee cake—
There were no better than she helped to make.
She heaped our plates when we could come to dine
And often gave us apples sliced real fine.

Then in her hours of rest she oft reclined
Upon the Ruhe-bank. There the window blind
Was drawn to keep the heat of summer day
And too-bright sunshine from the room away.
Or she would sit crocheting lengths of lace
A look of concentration on her face.
She'd tell about her youth in Germany;
Her voyage over on a rugged sea;
The things that she and Grandpa used to do
When they sere settling in this country new.
And all about her children on the farm—
Rememb'ring this, her face grew soft and warm.
Her hands would pause above her work-box brown—
Reflectively her thumbs would go around.

On Sundays, bound for church, she always dressed
In black wool gown and shawl—her very best.
She wore her brooch with Grandpa's face inside,
(He'd given it when she was just a bride.)
Her black hat on her head, song-book in hand,
She went to church in humble style, but grand!

(A tribute to a Prussian grandmother by her granddaughter,
Betty.)

MENU

Fruehstueck — Breakfast
    Homemade rye bread with butter and cheese,
        cheese being either homemade *Zwerg* or a *Muenster*
    Honey, apple butter, or plum jam
    Coffee and milk

Mittagessen — Dinner
    Fried *Klops* (meat balls)
    Mashed potatoes, with butter and cream added
    Fried apple slices, sprinkled with sugar
        or
    Red Cabbage
    Milk

Abendbrot — Supper
    Birnen-Suppe
    Rye bread
    Wurst; homemade sausage, such as liver sausage,
        Blutwurst, etc.

Vesper — Coffee Hour
    Schnittchen, Napfkuchen, or Butter Cookies
    Coffee, to which a spoon of whipped cream may be added

BREADS

Roggenbrot
Rye Bread

1 package yeast, dissolved in 3/4 c. warm water to which a little sugar has been added. Add to liquid.

2 c. warm water	"A"
1/2 c. melted lard	4 1/2 c. rye-graham flour
1/2 c. dark syrup	4 1/2 c. white flour
1 tbsp. salt	"B"
9 c. flour, either A or B	4 c. rye flour
	3 c. rye-graham flour
	2 c. white flour

Put the liquid into a large bowl and gradually stir in the flour. Knead well. Let rise until double in bulk. Knead down, divide into loaves, and put into greased tins. Let rise again until double. Bake at 350° for about 30 minutes, or until done.

Semmel
Buns #1

Dissolve 1 cake yeast in 1 c. warm water to which 1 tsp. sugar has been added.

Add 1 c. lukewarm water and 1 c. flour to the dissolved yeast. Mix well. Let rise until spongy, about 20 minutes. Beat sponge well.

Add:

6 tbsp. lard and butter	1 tbsp. salt
2 1/2 c. flour	

Mix well. Add a little more flour, if necessary, to make a soft dough.

Let rise again. Make small "buns" and put on greased pan, about 2 inches apart. Make a crease down center of bun. Let rise until light. Bake in moderate oven until browned.

Makes about 30 medium sized buns.

Semmel
Buns #2

4 c. flour	1/2 tsp. sugar
1 1/4 tsp. salt	1 1/2 c. water, part may
1 tbsp. lard	be milk
1 cake yeast	

Dissolve yeast in 1/2 c. of the water, to which the sugar has been added. Put flour and salt into mixing bowl. Add melted lard and the remaining c. of lukewarm liquid. Lastly add the dissolved yeast and beat vigourouly until batter is fairly smooth. Let rise 2-4 hours.

Spoon onto a greased baking sheet with a tbsp., placing the *Semmel* about 2 inches apart. (No need to let rise again.) Place in a preheated 425° oven and bake about 15-20 minutes, or until browned.

Serve warm with butter and honey.

For a variety add 1 tbs. poppy seeds to the top of the *Semmel* just before baking.

This *Semmel* is a hard crust type bun. Recipe makes 15 large buns. This can also be mixed late Saturday evening and allowed to rise overnight and be baked in time for Sunday breakfast.

Kringel fuer Gruen-Donnerstag
(A specialty for Maundy Thursday)

1 package yeast	1/4 c. lard, melted
1/2 c. warm water	1/3 c. sugar
1 c. milk	3 c. flour
1/2 tsp. salt	1/2 lb. butter
1 c. flour	slivered almonds
1 egg	egg yolk

Dissolve yeast in 1/2 c. warm water. Scald and cool to lukewarm the milk. Add the yeast, salt, and 1 c. flour to the cooled milk and beat well. Add the egg and beat again. Beat in the melted lard and continue beating until smooth. Then add the sugar and the 3 c. of flour, beat. Dough should be stiff enough to roll out.

Cover and let rise until double. Knead down and set aside to cool.

Roll dough out on a board to 1/2 inch thickness and spread the soft butter on 2/3 of the rolled out dough. Fold the unbuttered portion over 1/3 of the dough and bring the other 1/3 over this. Roll dough out again. Fold over again in thirds and repeat. Do this several more times and then roll out 1/2 inch thick. Cut into strips 1 inch wide by 9 inches long. Twist and form into a bow.

Brush with beaten egg yolk, mixed with 1 tsp. water. Dip into slivered almonds and put on a greased tin. Let rise until light. Bake at 400° about 10 to 12 minutes, or until nicely browned.

When baked, glaze with a regular powdered sugar icing while hot.

For a variety: Omit the almonds and brush an apricot jam glaze on top while *Kringel* is hot. Bring the jam to a boil and brush on.

Napfkuchen
Bundt Cake

Dissolve 1 package yeast in 1/2 c. water.

Scald 3/4 c. milk, and cool to lukewarm.

Cream 1 c. butter and 1 c. sugar until light.

Add 4 eggs, yeast mixture, grated rind of lemon, and 1/2 tsp. salt. Beat well. Gradually beat in the milk and about 4 c. flour. Dough will be rather stiff but still easy to work.

Lastly add 1 c. slivered almonds or raisins.

Let rise until double. Stir down. Put into a greased bundt cake form. Let rise till double.

Bake for 1 hour in a 325° oven.

Blechkuchen
(Pan-Cake) Coffee Cake

Dissolve 1 cake yeast or 1 package dry yeast, in 1/4 c. warm water and 1/4 c. sugar. Let rise until "spongy".

Add this to:

1 c. milk, scalded and cooled	3/4 c. sugar
	1 tsp. salt
2 eggs	1/2 c. melted butter

Gradually add approximately 4 c. sifted flour, beating well after each addition.

Add 1 c. floured raisins. Dough will not be too stiff, but soft enough to be spooned into pan.

Let rise till double. Spread thinly, about 3/4 to 1 inch thick, in a large, greased pan or cookie sheet. Brush top with melted butter or margarine and sprinkle with sugar.

Let rise until light.

Bake in moderate oven until golden brown.

Makes about 30 pieces. Best when fresh or warmed.

Rosinen-Stritzel
Raisin Bread — For special occasions!

Scald and cool till lukewarm 4 c. milk.

Dissolve 2 packages of dry yeast in 1/2 c. warm water with 1 tbsp. sugar added to it.

Add 1 1/2 c. melted shortening to the milk. Then add the yeast and 1 tbsp. salt.

Gradually add 11-12 c. flour, sifted, adding raisins towards the end. Use 1/2 c. raisins for 1 c. milk.

Knead dough. Let rise till double. Knead again and form into loaves. These are to be rather flat and so are placed on a cookie pan, which has been greased. Roll dough out about 1 inch thick in an oval shape. Brush lightly with melted butter and fold one half to almost cover the other half. Like "Stollen".

Cover and let rise in warm place till double.

Bake at 350° about 35 minutes, or until brown. Makes 3 or 4 loaves.

Berliner Pfannkuchen
(Bismarks)

1 lb. prunes, soaked, pitted, and then mashed or ground.
Scald 2 c. milk, cool to lukewarm.
Beat 2 whole eggs, and 10 egg yolks and add to the cooled milk.
Add 2/3 c. sugar, 2 tsp. salt, and 1/2 lb. melted butter. Beat well.
Soften 2 packages of dry yeast (or 2 cakes) and add to the above.
Gradually sift enough flour into the above sponge to make a soft dough, beating well. Do not knead dough.
Set in warm place and let rise until double. Then beat down and let rise again. Roll out 1/4 inch thick. With a fairly large glass mark the spots (faintly) where a tsp. of the prune paste will be placed, using half of the dough. Fold the other half over this and cut out both layers; or cut each circle separately, add prunes and cover with another circle. Pinch edges together. Place on greased pan or a floured board and let rise until double. Deep fry until golden brown. Sprinkle with sugar. Makes about 60 Pfannkuchen.

Portzeln
New Year's "Cookies"

Scald 2 c. milk and cool. Dissolve 1 cake yeast in 1/4 c. warm water and add to lukewarm milk.
Add 1/4 c. melted shortening, 1 1/2 tsp. salt, and 1/4 c. sugar.
Beat 2 eggs and add. Gradually sift in 3 to 3 1/2 c. flour, beating well. Lastly add 1 c. floured raisins.
Let rise about 30 minutes. Stir and beat a little, and let rise again until double. Then drop by tablespoonfuls into hot fat and fry until browned, like doughnuts.
If you dip the spoon into the hot fat to begin with the dough will slip off easily. Continue in same manner for remainder of dough.
Best served fresh, sprinkled with either white or powdered sugar. When some are left-over they may be warmed by steaming and then served with a white custard sauce.
For an added flavor add the grated rind of an orange or a lemon, and a little cinnamon.

Pflinzen
Thin Pancakes

Everyone's favorite! Good served with sugar, or syrup, or with thickened fruit sauce, hot or cold.

Beat until smooth:

2 c. milk	1 tsp. salt
2 c. flour	3 eggs

Melt about 1/2 c. shortening, part butter or margarine, in the frying pan to be used. Pour into a small container and keep on hand near the pan. Frying pan must be hot to begin.

For a large 9-10 inch pan use 1/2 c. of batter and pour it into pan, tilting pan so that the batter will flow evenly over the whole bottom. Set on a hot element. Add 1 tsp. melted fat around edges of cake. When browned turn the cake using a spatula or pancake turner. (Keep the cake whole.) Stack finished cakes.

For a beginner it might be well to use a smaller frying pan about 6-8 inch size and then gradually use a larger one.

Various ways to serve a batch of *Pflinzen:*

1. Roll one or two on a fork and put on your plate. Serve with sugar, syrup, or a thickened fruit sauce.
2. After finishing frying the first cake, put some cooked fruit (cherries, blue plums, rhubarb) on top of it and cover with the second cake. Continue this until the pancakes are finished. A layer-cake effect is the result. Cut the stack into pie-shaped wedges and serve.
3. *Apfelpflinzen* — Apple Pancakes
   Fry this on a cooler element, medium heat. After the pan has been filled with the batter, press some thinly sliced apples over the whole. Quickly cover the bare spots of the apples with a few dashes of dough. When brown, turn, and complete frying the other side. Add more shortening. This will take somewhat longer than without the filling, but it is delicious. Sprinkle with sugar. (For the above amount of dough, 3 apples, peeled, and cored, and thinly sliced are needed.)
4. Eat these *Pflinzen* cold as a snack. Sprinkle sugar on the cake and roll up. Good!
5. If there are several left after this, roll them up and cut similar to noodles and fry in margarine.

Potato Pancakes

6 medium raw potatoes,   2 tbsp. flour
    finely grated   1 tsp. salt
1 egg

Mix all ingredients thoroughly. Grease a hot skillet and put potato mixture into skillet with a tbsp. Flatten each cake. Add fat as needed to avoid sticking.

Fry till golden brown on both sides. (It's a good idea to stir batter occasionally.) Makes 18 pancakes.

To serve: 1. sprinkle with sugar, 2. apple sauce is a good accompaniment, and 3. serve with bacon and eggs.

If a blender is available. simply put 1 cut-up potato and egg into blender. Blend till well chopped. Add remainder of cut-up potatoes, flour, and salt. Blend well.

CAKES AND COOKIES

Streuselkuchen
Crumb Coffee Cake

Cream 3/4 c. margarine and 3/4 c. sugar. Add 2 eggs and beat well. Sift 3 c. flour, 5 tsp. baking powder, and 1/4 tsp. salt. Add dry ingredients alternately with 1 c. milk, ending with flour.

Dough will be rather stiff. Spread with a spoon into greased cake pan, large size, and even top with spoon dipped in water.

Spread jelly, jam, or cooked fruit on top of dough and cover with a crumb topping.

Topping:
1 1/4 c. flour   1/2 tsp. cinnamon
1/2 c. sugar   1/2 tsp. vanilla
1/2 c. margarine

Rub until crumbly. Spread evenly over cake.

Bake in moderate oven, 350°, about 40 minutes.

Sandkuchen

Have all ingredients at room temperature.

Beat 1 c. butter and 2 c. sugar until light and creamy. Add and beat well 1 tsp. vanilla and 1 lemon rind. Add 4 eggs, one at a time, beating about 5 minutes after each egg. Sift 2 c. cake flour and 1/2 tsp. baking powder. Add the sifted flour gradually, 2 tbsp. at a time and mix lightly. Continue until the whole amount is used.

Pour into a greased loaf pan, 9 by 5 by 2 1/2 inches, lined with waxed paper at the bottom of the pan. Sprinkle a little sugar along the center of the dough. Bake in a 300-325° oven approximately 1 hour or until done.

This cake keeps well.

E. Foth

Pfefferkuchen

An inexpensive treat for the family at Christmas time was a decorated *Pfefferkuchen*. In some homes this was also baked during the year, but then it was not decorated. At Christmas time, however, almonds, walnuts, and colored citron peel would be used to decorate the top before baking. The *Pfefferkuchen* then became a specialty to be put on the *Weihnachtsteller*.

As this kept well and tasted good even when dry, it was often served when unexpected company came weeks after the holidays.

Pfefferkuchen
"Spiced Squares" #1

1 c. sugar	1 tsp. soda
1 c. syrup	1 tsp. nutmeg
1 c. lard	1 tsp. cinnamon
1 c. milk	1 tsp. cloves
3 eggs	4 1/2 c. flour

Mix the sugar, syrup, and lard and bring to a boil. Dissolve the soda in a little vinegar and add to the somewhat cooled mixture. Beat the eggs and add. Sift the flour and spices and add alternately with the milk. Pour into a large pan, almost the size of the oven, and bake at moderate temperature for about 30 minutes. Cut into squares.

E. Foth

Pfefferkuchen No. 2

1/2 lb. honey
1 egg
1 tsp. ammonium
  carbonate
1/2 tsp. cardamon
1/4 lb. sugar
2 tbsp. sour cream

1/4 lb. butter or lard
1/4 tsp. cream of tartar
1/4 tsp. nutmeg
1 tsp. cinnamon
1/4 tsp. cloves
flour

Bring honey and sugar to a boil. Add the fat. Cool. Add spices, part of the flour, beaten egg, and sour cream. Dissolve the ammonium carbonate in 1 tsp. water and add with the remainder of the flour. Use enough flour to make a medium stiff dough, approximately 2 to 3 c. Knead dough a little and then place in a cool place for several days.

Roll dough out about 3/4 inch thick and put into a greased pan. Brush the top with water. Decorate with almond slices and cut peel, making floral designs.

Bake 20 minutes in 350° oven. Cut into squares while still warm.

If squares are not decorated, glaze when it comes out of the oven with the following:

Boil together 1 c. sugar and 1/2 c. water. When first sign of a "hair" appears, remove from heat and stir in 1/4 c. powdered sugar.

Peppernuts

Around mid-November the tantalizing aroma of cardamon and star anise began to fill our home. This was the time for the "noisy" procedure of pounding little bags filled with whole cardamon and star anise seeds. Sometimes on the edge of the kitchen cabinet, sometimes on the back steps, but the noise persisted until the seeds were fine as powder. Now it was time to begin mixing the dough, never a single recipe either. Each batch was added to a 5 gallon crock in the coolest part of the basement until at least one crock was filled. Often another one had to be started. Several weeks passed by to let the spices penetrate the whole dough; and then at last on a Saturday morning, when there was no school, all hands were busily engaged in baking these Christmas specialties. Rolling out dough in long thin rolls, cutting these into 1/2 inch pieces, placing them on the pans, checking the oven—it was a busy, exciting time. Several Saturdays would be used to bake the large amount of dough, but at last it was finished. In the pantry a large flour sack, filled with peppernuts, hung on a peg. On the shelf a jar was near at hand for all to grab a handful in passing; pockets were filled before going to school, or to town, or out to play.

Peppernuts were a MUST!

Peppernuts No. 1

A Special Christmas Treat

Cream:

1 c. butter	1 c. lard (or any good
1 c. white sugar	shortening)
1 c. brown sugar	

Add 3 beaten eggs and 1 pint syrup. Beat well.
Sift:

14 c. flour	1 tsp. cinnamon
2 to 3 tsp. ground	2 tsp. star anise
cardamon	1 tsp. salt

Add 1 tsp. vanilla to creamed mixture.

Add dry ingredients alternately with 1 c. sour cream, in which 1 tsp. baking soda has been dissolved.

Dough will be quite stiff and at the end may have to be kneaded by hand. When well mixed, cover and refrigerate overnight or for several days. This dough will keep even for several weeks in a cool place. Take out any amount of dough desired, and roll into long, narrow strips, about 1/2 inch thick. Cut into small pieces 1/3 inch wide. Place on a cookie sheet and bake until browned in a moderate oven, 350-375°.

Zerbrich den Kopf dir nicht zu sehr;
zerbrich den Willen das ist mehr.

Don't break (trouble) your head too much;
rather break your will.

Peppernuts No. 2

Heat, but do not boil:
1 1/2 c. syrup	1 c. sugar
1/4 c. lard	1/4 c. butter
1 c. sour cream	

Cool, and add:
1/2 tsp. almond extract	1 tsp. vanilla
1/2 tsp. soda	

Sift and add:
5 c. flour	1/4 tsp. cloves
1 tsp. baking powder	1/2 tsp. nutmeg
1 tsp. cinnamon	1/4 tsp. ginger

Add more flour, if needed, to make a stiff dough.

Roll out into long strips, cut into small pieces, 1/2 inch or size desired; and bake in a moderately warm oven.

Dough will keep in a cool place for several weeks. Bake as desired.

E. Foth

Raderkuchen No. 1
(Crullers)

Sift 4 c. flour, 1 tsp. baking powder, and 2/3 c. sugar. Cut 1/4 lb. butter or margarine into dry ingredients. Add grated lemon rind, and 3 well beaten eggs to which 1/4 c. milk has been added. Mix well.

Roll dough out quite thin, cut into 3 by 1 inch strips, using a pastry wheel. Cut a slit of about 1 inch in center, and draw the one end of dough through hole, forming a bow.

Fry in deep fat until well browned. Sprinkle with sugar, if desired, or leave plain.

Raderkuchen No. 2

1/2 c. egg yolks	1/2 c sugar
1/2 c cream	

Beat till light and creamy. Then add 1 tsp. almond or lemon flavoring, and 1/4 tsp. cinnamon.

Sift enough flour into the creamed mixture to make a soft dough.

Roll out 1/4 inch thick and cut with a pastry wheel or knife. Make a cookie 3 by 1 inches. Cut a slit in the center of cookie and pull the one end through this to form a "bow". Fry in deep fat.

Schichtkuchen

1 1/2 c. sugar	1 c. milk
1 c. butter	7 c. flour
4 eggs	3 tsp. baking powder

Cream sugar and butter. Add eggs. Alternately add milk and flour to which baking powder has been added. Bake in shallow round layer cake pans 10 minutes at 450°. This amount of batter makes 9 layers. Use three layers for one cake; putting filling of cherry sauce, plum sauce, chocolate sauce, almond paste, poppy seed, or whipped cream with almonds between them. These cakes can be baked a few days ahead and filled on the day they are to be used. They were frequently served at wedding or birthday celebrations.

Der Kluegste gibt nach.
The wiser one gives in.

Tortchen
(Puff Pastry)

Chill mixing bowl and all ingredients before starting to mix.

1 lb. flour	1 c. water
1 lb. oleo or butter	1 egg
1/2 tsp. salt	

Sift flour and salt into bowl. Flake in shortening, as for pie crust. Mix until mixture is like coarse cornmeal. Beat egg until fluffy, and combine with water. Add egg mixture to flour and shortening, mixing with fork. Roll out dough. Spread it with 2 tbsp. butter. Fold into 9 layers and roll out again. Fold again into 9 parts and chill for at least an hour. Can be chilled in refrigerator for a few days or frozen. When ready to use, roll out thin and cut with large round cookie cutter. Place on cookie sheet with a tsp. of filling— cherry, apricot, almond paste, poppy seed filling, or other. Bake at 450° until light golden color. These flaky tarts were frequently served at birthday parties or wedding celebrations.

Katrinchen
a crisp spice cookie

Katrinchen cookies got their name from the shape of the cutter which was used for them. They were always made in this particular form. This cookie is still made by the Prussian Mennonites living in Germany today, especially around Christmas time.

Heat 1 c. syrup or honey and 1/2 c. sugar, until sugar is melted. Add 3 tbsp. shortening. Cool a little and add:

1 1/2 tsp. cinnamon	1/4 tsp. nutmeg
1/4 tsp. cloves	1/2 tsp. cardamon

Beat in 1 egg.
Sift:

1/2 c. flour	1/2 tsp. cream of tartar
1/4 tsp. baking soda	

Set aside to be added later.

Dissolve 1/2 tsp. soda in 3 tbsp. hot water. Add this alternately with 3 c. flour to the creamed mixture. Add the 1/2 c. flour, which was set aside.

Knead dough a little until smooth.

Roll out fairly thin. Cut with cookie cutter. Decorate with almond halves, or brush lightly with a thin icing while still warm.

Bake at 375°, 8-10 minutes. Store in airtight container.

Butter Cookies
a delicate, crisp cookie

Cream until light 1 c. butter (or margarine) and 1 c. sugar.

Add 4 egg yolks or 2 whole eggs. Beat well. Add a dash of salt, 1 tsp. vanilla, and rind of an orange or lemon.

Sift 2 1/4 c. flour into mixture and stir till well blended. A little more flour may need to be added in order to prevent dough sticking while being rolled out. Do not make it too stiff. Cool dough for a short time.

Roll dough out quite thin and cut into "fancy" shapes. Put on cookie sheet and lightly brush cookies with 1 egg yolk and 1 tsp. water, lightly beaten together. Bake in 350° oven about 8 minutes. (Cookies must be very light in color, almost white.)

Flavor may be varied by using different extracts, such as vanilla, lemon, almond, etc.

Anisplaetzchen

Beat 3 eggs (electric mixer at medium speed) until fluffy.

Add 1 c. plus 2 tbsp. sugar, gradually, beating constantly. Continue to beat 30 minutes.

Add 1 3/4 c. sifted flour and beat 3 more minutes.

Drop by teaspoons on greased and floured cookie sheet.

Form into perfect rounds. Let stand overnight, or at least 8 hours.

Bake at 325° for 10 minutes. Cookies must be a very light creamy yellow. (They look as if they had been iced when baked.)

Store in an air tight jar.

These cookies are a Christmas favorite.

(Before electric mixers were used, the eggs were beaten by hand, which was quite a difficult task.)

DESSERTS

A dessert was not always part of a regular family meal and yet at times it would be a meal in itself. For a light supper Rice or Griess Puddings would be favorites. Buttered brown bread would be served with this.

Fruit Juice Pudding
Roter or *Blauer Pudding*

Sweeten to taste 2 1/2 c. fruit juice (grape, plum, cherry). Dissolve 3 tbsp. cornstarch with a little of the liquid and stir into the whole amount. Cook over medium heat, stirring constantly for 6-8 minutes. Remove from heat.

Gradually add a stiffly beaten egg white, stirring to blend. Cool.

Serve with Custard Sauce. (4-5 servings.)

Custard Sauce

Mix 1 tsp. cornstarch with a little milk. Beat 1 egg yolk and 1/4 c. sugar, pinch of salt. Pour into 1 c. milk and cook until thick. Add 1 tsp. vanilla.

Cool and serve over pudding.

(This pudding gets its name from the color of the juice, *Blauer* or blue, and *Roter* or red.)

E. Foth

Apple Custard

Put 1 gallon sweetened apple sauce in a large bowl.

Make the following custard:

Beat 4 egg yolks well. Add 1/2 c. sugar and stir in 2 tbsp. flour. Mix till smooth. Gradually stir in 2 c. sweet cream* and pour into double boiler. Cook until thickened, stirring frequently.

Fold in 4 egg whites, stiffly beaten. Cool a little. Pour on top of the chilled sauce.

Serve family style!

*Whole milk with a little cream or canned milk may also be used. Less calories!

Rice Pudding

Put 1 quart milk, pinch of salt, 1 tsp. butter, and 1/2 c. sugar in the top of a double boiler.

Add 1 c. washed, uncooked rice and cook until it is tender (about 45 minutes). Stir occasionally.

Beat 3 egg yolks and add to the hot mixture. Cook 2 more minutes, stirring constantly.

Remove from heat and add 1/2 tsp. vanilla and 1/4 tsp. almond extract. (Lemon is also good.)

Beat the 3 egg whites until stiff and fold into the rice mixture. Chill and serve.

Garnish with chopped almonds.

If desired, 1/4 c. raisins may be cooked with this pudding. Add lemon extract with this.

Griess-Pudding
(Cream of Wheat Pudding) 3-4 servings

Cook Cream of Wheat as directed on package. Or bring 2 c. milk to a boil. Slowly add 1/3 rounded c. of cream of wheat, stirring constantly. Add 1/4 tsp. salt. Cook 5 minutes or until thickened.

Beat 2 egg yolks, add 2/3 c. sugar and beat until light.

Add egg mixture slowly to cream of wheat mixture, stirring. Bring to a boil and cook for a few minutes. Remove from heat.

Add flavoring—vanilla, lemon, or almond (or put a small piece of a cinnamon stick into the milk for a different flavor).

Fold in the 2 egg whites, beaten stiff.

Pour into a mold, or a rounded bowl. Chill thoroughly, at least several hours. (If individual servings are desired, put into small individual molds.)

To serve: Unmold on plate and arrange a few colorful pieces of berries, or fruit around the pudding. Serve with fruit juice, fruit syrup, berries, etc. Cooked raspberries are excellent!

DUMPLINGS

Homemade Noodles

Beat 6 eggs and add 1/3 c. water, 2 tsp. salt. Gradually add flour enough to make a stiff dough, about 4 1/2 c. Knead dough well and divide into 5 portions. Roll out each part until it forms a large, thin sheet. Spread these out on a tea towel or cloth on table and allow to dry for awhile. Do not let the dough become brittle. Turn dough over in order to dry both sides.

The noodles are now ready to be cut. This can be done in 2 ways.
1. Cut the dough into long strips, about 2 inches wide, and stack one on top of the other. If the layers want to stick a little, add some flour between them. Cut the stacks (with a sharp knife) into thin noodles.
2. Leave the circle of dough whole, sprinkle a little flour on it, and roll up like a jelly roll. Cut very fine and after noodles have been cut. gently toss them up to separate them.

If noodles are to be stored, allow to dry on a cloth after they have been cut. When completely dry, store in tins or jars.

Kartoffel-Keilchen
Noodle-Potato Dish

Cook 4 large potatoes in salt water. In the meantime make the *Keilchen* or noodles.

Keilchen: 1 1/2 c. flour, 1/2 tsp. salt, 1 small egg may be added if desired, and enough water to make a dough stiff enough to roll out. Roll out quite thin and cut into long strips about 2 inches wide. Stack several strips, sprinkling a little flour between each layer. Cut into medium wide "noodles".

Cook the *Keilchen* in the salted potato water after the potatoes are done. Bring to a boil and cook for about 5 minutes or until done. Watch carefully, as this can easily boil over the top of the kettle.

Pour the noodle mixture over the cooked potatoes; and cover with 3 medium onions, sauted in 5 tbsp. fat, drippings or lard (a little butter is good for extra flavor).

Serve *Kartoffel-Keilchen* with fried, salted pork, or salted bacon slabs and pickles.

Storks

Having a stork build a nest on your barn was considered a sign of good luck. April was the month that the storks usually arrived. The manner of spotting a stork was often considered a sign of how your year would be. If you saw the first stork flying, you would have a busy year. If the stork was standing around, you would try to avoid seeing it, as it betokened laziness. If you heard the stork "clopping" his bill, it meant you would break many dishes during the year. However, all these predictions added a little more to the excitement of seeing the stork and would soon be forgotten.

Male storks arrived first to set their nests in order; so that when the females came, they had a good place in which to lay their eggs. It was always exciting for the children to see the head of the first baby stork pop up out of the nest. The parents were kept busy providing food for the brood of three or four babies. Frogs and mice were plentiful, and so the young storks grew rapidly. Evening was the time for lessons, when the parents taught the young storks to balance on the edge of the nest, to walk out on the roof, and, gradually, to fly. These "lessons" were eagerly watched by the children and they sighed with relief when the young storks returned safely to the nest.

Children, on hearing and seeing the storks, would sing out: *"Storch, Storch, bester, bring mir eine Schwester: Storch, Storch, guter, bring mir einen Bruder"*.

In October the storks left for their winter home in Africa. They would gather on a large field in the region where they had spent the summer and would seem to be receiving instruction about their flight. Then they would fly up into the air, circle each farm where they had lived, and head out on their long journey. Far below the children watched, waving good-bye, until the last white speck had vanished out of sight.

FOWL

Goose and Duck

In the early years, ducks and geese were usually found on a Mennonite farm. These served several purposes. The soft eiderdown feathers were necessary for the *Federbetten* (feather beds), comforters, pillows, etc. Then the fowl would be used for roasting, being served as a special treat for company, or on festive events such as Christmas. The fat was also saved and was rendered to be used for frying and baking. Some times this grease was also used as the basis for an ointment.

Roasted Goose or Duck

Wash a cleaned and drawn goose of about 9 pounds, and dry thoroughly. Sprinkle salt around inside cavity and fill with a fruit filling. Tie wings and neck portion to body and place in roasting pan, breast up, sprinkle salt over whole. Bake at 325° until done, 30 minutes per pound.

Occasionally dip out the fat and put into a container to be used later on for frying, baking, etc. Prick the skin at times to allow excess fat to escape. After the bird begins to brown, add about 1/3 c. water.

Remove from pan and make a gravy with the fat and liquid in pan. Remove the fruit filling from cavity and place around the goose, or serve in a separate dish.

Filling: 1. Wash, quarter, and core enough apples to fill. 2. Use 1 pound apples and 1 pound prunes, with 2 tbsp. sugar and 1 c. cubed, dried, rolls.

Duck: A duck is prepared in the same way as a goose, allowing the same amount of time per pound as for a goose.

Je mehr man hat, je mehr man will;
nie schweigen seine Wuensche still.

The more one has, the more one wants;
never are his wishes stilled.

MEATS

Koch-Kaese
Cooked Cottage Cheese Spread

1 quart dry curds, cottage cheese which has been ripened or cured.

Beat 2 eggs and add 2 tbsp. sour cream, a little salt, and 1/2 tsp. caraway seed.

Mix all the ingredients and put into the top of a double boiler, with water at boiling stage at all times. Stir occasionally and cook until mixture thickens.

Put into bowl and cool. Use as a spread on bread.

Another method: Put 1 tbsp. butter into frying pan, melt. Add the cheese mixture and cook very slowly over low heat, stirring constantly until thickened. Cool.

Prachersosse
So called "Beggar's Gravy"

This is a gravy made when no meat was used, and so called a beggar's gravy.

Saute 1 tbsp. minced onion in 2 tbsp. fat. Stir in 2-3 tbsp. flour and mix well.

Gradually add water in which the potatoes have been cooked, stirring constantly. When thickened and smooth, add 1/2 c. cream (or canned milk). Add pepper and more salt, if necessary.

Kasseler-Rippen
Pork Loin Roast

Use a lightly smoked 3 pound center-cut pork roast for this.

Score fatty outer part of roast and place in pan with the fatty side up. Put into a preheated 325° oven and roast until browned and almost done, approximately 1- 1 1/2 hours.

Add 1 c. water, 1 small onion, 1 tomato, and continue roasting for 15 minutes.

Remove the roast from pan and make the gravy.

Gravy: Thicken the liquid in the pan with 2 tsp. cornstarch, blended with a little water. Bring to a boil and cook a few minutes. Add 5 tbsp. sour cream (or canned milk).

Serves 5 or 6.

Serve with sauerkraut and (or) *Erbsen-Puree*, Pea Puree.

Sauerbraten
Beef Pot Roast

Combine:

3/4 c. vinegar	2 tsp. salt
3 tbsp. brown sugar	1 bay leaf
8 whole allspice	4 whole peppercorns

Boil 5 minutes. Cool and strain.

Put a 4-5 pound beef roast (boned beef rump pot roast) into a glass or earthenware bowl.

Add cooled marinade (or liquid), 1 medium raw onion, sliced and additional water to cover roast.

Refrigerate 3 or 4 days, turning daily. Remove from brine and wipe dry.

Brown meat in 2 tbsp. fat in a heavy skillet or Dutch oven, browning all sides.

Add 1 c. of the marinade and roast about 3 1/2 hours, or until done, in 325° oven. Add more liquid as needed. When meat is done remove it to a warmed platter and make the gravy.

Gravy: Strain the liquid from the roast, about 2 c. Remove the excess fat from the top of the liquid and thicken with a paste made of 1 1/2 tbsp. cornstarch mixed with a little water. Bring to a boil. Boil a few minutes, stirring constantly.

Slice roast into serving pieces and cover slices with gravy.

Serve with parsley potatoes, peas, and carrots.

This *Sauerbraten* may also be prepared in a Dutch oven on top of the range. Add the marinade to the meat and simmer, covered, until done, approximately 3 hours.

Rippspeer
Spare Ribs with Sauerkraut

Use 2 pounds country-style spare ribs.

Preheat oven to 325°.

Put 1 quart sauerkraut into roasting pan with 2 c. water. Place the salted spareribs on top of kraut and put into the preheated oven. Bake until done, about 45 minutes.

Remove the spareribs and put on a platter. Thicken the sauerkraut with 3 tbsp. flour mixed with 1 c. cream. Bring to a boil and pour over the meat.

Serve with boiled potatoes.

When sauerkraut was the main meal, the meat was cooked with it, and the sauerkraut thickened. Then boiled potatoes were served. If the kraut was cooked separately, fried potatoes were used.

Gedaempfter Schinken
Steamed Ham

Cut ham into medium thin slices, allowing 2 or 3 slices per person. Brown in a little fat, and barely cover with water. Cover pan with a lid and steam about 20 minutes on low heat.

Remove meat to a platter and make the gravy.

Gravy: 1 c. liquid from ham. Thicken with 4 tbsp. flour mixed with 1 c. cream. Add to liquid and bring to a boil. Cook for about 5 minutes. Add more salt and pepper, if needed. Pour over ham slices and serve.

Serve with boiled parsley potatoes and green beans.

Wild Hasen-Braten
(Wild Jack Rabbit Roast)

For this roast use the tenderloin strip, and, if desired, also the thighs and legs.

Soak the meat in buttermilk overnight. Dry thoroughly.

Salt and pepper the meat to taste. Wrap strips of bacon over the whole back, legs, etc. If the legs are used, put these into the oven without the tenderloin part and roast for 15 minutes. Then add the remainder. Bake 1 to 1 1/2 hours at 350°.

If the meat seems to brown too rapidly, add a little water.

10 minutes before the rabbit is done, add 1 c. cream (or canned milk). Continue roasting until done. Remove meat and place on a deep platter. Pour gravy over meat and serve.

Gravy: Mix 1 tbsp. cornstarch with 2 tbsp. water and stir into the hot liquid in roasting pan. Bring to a boil and cook a few minutes or until clear.

Alles in der Welt laesst sich ertragen,
nur nicht eine Reihe von guten Tagen.

Anything in the world you can endure,
except a series of good days.

Rabbit Hunt

During the winter months in Prussia, a community event of great interest was the *"Treibjagd"* or "Rabbit Hunt". Most of the rabbits shot were sold to restaurants or grocery stores. Each farmer, however, would receive one free and could buy more if he so desired. After coming to America rabbit hunts were no longer organized, but hunters went out on their own, alone or in small groups.

MISCELLANEOUS

Marzipan
A Christmas Candy

Sift 1 1/2 lbs. powdered sugar into 1 pound almond paste and 1 egg white. Add 2 or 3 drops rose water and 1/4 tsp. almond extract. Knead all ingredients by hand. Dough will be quite stiff. Form into different shapes: tiny loaves, apples, hearts, pears, etc. Put on a tin and place under the broiler for a very brief time. Watch the Marzipan very carefully, as it should not be baked, only delicately tinted a little brown.

Marzipan No. 2

Roll 1/2 pound icing sugar until fine, and mix with 1/2 pound almond paste. Add juice of lemon. Knead well. Shape into a long roll 1 inch thick, and let set 1 hour. Then shape into desired forms.
    These may be tinted with diluted food color to give a red cheek to an apple, a green tint to a leaf, etc. Allow to dry.

Kraeutertee
Tea Brewed from Herbs

Herb teas would be used for colds, upset stomach, coughs, and also as a regular drink. Often many of the herbs would be grown in the kitchen garden, while at other times the leaves and seeds would have to be gathered elsewhere.
    The seeds and leaves were dried and stored for winter use. Some of the most common herbs were: peppermint, camomile,

fennel seed, and the rose hips. The dried leaves from strawberries, raspberries, cherries, thyme, and others were also blended together and used as needed.

Peppermint tea is good for colds; camomile tea for upset stomach, as well as a hot compress in cases of infection; fennel seed tea, with a little honey added to it, for coughs; rose hip tea, either sweetened or unsweetened, is a delicious drink at supper time.

To make these herb teas use: 2 tbsp. dried herbs over which 1 quart of boiling water is poured. Steep 5 minutes. Strain and serve. Use sugar, if desired.

Butter Mold "Rubbing" by E. Foth

PASTRY

Cherry Tarts
A very pretty, tasty dessert

Mix with hands, similar to a pie dough, until crumbly:

3 c. flour	1 c. butter
3/4 scant c. sugar	1/4 c. lard (margarine may
1 lightly beaten egg	be used for the whole)

Mix well, dough will be somewhat stiff, but by kneading a little, it will be soft enough to be rolled out.

Cut into large circles to fit tart or muffin tins.

Prick with a fork to prevent bubbles from forming.

Bake at 325° about 15 minutes. Tarts must be almost white when done.

These shells may be stored and used as needed. Fill tart shells with a thickened (sour) cherry sauce. A prepared pie filling mix may be used for this. Top with a spoon of whipped, sweetened cream or a prepared whipped topping.

Frucht-Torte

with *Muerbeteig* bottom

Crumbs:

3 c. flour	1/2 c. sugar
1 c. butter (or margarine)	1 tsp. baking powder

Add a lightly beaten egg and 1 1/2 tbsp. cream. Mix well.

Roll out and press into a Torte pan. (If this is not available use 2 layer cake pans, pressing up on sides so filling can be put into torte.)

Bake at 325° about 25 minutes, or until golden brown.

Fill with a thickened fruit filling. A pie filling is good. If canned fruit is used, such as peaches, cherries, etc. drain the syrup from the fruit and thicken with cornstarch and a little more sugar to taste. Put fruit into torte shell, pour thickened syrup over the whole.

Top with whipped topping. Cut into small pie shaped pieces.

This *Muerbeteig* dough can also be used for individual tarts and cookies, if rolled out fairly thin.

Streusselkuchen

(Crumb Cake) made with *Muerbeteig* dough

See recipe for *Frucht Torte*. Roll dough out about 1/2 inch thick and press into layer cake pan, pushing up edges like a pie crust.

Fill with a colorful jam or mashed cooked fruit.

Top with crumb topping:

1 c. sugar	1 3/4 c. flour
1 c. margarine	

Add 1/4 c. slivered almonds to crumb mixture.

Bake at 325° about 35-40 minutes until a golden brown color. To serve cut into narrow pie shaped wedges.

Schnittchen

Puff Pastry—They melt in your mouth!

Sift 1/2 pound flour (2 c.) into a mixing bowl.

Add 1/4 pound butter and work like a pie dough, to a crumbly stage.

Add 1 egg, lightly beaten, and about 2/3 c. water to which 1 tbsp. vinegar has been added.

Knead dough a little. Roll out, turn over in half and roll out again. Repeat a few times. Chill at least 1 hour.

Roll out again, add a little of 1/4 pound additional butter. Fold over in half, roll out again. Add more butter, repeat, until all butter is used. Chill overnight.

Next day roll out again, fold over, etc. Repeat 3 or 4 times. At the end have the dough about 1/4 inch thick. Brush top with mixture of 1 egg yolk and 1/2 tsp. water. Cut with a pastry wheel into oblong pieces, and sprinkle with sugar.

Bake in a hot oven, 425-450°, about 12-15 minutes.

Hint: Keep dough cool at all times.

PRESERVING

Meat Preserving

Three ways of preserving meat were used in West Prussia: salting down, smoking, and covering with hot fat.

SALTING: Meat for salting was laid out on a clean sheet on the cellar floor to cool. The next day the father would rub salt on it, and pack the pieces of meat into a large crock. He would add a layer of salt and then a layer of meat, until all the meat was packed. A close fitting lid was put on top and a heavy stone would be placed on top to weigh it down. The meat would keep a long time in the salt brine, which formed during this process. Before using, the meat was put into a large pan and soaked overnight in cold water. In the morning it would be thoroughly dried and then fried.

SMOKING: Sausages, hams, and bacon were smoked in the smokehouse. This was a little room made of bricks, located on the third floor (or attic), *Der Oberboden.* This was also the place where the grain was stored. The smoke from the kitchen fires passed through the smokehouse or *Raeucherkammer* and could be regulated. The wood for smoking was specially selected as it had to burn with a low flame. Once each day a fire for smoking was made under the *Grapen* and this would keep going until the meat was ready. Sausages usually had to be smoked for 10 to 14 days, depending on the size of the pieces. Bacon and hams were salted before being smoked, and so kept well.

HOT FAT: The hot fat method was used to preserve fried meat, such as *Klopse,* ribs, and small roasts. After the meat was fried, it was put into crocks and then covered with hot lard. This was done on butchering day so the meat would be very fresh. After the lard had cooled and set, the crocks were closed with parchment paper and stored in a cool pantry. When the meat was to be used, it was placed in a hot oven and the lard gradually would melt. The hot fat would be poured off and the meat would be ready to be used.

Fried potatoes and apple sauce were often served with this kind of meat.

Pickled Plums
(or small pears)

Wash 6 pounds of plums (blue plums) and prick skin here and there with a toothpick to prevent the skin from breaking when the fruit is boiled.

Syrup:

2 c. vinegar	small cinnamon stick
1 c. water	4 to 5 cloves
5 c. sugar	

Bring syrup to a boil. Boil a few minutes. Add plums. Cook slowly until tender but still whole.

Remove plums carefully from syrup and put into sterile jars. Pour hot syrup over plums and seal.

Small pears may be treated the same way.

Straemel-Gurken
Ripe Cucumber Slices

Pick long, ripe cucumbers. Peel, cut in half. Scrape the seeds out of each portion and cut into long wedges. To a gallon of sliced cucumbers add 2 tbsp. salt. Let stand overnight. Then drain and rinse.

Method: Add 1/2 c. white vinegar to enough boiling water to cover cucumbers. Bring to a boil and remove from heat. Drain.

Syrup:

1 c. white vinegar	2 to 3 c. water, depending
1 c. sugar	on strength desired
1 tbsp. white mustard seed	

Boil all together. Then add the drained cucumbers and bring to a boil. Immediately pack into sterile jars and seal.

West Prussian Weddings

Weddings among the West Prussian Mennonites were real family celebrations. A calf or young beef would be butchered. The house would be thoroughly cleaned, and on the day before the wedding, neighbor ladies and relatives would come to weave evergreen garlands to decorate the verandas and the front door.

On the morning of the wedding day, the bridal couple would go to the court house for the civil ceremony, which was only attended by the witnesses. This was followed by a simple dinner in the bride's home. The religious ceremony was held in the church in the afternoon, and here the relatives and friends were invited. All guests were asked to the home of the bride, where coffee and cakes *(Kuchen)* of all kinds were served: *Blechkuchen, Rosinen-stritzel, Schnittchen,* etc. The bridal couple were seated on chairs decorated with greens, often myrtle branches; there personal greetings were received, followed by entertainment, both serious and comic, skits and recitations and inbetween there was singing.

At 9:00 p.m. a buffet supper was served: veal or beef roast, cooked potatoes, gravy, vegetables (mostly peas and carrots), and pickles—cucumbers, beets, and plums. For dessert there was *Griess Pudding* served with cherry or raspberry juice.

Several hours of fellowship followed until around midnight, when *Torten* and wine were served. The celebration usually lasted until the early morning hours when, again, the guests were served a meal—"breakfast". This consisted of herring salad served with open faced sandwiches and coffee.

And then, at last, the young couple would be free to depart for their own home!

Silver and Golden Weddings

Upon such special wedding anniversaries as the Silver and Golden weddings, the celebrating began early in the morning. Then a choir of neighbors and friends serenaded the couple with familiar chorales such as *Lobe den Herrn* and *Bis hieher hat dich Gott gebracht.* A short talk was given, followed by the children or close relatives presenting the honored couple with a silver or golden wreath. The singers were then treated to *Broetchen* and *Blechkuchen.* In the afternoon the guests arrived and after a short service, a light lunch or supper was served. Coffee, bread, *Torten, Kuchen,* etc. It was a time of joyful fellowship!

SALADS

Herring Salad
A Wedding Breakfast Specialty

1 small jar pickled herring
  or few pieces *Rollmops*
1 c. diced cooked potatoes
1 c. diced cooked chicken
1 dill pickle, diced (or
  any cucumber pickle)

2 apples, peeled and diced
3 hard cooked eggs
3/4 c. salad dressing or
  mayonnaise, more if
  desired
1 tsp. mustard and salt
  may be added

Mix well. Put 2 eggs into salad and grate the other one on top for decoration.

Serve this salad with buttered bread.

Apple Sauce Deluxe

Pour 4-5 c. sweetened apple sauce into a serving dish.

Wash 1/2 c. (more if desired) dried currants, drain well. Add to the sauce. Chill.

Served instead of a salad.

Simple, but different!

Sour Milk and Lettuce Salad

Let 4 c. of whole, raw milk stand in a warm room until thick. When clabbered, beat with 1/3 c. sour cream. Add a little salt and pepper to taste. If desired, 1 tsp. sugar and a little vinegar may be added.

Wash fresh leaf lettuce well and tear into smaller pieces. Add to the beaten milk mixture. Slice 5 hard boiled eggs on top of lettuce. Serve in sauce dishes, as cold as possible.

This sour milk mixture may also be used with thinly sliced cucumbers, to which a few slices of green onions have been added.

Hospitality

One characteristic of Mennonites is their hospitality, and so in Prussian Mennonite homes guests were always welcome. It was the pride of the *Hausfrau* to serve refreshments to any visitor at any time of the day. Often unexpected guests would come, but there was always something to be served even in such cases.

During the spring, summer, and fall, when the farmers were busy, company was usually invited for Sunday afternoons. *Kaffee* and *Blechkuchen* or *Rosinenstritzel*, were served soon after the guests arrived. After this the womenfolk would enjoy a walk in the garden to admire the flowers and see how the vegetables were progressing. The men, with their walking sticks, would go out into the fields to view the crops or look at the cattle. Politics would also be interspersed in their talk and many lively discussions took place during these outings.

In the meantime the children would be enjoying themselves by playing games of various kinds until they were called inside for an early supper. This would consist of bread and butter, cheese, meat, milk, and coffee.

During the winter months, when the livestock was kept in the barn, there wasn't much work to be done outside and so more time was spent in visiting. Each family had a *Nachbarabend*, evening with the neighbors, to which the children were not invited. The women would bring their knitting and many socks were completed during these visits. A common saying stated, "Close a sock in the evening, and a young hen will start to lay eggs the next day."

On special occasions, such as birthdays, a large number of relatives and friends would be invited. Some came early for dinner, others later on, and so it seemed as if *Kaffee* was served all afternoon. Later a supper would be served to all the guests which usually consisted of *Klopse* (meatballs), or beef roast, or cooked ham or sausage, hot potatoes, pickles, and apple sauce with currants. A *Griess-Pudding* (Cream of Wheat Pudding) with fruit juice would finish the feast.

This hospitality was carried over to the Prussian Mennonite homes in America and foods served were like those of the old country. But let us "listen" to a Kansan describe the early fellowship in her home.

"When guests came for *Vesper*, the red tablecloth with the big white flowers was spread over the oilcloth on the table. Only on very special occasions did we use the white damask tablecloth, which was part of Mother's dowry. Mother also had a large dinnerware set, white with small blue flowers, and for *Vesper* the small plates of this set were used. On very special festive occasions the large dinner plates were set on the table. At such a time the large tureen, which was seldom used, would be filled with creamy mashed potatoes. Then there would be either fried chicken, boiled ham, or *Klopse* (meatballs) with a dish of pickled cucumbers or peaches. Salads and vegetables were rarely used. A vegetable soup, such as carrot soup, was made for everyday when it was the main dish. However, fresh rye bread was often on hand for this day and with a dessert of *Roter Pudding*, topped with a custard sauce, no one left the table the least bit hungry.

In setting the table for a dinner, the knives, forks, and teaspoons were all placed on the right hand side of the plate. If soup spoons were needed, they were put above the plates. We did not have silver cutlery or stainless steel, but a steel that rusted easily, with wooden handles. When these were washed, we were not to put them into the water, for the wood would lose its shape or come off. These knives and forks had to be dried carefully, otherwise they would get rusty and it took a lot of elbow grease to polish them with brick dust.

Our meals were always very simple. For Sunday dinners Mother usually prepared a kettle of *Mus*, a fruit soup made from any available fruit; apricot, cherry, apple, or gooseberry were our favorites. This *Mus* would be served with cold ham and fried potatoes. One great treat for the girls of the family was that the Sunday dishes were washed only at breakfast. At noon and in the evening, they were stacked and not washed until Monday morning . . . Only the knives and forks, of course, had to be wiped and thoroughly dried.

For special days, such as Christmas, Easter, and so on, *Pflaumenkeilchen* was served. This soup is still a favorite dish of the younger members of our family, even though they are scattered a long distance from the old 'Parental home.'"

SOUPS

Soups play an important part in the menu of a Prussian Mennonite family. Often these soups are a meal in themselves: *Koenigsberger Klops*, chicken noodle, fish soup, etc. Lighter, thinner soups are served at supper time, when no heavy meal is wanted. Milk soups belong in this class. These are easily made and are also very nourishing. When our mothers or grandmothers made such soups, very few of the ingredients were measured. If they preferred a thicker soup, more flour would be used; if a thinner one, less flour or more milk. Always these dishes seemed to turn out satisfactorily and tasteful. So in trying to make soups from some of these recipes, it is not absolutely necessary to follow the measurements to a "T". Make according to your own individual taste or preference.

Although *Klueter-Suppe* or *Eier-Mus* were enjoyed by a great many families, there were some who did not find this milk soup too interesting. One Mennonite mother often cooked this soup for supper as she thought it was nourishing for her children. But her children did not like it. One evening when some soup was left over, two of the older children went into cahoots and dumped the whole thing into the "slop" bucket for the pigs, right under their mother's nose. That made her think. She realized that she did not like this *Mus*, neither did the father, so why cook it? But it had just seemed the proper thing to do ever so often. From that time on there was no more *Eier-Mus* served.

Klueter-Mus (Eier-Mus)
A milk soup #1

Gradually bring to a boiling point, 3 c. milk and 1/2 tsp. salt. In a bowl mix:

    4 rounded tbsp. flour   6 to 7 tbsp. milk
    1 egg

Beat until smooth but somewhat thick.

When the milk begins to boil, add the flour mixture gradually in a "shaky" method, about 1 tsp. at a time. The result will be a small dumpling effect throughout the soup. The texture should not be smooth.

Allow to come to a boil and remove from heat.

To serve, add sugar, if desired, and a little cold milk.

— a good dish for a bachelor to make!

Klueter-Mus No. 2

Gradually bring to a boil 6 c. milk and 1/2 tsp. salt.

In the meantime sift 1/2 c. flour into a mixing bowl. Add 1 tbsp. of water at a time to the flour, mixing or rubbing the dough with your hands. Make pea-sized crumbs. Add just enough liquid to use all the flour.

Add these crumbs slowly to the boiling milk. Let come to a boil, simmer a few minutes, stirring constantly and then serve.

Makes 6 servings.

For a variety add an egg to the flour mixture. Then less flour will be needed.

Also try buttermilk as a substitute for the sweet milk. Add sugar if desired.

Birnen-Suppe
Pear Soup
— a delicious Milk Soup

METHOD 1. Add 1 1/2 to 2 c. uncooked noodles, 1/2 tsp. salt to 5 c. milk. Heat over a low heat, stirring occasionally.

In the meantime peel, core, and quarter 3 large pears, or more smaller ones. Cover with water and cook until done, adding 4 tbsp. sugar near the end.

When the noodles are done, add the cooked pears. Stir to mix evenly. Serve hot.

METHOD 2. Cook noodles separately or use left-over noodles. Heat milk and add the cooked noodles. Dice canned pears to make 1 to 1 1/2 c. and add, using about 1/2 c. of the syrup in which the pears were preserved. A piece of butter, the size of a walnut may be added at the end.

Serve *Birnen-Suppe* with cold cuts. A complete meal!

Kleine Toepfe haben auch Ohren.

Little pitchers also have ears.

Pflaumen-Keilchen
Prunes and Noodles

1. Wash 1 pound dried prunes and cover with 4 c. water. Add 1 cinnamon stick and simmer until prunes are done. Add 1/2 c. sugar and 2 c. uncooked noodles. Cook until noodles are soft. Add 1 1/2 tbsp. vinegar or lemon juice.

2. *Einlegs-keilchen*, or small "dumplings" which can be used instead of the noodles in the above recipe.
Mix 1 c. flour, 1 egg, 1/2 tsp. salt, and just enough water to make a medium stiff dough.
Put a small part of this dough on a saucer, dip a serving spoon into the boiling soup, and quickly scrape small pieces of the dough into the water. Dip the spoon into the liquid often to prevent sticking. These little *Keilchen* should be about the size of a large pea.
Bring the soup to a boil, cook a few minutes and remove from the heat.
Serve with fried ham or bacon.

Fish Soup

Use a mild fish, such as white, Jack, or salmon.
Prepare a fish of about 2-3 pounds, removing head, fins, etc. Cover with cold water and bring to a boil. Add 1 tsp. salt, 1 tsp. peppercorns, 10 whole allspice, little parsley, small bay leaf, and a small onion. Add water as needed during cooking to keep fish covered.
When fish is tender, carefully remove the "bones", leaving fish in large pieces. Set aside.
In the meantime boil separately, 4 medium potatoes in salt water.
Strain the fish broth to remove spices. Return to heat and add enough water (or potato water) to make 1 quart. Thicken this with a paste made of 4 tbsp. flour and 1/2 c. thick cream. Bring to a boil and continue cooking until thickened. Add the cooked, diced potatoes and fish, adding 2 tbsp. butter. Serve hot. Delicious with buttered bread.

Quick Method for Fish Soup

Put the diced potatoes in a kettle of cold water, adding the spices as given. Cook until potatoes are done. Then thicken the soup, adding a can of salmon (drained), and heat just enough so the fish is warmed thoroughly. Add butter.

Tauben-Suppe
Squab Soup with Rice

Prepare 3 squabs, 1 for a serving.

Make a stuffing for each by using the liver, heart, and gizzard, cut fine, 3 tsp. raw rice, and a little salt.

Put the birds into a kettle and add 4 to 5 c. water to which the following spices have been added:

1 bay leaf	sprig of parsley
3 slices onion	1 tsp. salt (or to taste)
1/2 tsp. whole allspice	pepper

Cook slowly until done, about 1 to 1 1/2 hours. When almost done add about 1/2 c. rice to the soup and finish cooking until the rice is tender. (Add more rice, if desired.)

Tauben-Suppe was often made just for sick people as it did take more patience to make it then other soups.

Koenigsberger Klops
Saure Klops
Sour Meatballs with Potatoes

Use your favorite recipe for meatballs, or use the following:

1 lb. ground beef or beef	1 tsp. salt
and pork mixed	1/8 tsp. pepper
1 egg	1 tbsp. chopped onion
2/3 c. dried bread crumbs	1/4 c. water

Mix all together and form into medium sized meatballs.

SOUP: Boil the following for 10 minutes:

1 small bay leaf	1/4 tsp. whole allspice
1 tbsp. chopped onion	1 tbsp. vinegar
1 tsp. salt	4 to 5 c. water

Add the meatballs and simmer until done, about 20 minutes. When meatballs are done, remove from liquid and thicken soup. Make a paste of 1/4 c. flour and 1 c. sour cream. (For less calories use canned milk for half. Add 1-2 tsp. vinegar with canned milk.) Add paste gradually to hot liquid and continue stirring until it comes to a boil. Cook a few more minutes. Add 1 tbsp. butter.

Potatoes: Allow 1-2 potatoes per person, cut in half. Cook in salted water until done.

To serve, put a cooked potato in a soup bowl, add a meatball and pour the soup over these.

Method #2. A simple method— Add the diced potatoes to the liquid at the same time the meatballs are added. Cook everything together. When done remove the meat and thicken the liquid as in the first method.

This dish is a great favorite among Prussian Mennonites, and is even served for company.

Chicken Noodle Soup

Cut a 3-4 pound chicken (at least 1 year old to give a better flavor), into serving sized pieces. Cover with water, about 2 1/2 quarts and bring to a boil. Remove the "scum" as it forms.

Add spices:

1 small onion	1 sliced carrot
1 bay leaf	1 tsp. peppercorns
1/2 tsp. whole allspice	little sprig of parsley,
2 tsp. salt	may be added

Simmer until done. Skim off excess fat and replace it with 4 tbsp. butter at serving time.

Remove the chicken and strain the liquid.

Return liquid to heat, bring to a boil, and add the homemade, fine cut noodles. Cook about 8-10 minutes or until tender.

The noodles may also be boiled separately and added to the hot soup.

For a variety cook 1 to 2 c. rice and add instead of noodles.

Pastinake Suppe
Parsnip Soup

Cook fresh pork hocks or 2 1/2 pounds fresh country-style spare ribs in about 2 quarts water, to which 1 tsp. salt and a few peppercorns have been added. Cook until meat is almost done, adding more water if necessary to keep meat covered.

Add 3 large parsnips, peeled and sliced, and 4-5 potatoes, diced. Cook until vegetables are tender. Remove the meat and mash the vegetables. Add 3 tbsp. butter and serve.

If cream is desired, add about 1/3 c. just before serving.

Green Bean Soup with Pears

Cook together:
— 2 quarts cut raw green beans
— smoked ham bone or ham hocks, with enough meat to make several good sized pieces
— 6 sugar pears (a hard type pear rather small in size. If larger ones are used, add only 3, eg. Keefer pears.)
— 1 quart water
— 1 tsp. dried savory or a sprig of fresh
— salt and pepper to taste

Boil together until beans are done. The soup will be rather thick.

If canned or frozen beans are used, cook the meat alone for about 15 minutes.

Serve with boiled *salz Kartoffel* (plain boiled potatoes).

Obst-Mus
A Fruit Soup

Mus can be made from dried, raw, or canned fruit, and served either warm or cold. It is convenient for Sunday dinner or for any special event, as it can be prepared ahead of time. Some popular fruits used for *Mus* are: apricots, cherries, plums, rhubarb, apple, and gooseberry.

METHOD: Cook 1 quart fruit with 6-8 c. water until tender. Thicken with a paste made of 3 tbsp. flour or 2 tbsp. cornstarch, 3/4 c. sugar (or to taste), and 1/2 c. cream. Gradually add to the boiling liquid, stirring constantly. Remove from heat. Set aside to cool.

1. For rhubarb: cut rhubarb into pieces about 1 inch thick and then boil.
2. For gooseberry: pick off the stems and blossom-end, and cook until done. Make the thickening for this by adding 1 egg to the mixture. This makes the soup less tart.
3. If preserved fruit is used the method will be the same, but will be a little quicker. Add 3 to 4 c. water to 1 quart of canned fruit to make enough liquid. Thicken as for the other mixtures, using a little less sugar.
4. For *Apfel-Mus*, dice the apples which may be peeled or unpeeled. Add a stick of cinnamon and cover all with water. Cook until apples are done. Thicken with flour and cream paste. Serve either hot or cold.

VEGETABLES

Navy Beans with Sweet-Sour Sauce

In a frying pan put 3 tbsp. fat and 3 tbsp. flour. Brown a little. Gradually add:

1/4 c. brown or white sugar	1/2 tsp. salt
1/4 c. syrup	1 tbsp. vinegar

Stir until blended; then add 2 c. liquid, gradually, either hot water or the liquid in which the beans have been cooked. Boil a few minutes. Pour over beans.

Beans: Cook either dried beans as directed or use 2 tins of commercially canned white beans, navy or Northern. Heat these and serve with the sauce.

Serve with ham or sausages and a green salad.

Erbsen-Pueree
Split Pea Puree

Soak 3/4 pound split peas in 3 c. water overnight. In morning cook slowly for about 2 to 2 1/2 hours, adding 1 tsp. salt, 1 small onion, and 1 tbsp. butter; or use 2 slices crisply fried bacon strips, crumbled, instead of the butter.

When done the mixture will be rather mushy.

Good served with *Kasseler Rippen* Roast.

Red Cabbage

1 small head red cabbge, coarsely cut.

Melt 3 tbsp. shortening in pot and add the sliced cabbage.

Core and quarter 3 tart apples and add. Cover and steam, or simmer, until the cabbage is tender, stirring occasionally.

When almost done add:

    1 tsp. salt   1 tbsp. sugar

    2 tbsp. vinegar

In Prussia the green cabbage was used out of the garden, and was not stored over winter as it did not keep as well as the red cabbage. The latter would then be used mostly in the winter time, and would often be served for company or special occasions.

Fried Apples

Served as "Vegetable"

#1. Allow 1 apple per person. Quarter each apple and remove core. Cut pieces in half. Put into frying pan with:

    1 tsp. butter   1 tsp. water   1 tsp. sugar

per apple. Sprinkle with salt. Cover. Set on medium low heat and cook till done. Add more water if necessary. Serve hot.

#2. Core apples. Cut into slices. Melt butter in pan and add the appleslices. Turn to brown both sides. Put into serving dish and sprinkle with sugar. Serve hot.

Rice With Milk
(Quick Method) 3-4 servings

1 c. rice, cooked as directed on package. Or bring 6 c. water to boiling stage, add 1 tsp. salt and the rice. Stir well. Cook until rice is done, about 15 minutes. Drain.

Add 3 c. milk. Heat and simmer slowly until well blended, approximately 15 minutes.

Serve in bowls with a cinnamon and sugar mixture. Add cold milk, if desired. (Mixture: 1/3 c. sugar and 1 tsp. cinnamon, stir well.)

This dish was and is usually served for supper, especially during the winter. Years ago when the kitchen range was in use, the milk and rice were put on the back of the range and cooked slowly for several hours. Off and on it would be stirred to prevent sticking.

Buttermilch-Gruetze
Barley Porridge with Buttermilk

Soak 1 c. regular pearl barley in 2 c. water for several hours or overnight.

Add 4 c. buttermilk and cook slowly over a low heat until done, several hours. Stir often.

This barley porridge is usually served cold but it is also good warmed. Top with whole sweet milk and add sugar, if desired. Served with cold sliced meat, it is a good supper dish.

QUICK METHOD: Add 1 c. quick barley to 2 c. boiling water, 1/4 tsp. salt. Simmer about 10 minutes or until thick, stirring frequently.

Add 3 c. buttermilk and continue cooking until done, about 25 minutes. Stir often. 4 servings.

Hans haut Holz	Hans is chopping wood
Hinter Harders Haus.	Behind Harder's house.
Hinter Harders Hinterhaus	Behind Harder's backhouse,
Haut Hans Holz.	Hans is cutting wood.

Der Faule wird Abends fleissig.
  (The lazy person becomes diligent in the evening.)

Wenn der Hahn kraeht auf dem Mist
 Aenderts sich's Wetter -
Oder bleibt wie es ist!

    (When the rooster crows on the manure pile
      The weather will change -
      Or remain as it is.)

Wer lauft der sieht es nicht.
Wer langsam geht der denkt es muss so sein.

    (He who runs does not see it.
      He who walks slowly thinks it has to be that way.)

9

The Polish Mennonites

HISTORY

Mennonites In Poland

Poland, located between Germany and Russia, has undergone many changes in its history and played a significant role in the history of the Mennonites who moved eastward from the Netherlands. West and East Prussia were added to Poland in 1466 under the Jagellon dynasty (1386-1572) in a conflict with the Teutonic Knights. After 1530, therefore, when the Mennonites started to come from the Low Countries to settle along the Vistula River, they settled in Polish territory. Both privileges permitting them to settle under certain conditions, and edicts prohibiting their settlement as "heretics" were issued in early times, primarily by Polish rulers. They were mostly valid only during the lifetime of a ruler. The Mennonites were tolerated only because some estate owners or officials derived benefits from them as expert farmers and drainers of the swampy areas along the Vistula River. The Mennonites and other Dutch immigrants became known as experts in various trades, particularly in draining swamps. Numerous favorable privileges and restricting edicts were issued in the following years. A special manner of settling, i.e., the pattern by which the "Hollanders" settled and rented their land, became known throughout Poland.

Starting in Danzig around 1535, Mennonite settlers moved into the unoccupied areas along the Vistula River establishing "Hollaender" villages in the triangle between Danzig and Elbing and Marienburg. As the land in this triangle became occupied the

248

descendants and newcomers proceeded south along the Vistula River, establishing themselves in Schwetz, Graudenz, and Culm. From here, they proceeded into the interior of Poland. During the late 18th century, they established the Mennonite settlements of Deutsch-Kazun and Deutsch-Wymysle near Warsaw, and farther southeast Michalin near Makhnovka, Karolswalde near Ostrog in Volhynia, which meanwhile had become Russian Poland.

During the first partition of Poland (1772), West Prussia, not including Danzig and Thorn, became a part of Germany and East Galicia, of Austria. During the partitions of 1793 and 1795, other parts of Poland—Danzig, Thorn, Plock, and Warsaw—were added to Germany, and Volhynia to Russia. The Volhynian and some other Mennonite settlements were in Russian Poland when the great migration of Mennonites to America took place in 1874.

After World War I, Poland again became independent, and Danzig became a free city. Many of the Mennonite settlements were located in Polish territory or the Polish Corridor. At the beginning of World War II, Germany and Russia divided Poland once more, and the Mennonite population in Russian-occupied Poland was transferred to the German part. Since 1945, all of the areas in which Mennonites lived in Danzig, Prussia (except the Koenigsberg-Memel area, now Russian), and Poland belong to Poland and are under Polish rule. The Mennonite population either fled from this territory during World War II or the German collapse in 1943-45, or they were evacuated or have fled since that time. No organized Mennonite community or church exists today along the Vistula River or any other part of Poland.

Cornelius Krahn, *Mennonite Encyclopedia*, Vol. IV, Pages 199-200.

The Michalin Mennonites

The forefathers of the settlement today known as Grace Hill *(Gnadenberg)*, of Harvey County, Kansas, originally came from West Prussia and accepted the invitation to settle on marshy land on the Vistula River in the Graudenz area.

This particular group left in 1791 for Makhnovka, southwest of Kiev. Some of the common names of families were Nickel, Kliewer, and Harms.

The precarious journey by horse and wagon of at least four weeks depended very much on the ingenuity and foresight of the women. How to pack? What food would keep best? How much clothing should be taken? What heirlooms? And maybe a few tulip bulbs and other seeds tucked into small spaces?

This small group built the village of Michalin on the estate of Count Potocki and lived here for about 80 years. In 1793, this part of Volhynia became Russian. The soil was rich. The ready supply of firewood made the brick hearth, with built-in oven, a source of comfort and convenience. The huge chimney made a fine meat curing chamber, and the loft above the granary offered a good cold storage room.

Ministers from the Graudenz region and Southern Russia visited the group several times, giving them assistance in their church organization.

The group joined those Mennonites who, because of nonresistance, chose to come to America. The families purchased their farms mostly from the Santa Fe Railway with a bonus gift of forty acres from the railway for a church. The Register of Deeds office shows many of these plots to be heavily mortgaged, renewed, and foreclosed, but they had tenacity, persistence, and resourcefulness.

This group of Mennonites, as is true of many others, has a strong feeling of togetherness. To this day their great concern is to remain true to the precepts of Menno, *"Unser Ausgaenger!"*

Table Grace

1. *Dankt dem Herrn denn Er ist freundlich*
    Und Seine Guete waehret ewiglich. Amen.

2. *Komm Herr Jesu sei unser Gast*
    Und segne was Du bescheret hast. Amen.

MENU

Polish-Russian Menu for a Day

Breakfast
 Oatmeal
 Bread and butter
 Cracklings and syrup (in winter)
 Coffee and milk

Noon Meal
 Chicken Noodle Soup or *Borscht*
 Apple Dumplings
 Water

Evening Meal
 Fried potatoes
 Vegetables
 Fruit
 Cookies
 Coffee or tea

BREADS

Zwieback

2 c. milk	1 1/2 packages yeast
2/3 c. butter or part lard	1/4 c. warm water
2 tsp. salt	1 tsp. sugar
2 tbsp. sugar	6 c. flour

Scald the milk and add the butter or lard, salt, and 2 tbsp. sugar. Cool.

Dissolve the yeast in the warm water. Add 1 tsp. sugar.

Add the dissolved yeast and 4 c. of the flour to the milk mixture. Mix well.

Add the rest of the flour and knead until smooth. Let rise until double in bulk.

Pinch off small portions of dough, and form into balls size of a small egg.

Place on a greased cookie sheet, and put a slightly smaller ball on top of the bottom ball. Press down in the center with the finger.

Let rise until double in bulk.

Bake at 375° for about 20 minutes.

Fett-Platz
(Fritters)

1 1/4 c. flour	2 tbsp. sugar
1 tsp. baking powder	1 egg, beaten
1/2 tsp. salt	1 c. milk

Beat the egg well, add the sugar and salt, then the milk alternately with the sifted flour and baking powder.

Drop spoonfuls of batter into deep hot fat at 375°, till the fritters are golden brown all around.

Don't prick them or they will absorb fat. Drain on absorbent paper.

Serve them with sugar sprinkled on top, or with syrup poured over them.

Apfel-Fett-Platz
(Apple Fritters)

Use the above recipe for fritters, but add 1 c. cut up apples to the batter before frying.

Quick Cream Biscuits

2 c. flour, sifted before
   measuring
3 tsp. baking powder

3/4 tsp. salt
1 c. sweet cream

Sift dry ingredients into a bowl.

Mix in the cream to make a soft dough. Transfer to a well floured board or pastry cloth, and pat or roll out to one-inch thickness. Cut with a biscuit cutter, first dipped in flour.

Place close together on a greased pan and bake at 425° for 12-15 minutes.

Roll-Koke
(Crullers)

3 eggs
1/3 c. sweet cream
2/3 c. sweet milk
1 tsp. sugar

3 1/2 to 4 c. flour (to make a
   soft dough)
1 tsp. salt
3 tsp. baking powder

Beat eggs, add cream and milk.

Sift all dry ingredients together, add to mixture.

On a floured board or pastry cloth, roll out to about 1/4 inch thickness.

Cut into strips about 2 by 4 inches.

Cut two slashes through the strips.

Fry in hot fat (or vegetable oil) at 375°.

Drain on absorbent paper.

Pancakes

1 egg
1 c. buttermilk or
   sour milk
2 tbsp. soft shortening

1 tsp. sugar
1 tsp. soda
1/2 tsp. salt
1 c. sifted flour

Beat the egg well, dissolve the soda in the buttermilk. Mix all ingredients together with beater until smooth.

A heavy griddle is best. If necessary, grease the griddle lightly. Pour batter from tip of spoon or from a pitcher. Turn pancakes as soon as they are bubbly and brown the other side.

Coffee Cake With Prune Topping

2 packages dry yeast	1 1/2 c. milk
1/2 c. warm water	2 tsp. salt
2 eggs	1 c. shortening
3/4 c. sugar	5 c. flour

Dissolve the yeast in warm water.

Scald the milk, and melt the shortening in it. Allow to cool. Stir in the beaten eggs, sugar, and salt.

Add 3 c. of the flour and mix. Stir in the dissolved yeast and beat thoroughly. Stir in the remaining flour.

Let rise until double in bulk; then stir and let rise again. Divide the dough into three 8 by 8-inch squares or 9-inch rounds, greased pans.

Before baking, spread the top with a Prune Topping:

Soak approximately 4 c. of prunes in warm water for 3 or 4 hours or overnight. Cook until tender and remove pits. Press the prunes through a strainer. Add sugar to taste, approximately 1/4 c.

Bake at 375° for 30-35 minutes.

Pummelchen
(New Year's Cookies)

1 1/2 c. milk	1 package yeast
1/2 c. shortening	1/2 c. warm water
1/2 c. sugar	1 tsp. sugar
2 tsp. salt	7 c. flour
2 eggs	

Dissolve the yeast and 1 tsp. sugar in 1/2 c. warm water. Scald the milk. Remove from heat and add shortening, sugar, and salt. Cool.

Gradually add 4 c. of the flour to the milk mixture and stir. Add the dissolved yeast and beat. Add the eggs, one at a time. Add the rest of the flour and knead until smooth. Let rise until double in bulk. Punch down and let rise again.

Pinch off small portions of dough, and press a stewed, sweetened, pitted prune in the center, wrapping dough around, forming a ball.

Place on a lightly floured bread board, and let rise until double in bulk.

Drop into hot fat, 375°, raised side down, so top will rise while underside cooks. Turn, but be careful not to prick them. Drain on absorbent paper.

Roll in granulated sugar while hot, if desired.

Harvesting and Threshing

Preparations for the harvesting of wheat, barley and oats were usually made in advance. Bins and machinery had to be checked and repaired, binder canvases checked and mended. Harvest involved the entire family. Usually the father or an older person operated the horsedrawn binder. The binder cut the standing, ripe grain, tied it into bundles with twine, then dropped the bundles onto a carrier on the side of the binder. When the carrier was full, the bundles were dumped in neat rows by the person operating the binder.

The older children were taught the art of standing up the bundles to form shocks. The younger children, not strong enough to set up the bundles, provided cool drinking water and carried out the mid-afternoon lunch to the workers in the field. Mother was busy at home cooking the meals, to which the hungry appetites did full justice.

After the grain was all cut and shocked, the farmers formed a threshing ring, and awaited their turn for the threshing outfit, which consisted of a big steam engine, a grain separator, and a water tank. As a rule a threshing crew consisted of about twelve to fourteen men. Farmers helped each other by loading the bundles onto hayracks, then hauling them to the grain separator. Two men, on racks, one at each side, pitched the bundles onto the separator bundle carrier. This work required about six men with teams and racks, and usually several extra field pitchers, to help load. It required two men to take care of the loads of grain, one man to tend the steam engine, one man to haul the water for the steam engine (which usually was hauled from a creek or pond), and, if no water was available from that source, the farmer had to supply the water from the stock tank. The farmer had to hope for enough wind to run his windmill to supply the water for the horses and, if need be, for the steam engine.

The farmer's wife usually had extra help from a neighbor to assist with the cooking. Provisions were made for the men to wash up at noon by setting out some benches under a shade tree, and providing several wash basins, towels, soap, combs, a mirror, and several pails of water. Mid-afternoon lunches were taken out and served in the field.

Threshing meant long days of hard work, but it also afforded neighbors an opportunity to get together and work together, thereby knitting a closer community fellowship.

Raised Doughnuts

1 package dry yeast	1 tsp. salt
1/4 c. warm water	3 eggs, beaten
1 c. milk	1 tsp. vanilla
1/4 c. shortening	5 c. flour
2/3 c. sugar	

Dissolve the yeast in the warm water. Scald the milk, add the shortening, sugar, and salt. Let cool to lukewarm. Add the beaten eggs, the vanilla, dissolved yeast, and flour. Mix and knead well.

Let rise until light. Roll dough out on a floured board or pastry cloth 1/3 to 1/2 inch thick. Cut with a doughnut cutter and let rise on a board until very light (30-45 minutes). Leave uncovered so crust will form on the dough.

Fry in deep fat at 375°, with the raised side down to allow the top side to rise while the under side cooks.

Drain on absorbent paper.

Roll the hot doughnuts in powdered or granulated sugar, or glaze them with 1 c. powdered sugar, 5 tbsp. water and 1 tsp. vanilla, if desired.

NOTE: Raised doughnuts, *Roll Koke* and *Apel Pirogy* were frequently served to threshing crews for midafternoon lunches.

Stretzel

(*Streusel* Coffee Cake)

2 packages dry yeast
1/2 c. warm water
1 1/2 c. scalded milk
1/2 c. shortening
1/2 c. sugar

2 tsp. salt
2 eggs
2 c. raisins (optional)
6 c. flour (approx.)

Dissolve the yeast in the warm water.

Melt the shortening in the scalded milk. Let cool to lukewarm.

Add the beaten eggs, sugar, salt, and 3 1/2 c. of flour to the warm milk. Mix with a spoon, then add the yeast mixture and mix well until smooth. Then add the raisins (if desired) and enough remaining flour to handle easily.

Turn dough out on a floured board and knead until smooth. Then place it in a greased bowl and cover with a damp cloth. Let rise until double in bulk. Punch down, and let rise again for about 30 minutes.

Divide dough into 4 parts and pat each into greased round pans. Sprinkle *Streusel* topping over dough (recipe below). Cover. Let rise until double in bulk, about 30 minutes. Bake in oven at 375° for 25-30 minutes.

Streusel Topping: Rub together until crumbly: 3/4 c. sugar, 1/2 c. flour, 3/4 tsp. cinnamon, and 1/2 c. butter.

CAKES AND COOKIES

Old Fashioned Sugar Cookies

1 c. sugar
1 c. butter
2 eggs
1/4 c. sweet milk
1 tsp. vanilla

3 c. flour
2 tsp. baking powder
1 scant tsp. soda
1/4 tsp. nutmeg
1/2 tsp. salt

Cream the butter and sugar; add eggs, then milk, and vanilla.

Sift all the dry ingredients together. Add to the first mixture.

Thoroughly chill the dough, then roll out on a lightly floured board to 1/8 inch thickness.

Sprinkle top with sugar and lightly run a rolling pin over the sugar.

Cut with a 3-inch cookie cutter. Place on greased cookie sheets. Bake at 350° for about 15 minutes, or until light brown.

Pfeffernuesse
(Peppernuts)

1 c. butter (or part lard)	1 tbsp. cinnamon
2 c. sugar	1 tbsp. powdered anise
1 1/2 c dark syrup	seed
1 c. sour cream	1 tbsp. powdered star
1 1/2 tsp. soda	anise seed
1 tsp. salt	2 tsp. vanilla
9 c. flour	

Cream the butter with the sugar.

Add the syrup and the sour cream, to which the soda has been added, and the vanilla. Sift the salt, soda, and spices with 5 c. flour and add to the creamed mixture. Mix well. Work in the remaining flour.

Chill dough in refrigerator.

Cut off portions of dough and make long thin rolls.

Slice the rolls with a knife about 1/2 inch apart.

Place cut side down on greased baking sheet. Bake at 350°.

CHEESE

Gloms-Pirogy
(Cottage Cheese Dumplings)

2 egg whites	1 tsp. salt
1/2 c. milk	2 c. flour

Filling:

1 pint dry cottage cheese	1/8 tsp. pepper
1 tsp. salt	2 egg yolks

Make a stiff dough with the egg whites, salt, milk, and flour. Roll thin as for pie dough on floured board. Cut dough into 4 inch circles.

Place 1 or 2 tbsp. of cottage cheese filling on each round of dough, and tightly press the edges together.

Place in boiling water and boil slowly for about 15 minutes.

TO SERVE: Add 1/2 c. sour cream to hot bacon or sausage drippings and pour over the dumplings.

NOTE: Sauerkraut may be used in place of cottage cheese.

Gloms
(Cottage Cheese)

Place thick, freshly-soured, raw, clabbered milk over a pan of hot water, not boiling, or on low heat to about 115°. When the milk is warm and the curd separates from the whey, cool, drain in a cheesecloth or a strainer. Put the curd into a bowl and add salt, pepper, and cream to taste, mixing with a fork. The whey may be saved and used cold as a beverage.

DESSERTS

Apfel Pirogy
(Apple Dumplings #1)

2 c. flour
3 tsp. baking powder
1 tsp. salt
1/4 c. sugar

1/3 c. shortening
1 egg
1/3 c. milk
2 or 3 apples

Sift the dry ingredients into a bowl.

Cut in the shortening.

Add the milk mixed with the beaten egg.

Turn dough out on a lightly floured board and gather up into a ball; knead lightly until dough is somewhat smooth. Roll to 1/4 inch thickness. Cut into four or five inch squares.

Place the diced or sliced apples in the center of the squares. Sprinkle 1 tsp. of sugar on the apples.

Bring the four corners of dough together in the center and firmly seal the edges.

Bake at 375°, until browned.

Apfel Pirogy
(Apple Dumplings #2)

3 c. flour
4 tsp. baking powder
1/2 tsp. salt
1/2 c. shortening
3/4 c. milk
2 tbsp. butter

1 egg
3 or 4 apples
1 c. brown sugar (or 1/2 c.
   brown and 1/2 white)
1 c. water

Sift the flour, baking powder, and salt together. Cut in the shortening.

Add the beaten egg to the milk, and add this to the flour mixture. Roll 1/4 inch thick.

Cut the dough to fit apple quarters or halves.

Sprinkle the apples with a tsp. of sugar. Fold the dough around the apples and place in a greased pan, about 1 inch apart.

Combine the sugar, water, and butter and bring to a boil for about 3 minutes. Spoon the hot syrup over the dumplings after they have been in the oven 10 minutes.

Bake at 375° for 30-35 minutes.

Plume Pirogy

Use the recipe for *Apfel Pirogy* but use cooked, pitted, and sweetened prunes in place of apples.

Bread Pudding

2 eggs	2 c. scalded milk
1/2 c. sugar	3 1/2 c. soft or stale bread
1/4 tsp. salt	crumbs
1 tsp. cinnamon or vanilla	1/2 c. raisins

Beat the eggs, add the sugar, milk, salt, and cinnamon (or vanilla). Mix and pour over the bread crumbs. Add the raisins and blend all together.

Pour into a 1 1/2 quart greased baking dish. Place the baking dish in a pan of hot water (1 inch deep). Bake at 350° for 40-50 minutes, or until a knife inserted an inch from edge comes out clean.

Serve warm with milk or cream.

Apple Coffee Cake

2 c. flour, sifted	1 egg
1 tsp. salt	2/3 c. milk
3 tsp. baking powder	3 sour apples
1/4 c. sugar	2 tbsp. sugar
1/4 c. shortening	1/4 tsp. cinnamon

Sift the dry ingredients together; cut in the shortening. Add the milk and beaten egg. Spread in a greased shallow pan 7 by 11 inches. Pare and cut the apples into quarter sections. Slice each section into 4 slices lengthwise and set in rows on the dough, with the sharp edges pressed lightly into the dough.

Sprinkle the top with the mixed sugar and cinnamon.

Bake in a hot oven, 400°, for 25-30 minutes. Serve hot with vanilla sauce.

Vanilla Sauce

1/2 scant c. sugar
1 tbsp. cornstarch or
2 tbsp. flour

1 c. boiling water
1 tsp. vanilla
1 tbsp. butter

Mix sugar and cornstarch (or flour) in a sauce pan. Pour on the boiling water slowly, stirring rapidly. Boil and stir until clear. Remove from heat and add the butter and vanilla.

MEATS

Cabbage Rolls

1 firm head of cabbage
1/2 lb. ground beef
1 tsp. salt
1/8 tsp. pepper

1 small onion, minced
1 1/2 c. cooked rice
4 strips bacon
1 1/4 c. tomatoes, put through a strainer

With a sharp knife remove the core from the head of cabbage, and place it in a deep kettle. Cover the cabbage with boiling water, and bring to a boil. Remove the cabbage and drain thoroughly. Separate the leaves.

Fry the meat until it is cooked (not browned).

Mix in a bowl the meat, onion, and seasoning.

Add the cooked rice, stirring until well blended.

Place 2 tbsp. of the mixture on each cabbage leaf, rolling tightly and binding with tooth picks.

Place in a baking dish, spreading the bacon slices over the rolls. Pour the strained tomato juice over all.

Bake at 350°, basting several times with the soup.

Old Fashioned Hash

3 c. left-over roast meat
1 c. mashed potatoes
1 medium onion
1 1/2 tsp. salt

1 1/2 c. milk
1/2 c. bread crumbs
3 tbsp. butter

Grind the meat and onion in a food chopper.

Add the mashed potatoes, salt, and milk. Mix well.

Place in a baking dish and sprinkle buttered crumbs over the top. Bake at 350° for about 40 minutes.

Cracklings

Cracklings are made by rendering the hog fat, which has been coarsely ground or cut into approximately 1 inch cubes.

Drain the lard from the cracklings through a colander or a strainer.

Reserve the cracklings for later use.

Heat the desired amount of cracklings in a frying pan over medium heat, stirring while heating. Allow them to fry several minutes.

Drain off the accumulated fat.

Sprinkle with salt and serve hot.

Good served with fried potatoes or with syrup and bread.

Bobbat With Sausages

1 package dry yeast	3 tbsp. sugar
1/4 c. warm water	2 tsp. salt
1 1/2 c. milk	1 pound sausage
1 egg	3 1/2 to 4 c. flour

Dissolve the yeast in 1/4 c. warm water.

Scald the milk. Cool to lukewarm, then add the dissolved yeast, beaten egg, salt, sugar, and flour. Mix well. Let rise until double in bulk.

Spread the dough in a greased pan, 10 by 14 inches, then press 3 inch lengths of sausage at intervals. Let rise again.

Bake at 375° for 45-50 minutes.

PRESERVING

Beef Steak Salted Down in Sweet Brine

1 c. pickling salt	1 gallon water
1 c. sugar	

Boil together until salt and sugar are dissolved. Let cool. This makes enough brine for 16 quarts of beef steak.

To prepare the steak, cut into about 1/2 inch thick slices. Pound lightly. Pour 1 c. of the brine in each quart jar. Add the raw, sliced, steak up to the neck of the jar. Seal the jars, and cold pack in hot water bath for 1 hour.

To use meat: Take from jar and smooth out the crumpled slices. Flour and fry as usual. The brine can be used for gravy.

Sauerkraut

Shred kraut cabbage very finely on a board or with a shredder. Weigh off 5 pounds of the shredded cabbage and place in a large glass bowl or enameled pan.

Sprinkle 3 tbsp. of pickling salt over the shredded cabbage. Mix and let stand for 1 or 2 hours.

Pack a small amount of the cabbage into quart jars, pressing it down with a wooden spoon or potato masher, to make its own juice; continue adding cabbage and pressing down until jar is filled to the neck, being sure the juice covers the kraut.

Let stand, unsealed, at room temperature until it ferments. Seal the jars, then boil them in water for 3 to 5 minutes.

Store in the basement or a dark room.

Silt-Fleesh

Place the head and the feet of a fully dressed hog in a large kettle and cover with cold water; bring to a boil. Cook until the meat falls off the bones and the stock cooks down somewhat. Drain off the stock, and skim off the fat. Separate the meat from the bones.

Grind the meat, add salt and pepper to taste; then add the stock and mix well.

Press the meat mixture to form a loaf. When the loaf is cold and jelled, slice and serve plain, or allow the sliced meat to remain in vinegar for several hours before serving.

(This is good when served with fried potatoes.)

Pickled Beets

Boil the beets until they are tender, but not too soft; plunge them in cold water and slip off their skins.

Mix the following and boil a few minutes:

2 c. vinegar	1/2 tsp. salt
1/2 c. water	1 or 2 sticks of cinnamon
1/2 c. beet juice	(broken up)
1 c. sugar	1 tsp. whole cloves

Tie the spices in a small cloth. Add to boiling syrup.

Immerse the beets in the boiling syrup and bring to a boil again. Drop the beets into sterilized jars, and pour the syrup over them and seal the jars tightly.

After having used all the beets out of the jars, keep the syrup to make Pickled Eggs.

Pickled Eggs

Drop whole, hard-cooked shelled eggs into the beet liquid and let stand to pickle for 2 days before serving.

Dill Pickles
(for summer)

Cucumbers of any size may be used as long as they have not turned yellow.

Wash cucumbers in cold water.

In bottom of a 2-or 3-gallon stone jar place dill stems with seeds, then grape leaves, and cherry leaves.

Next place several layers of cucumbers, another layer of dill and leaves.

Add more cucumbers.

Finish with a layer of leaves, topping with dill.

Over this pour a brine made by using 1/2 c. pickling salt to 1 gallon of cold water.

Weight down to cover with the brine.

Cover the top with a clean cloth, change the cloth every other day to keep it from molding.

If possible keep it in the basement.

It will be ready for table use in about two weeks.

(Cabbage heads cut into sections may be added to this brine with cucumbers.)

Dill Pickles
(for winter)

Soak a gallon of small or medium sized cucumbers in a brine made of 1/4 c. pickling salt and 1 quart cold water over night. In the morning take cucumbers out of the brine and pack in jars perpendicularly.

Put dill, cherry, and grape leaves at the bottom, center, and top of jar.

Also add a small red pepper in each jar and 1 clove of garlic, if desired.

Put boiling juice over cucumbers:

2 1/2 quarts (10c.) water   1 c. white vinegar
1/2 c. pickling salt

Let jars stand at room temperature for 2 or 3 days, until just right and sour.

Then seal the jars and boil in water for 3 to 5 minutes.

Remove from heat, but leave jars in the water 3 minutes longer. Store in the basement.

SALADS

Cucumber Salad

2 large cucumbers   salt
1 small onion

Dressing:
3/4 c. sour cream   1 tsp. vinegar (or less)
1 tsp. sugar   pepper

Peel the cucumbers and slice thinly. Sprinkle the slices with salt and stir a bit so the salt is well distributed. Peel the onion and slice it finely. Sprinkle salt over onion slices.

Let both cucumber and onion stand in their separate dishes for about 15 minutes, stirring occasionally. Drain thoroughly. Combine the onion and cucumbers and cover with dressing.

Summer Lettuce Salad

1 quart raw, thick sour
    milk
2 or 3 hard boiled eggs
1/2 tsp. salt

1 tbsp. sugar
3 tbsp. sweet or sour
    cream
fresh garden lettuce

Cut the eggs into the clabbered milk. Add salt, sugar, and cream. Mix lightly.

Cut, and mix in the lettuce.

Prepare shortly before serving.

NOTE: Sour milk was considered very healthy and was used extensively in cooking, in cottage cheese, or to eat with a spoon.

SOUPS

Chicken Noodle Soup

1 cut-up stewing hen
2 tsp. salt
2 sprigs parsley (or dried
    parsley flakes)

1/4 tsp. whole allspice,
    approx.
1/2 tsp. whole pepper

Place the chicken in a kettle with enough water to cover. Add salt and sprigs of parsley. Tie the allspice, whole pepper, and parsley flakes (if used) in a small clean cloth and add. Cover. Then simmer until the meat is tender (about 2 or 3 hours). Add more water if necessary.

Remove the meat from the stock and discard the spice bag. Remove the meat from the bones and cut into desired pieces. Add the meat, the cooked noodles, and 1/2 c. sweet cream to the stock and serve.

Homemade Noodles

3 egg yolks
1 whole egg
3 tbsp. cold water

1 tsp. salt
2 c. flour

Beat until light, the yolks and whole egg. Beat in water and salt. Work in flour. Divide dough into 3 parts. Roll out each piece as thin as possible. Place between 2 towels until dough is partially dry. Roll up the dough as for jelly roll; or cut the dough into about 1 1/2 inch wide strips, placing the strips one on top of each other. In either case, cut with a sharp knife into desired widths (1/8 inch for thin, up to 1/2 inch for broad noodles). Shake out the cut pieces and allow to dry before using or storing.

Cook noodles in salted water for 20 minutes. Then drain and rinse with warm water.

Plume-Moos

1 pound prunes (or less)   1 c. raisins

Cook the fruit in 2 c. water, let stand several hours.

1 c. sugar or 1/2 white
   and 1/2 brown)
1/4 c. flour
1/4 tsp. cinnamon
1/4 tsp. powdered star anise
1 c. fruit juice (drained
   from above fruit)

1 c. lightcream (or half
   and half
1 quart buttermilk
1/2 tsp. salt
2 c. noodles

Mix sugar, flour, salt, cinnamon, and star anise. Gradually add the fruit juice, stir until smooth.

Add cream and buttermilk. Whip until well mixed and smooth.

Cook slowly on medium heat and continue whipping or stirring continuously until it thickens.

Remove from heat and add the fruit while this is hot.

Add the cooked noodles just before serving.

Variations for Plume-Moos

Some prefer to add a little juice of cooked sandhill plums, as part of the liquid to the recipe.

Another variation is to use mixed dry fruit, such as dried prunes, raisins, peaches, and apricots.

Buttamalch-Kielke
(Buttermilk Dumplings)

1 c. flour	1 large egg
1/2 tsp. salt	4 c. buttermilk

Beat the egg, add the flour and salt. Mix with 2 knives, then rub the mixture between your fingers until it forms small lumps.

Heat the buttermilk slowly, stirring continuously to prevent curdling.

When the buttermilk comes to a boil, continue stirring while dropping in the small dumplings.

After all has been added, continue to boil for 5 minutes longer, until the dumplings have blended with the buttermilk.

Pastinak-Supp
(Parsnip Soup)

1 1/2 lbs spare ribs
1 1/2 tsp. salt
1/8 tsp. pepper
1 pound parsnips, cut up

3 c. potatoes, (more or less) cut up
1 small onion, cut up

Cover meat with cold water, and bring to a boil. Continue cooking slowly, until meat is almost tender. Remove the meat from the broth. Take out the bones and cut up the meat. Skim off fat from the broth, and add more water, if needed.

Add to the broth: the meat, parsnips, potatoes, onion, and seasonings.

Cook until vegetables are tender.

Slightly mash the vegetables with a wire potato masher.

Sauerkraut-Dumpling Soup

Take approximately 1 1/2 pounds pork or beef.

Cover with water and bring to a boil.

Add 1 tsp. salt and cook until meat is tender.

Add 2 c. sauerkraut and boil 5 minutes longer. Lay the dumplings on top of the meat and sauerkraut. Cook slowly 10 minutes with kettle uncovered, and 10 minutes tightly covered.

Dumplings:

1 c. sifted flour
2 tsp. baking powder
1/2 tsp. salt

1 tbsp. melted shortening
1 egg
1/4 c. milk

Sift together the flour, baking powder, and salt.

Beat the egg, add the milk and melted shortening; then blend the liquid with the flour mixture.

Roll the dough out on a floured board to 1/3 or 1/2 inch thickness and cut into strips approximately 1 by 2 inches, or as desired.

These dumplings may be dropped by spoonfuls, if preferred.

TO SERVE: Take out the fluffy dumplings; cut the meat into smaller pieces and return it to the sauerkraut soup. Dish out into serving bowls, and place dumplings on top of the soup.

Summer Borscht

2 lbs. soup bone (or
    piece of ham)
1 medium cabbage head,
    shredded
3 green onions, tops and
    all, cut up
6 new potatoes, cut up
1/2 c. tomatoes (fresh or
    canned)

1 c. beets, peeled and
    cut up
1 c. beet leaves, stems
    and all, cut up
    few sprigs of dill
1/8 tsp. pepper
2 tsp. salt
1/2 c. sour cream

Cover the meat with cold water and bring to a boil. Cook slowly until meat is almost tender. Add the cabbage, beets, potatoes, tomatoes, and seasonings.

Cook until vegetables are almost tender. Add the onions, beet leaves, and dill. Cook for about 10 minutes more. Remove from heat and add the sour cream just before serving.

Schauble-Supp
(Bean Soup)

2 c. navy beans
2 quarts water

1 small onion, cut up

Soak beans in the water overnight.

Drain in the morning.

Cover a 2-pound soup bone with cold water and bring to a boil. Add the drained beans and onion. Cook slowly for about 3 hours or until beans are soft. Add more water if necessary, to make a soup.

Klache Kielche
(Minature Milk Dumplings)

Beat 2 large eggs, add 1/2 tsp. salt, 1/4 c. water, and beat.

Add 1 c. flour and beat until smooth.

Heat to boiling point, 1 quart of milk, stirring constantly to avoid scorching.

Add 1/2 tsp. salt.

Keep the milk boiling while slowly dribbling the soft dough into the boiling milk. Continue boiling for about 2 minutes after all the dough has been added.

Mashed Potato Soup

5 medium potatoes	2 small or 1 medium onion
1 tsp. salt	1/2 tsp. salt
2 tbsp. fat	dash of pepper
2 c. milk	

Boil potatoes in salted water. Drain and mash. Yields about 3 c.

Heat the fat in a skillet, slice in the onion, stir and cook the onion until it is light brown.

Add salt and pepper.

Add the milk and heat.

Pack mashed potatoes in the center of a serving bowl, forming a peak.

Pour the onion-milk over this to surround the potatoes.

VEGETABLES

Gebrodne-Pastinak
(Fried Parsnips)

6 medium parsnips	2 tbsp. butter
1 tsp. salt	

Wash and scrape parsnips.

Cook in salted water until tender, but not soft.

Cut in halves, lengthwise.

Fry in hot butter until brown on both sides.

Gebrodne-Edchoke
(Fried Potatoes #1)

4 good-sized potatoes	3 tbsp. fat
(1 1/2 pounds)	1 tsp. salt
dash of pepper	

Wash, pare, and slice the potatoes.

Heat the fat in a skillet.

Add the raw sliced potatoes, add the salt and pepper.

Allow the potatoes to fry, turning bottom side up, occasionally.

Fry until the potatoes are cooked, for about 25 minutes.

Keep covered while frying.

Gebrodne-Edchoke
(Fried Potatoes #2)

4 c. small potatoes,   dash of pepper
   approx.   1/4 c. fat
1 tsp. salt

Wash and cook the potatoes, in their jackets, until tender. Drain.
Remove the jackets and slice.

Heat the fat in a frying pan; add the sliced potatoes, salt, and
pepper. Allow the potatoes to fry, turning bottom side up occasionally.

They are ready to serve when nicely browned.

Mashed Potato Cakes

Add beaten egg to left-over seasoned mashed potatoes, and mix
while they are warm. Chill. When ready to use, shape into cakes,
dip into flour and fry slowly in hot fat until brown. Turn and
brown the other side.

The Ostrog Mennonites

Many Mennonites of the Netherlands who were persecuted for religious convictions found refuge in the Vistula River area of Danzig and West Prussia. Thriving villages sprang up where swamps had previously existed. After years of progress, it again seemed as if their religious freedom would be in danger. Some moved into the area near Ostrog, Poland in the province of Volhynia which later became Russian. Among the places of settlement were Karolswalde, Karolsberge, Antonovka, Waldheim, Gruental, and Fuerstendorf.

In 1870 the Mennonites became aware that the Russian government was considering the cancellation of the special privileges promised them and so they looked for other lands to which they could go. A group, representing Mennonites from different areas, was sent to America to investigate the conditions. The first group left in 1874, taking tools, bedding, cooking utensils and clothing with them in large crates or chests, sealed with iron straps. These are not all from Ostrog.

A few of these immigrants stayed in the Eastern states to work for a period of time, others went directly to Kansas.

As a whole this group was somewhat impoverished, although a smaller number did obtain some money from land sales in Poland. Some arrived in Kansas unannounced during the winter. Shelter was found in empty warehouses in the Peabody-Florence area. Conditions were "terrible"; food was scarce, the buildings were cold and very crowded. Many children died during these winter months.

The Mennonite churches in America assisted these people and in the spring of 1875, a Kansas Relief Committee with the assistance of the Santa Fe Railway Company made it possible for them to leave their crowded, impoverished conditions. Each family was given forty acres of land in the Lone Tree Township, McPherson County, Kansas and a small loan with which they could purchase oxen, seeds, and other necessities to make a new beginning.

Many of the descendants of these early settlers, except for those who moved to Meno and Enid, Oklahoma, still live in this same area. Many have joined the Church of God in Christ, Mennonite, founded by John Holdeman. Another group moved westward to Pawnee Rock and Dundee, Kansas in the spring of 1875.

Some of the early settlers had learned certain trades while living in Europe. One settler, Christian Schultz, was able to build carriages, do blacksmith work and build cabinets. These skills enabled him to make tools with which to farm and do housekeeping.

Wagons, header barges, buggies, wooden churns, butter paddles, bowls, rolling pins, chests, and coffins were some of his contributions. He also became (in the settlement) somewhat of a doctor, setting bones and blood letting.

Among the hardships the early pioneers endured were prairie fire, grasshopper plagues, interest on their loans at the rate of 36 per cent, a selling price of fifty cents per bushel for wheat, five or six cents per pound for butter, five to ten cents per dozen for eggs.

MENU

Menu for a Day
(in winter)

Breakfast
Bread (homemade)
Butter (homemade)
Cracklings or head cheese
Oatmeal (with cream or milk)
Coffee (with cream)

Dinner
Fried ham
Boiled potatoes
Fried onions in gravy
Bread and butter
Baked apple

Supper
Beef soup with potatoes (home canned meat)
Tomato stew
Bread
Butter, jelly, molasses
Coffee

Seeds

Our forefathers were mostly "tillers of the soil". They believed in living close to nature. They had the art of turning unproductive soil into bread baskets and bringing about a good livelihood for themselves. Many families brought with them seed wheat (turkey red wheat) from the old country. Mother and children picked out the very best seeds to bring. Other seeds too were brought— vegetable seed, fruit and flower seed. Careful selection brought about plenty of food for the early pioneers. Many of these seeds have been kept up to this time by passing fresh seeds down through the generations.

At first, holes were dug by hand and seed was planted that way. Later the plow became the important tool. It was drawn by oxen. Seed was scattered by hand.

BREADS

Mother's Homemade Bread

Mother had received a beer yeast, from a lady in a cook shack, which she used as her bread starter. This was also called "everlasting yeast". The night before bread baking, Mother would get this yeast from the "butter well" where it was kept cool. To this she would add 2 c. cooled, boiled potato water and 1 or 2 mashed potatoes. The 2 tbsp. sugar would be added and the mixture would be left standing over night.

In the morning 2 c. of this mixture was taken out for the bread making and the other cup would be saved in a quart jar for the next baking, being kept cool in the well as before.

Water, sugar, and salt would be added to this yeast and then flour would gradually be added to make a soft dough. This would then be beaten vigorously, left to rise for a while, and then more flour added so it could be kneaded well. The dough would then be left to rise until double in bulk, after which it would be formed into loaves. Mother would place the loaves on a deep, round tin. When doubled in size the bread was baked in a moderate oven for 40-55 minutes or until golden brown. The aroma and taste of fresh bread was something never to be forgotten!

Often on baking days there would be no bread for lunch, so Mother would keep out part of the bread dough when shaping it into loaves. This dough was cut into strips and dropped into hot fat and deep fried until golden brown. These were good dipped in powdered sugar or jelly or just plain.

White Bread No. 1

2 cakes yeast foam	1 tbsp. sugar
enough flour to make a soft sponge	4 c. potato water

Let set over night.

Add 1 tbsp. salt, 1 tbsp. sugar, and flour to make nice firm dough. Knead about 10 minutes. Grease bowl and bread. Let rise, work down. Let rise again and shape into loaves.

White Bread No. 2

2 packages yeast foam and 1 tsp. sugar in 1/2 c. warm water till it foams.

Mix 2 tsp. salt and 2 c. potato water. Use enough flour to make dough like cake batter, then add yeast. Add more flour to make medium stiff dough. Let rise 2 times, then shape into loaves. 2 loaves.

Oats were heated in oven then bread dough was warmed in oats. Corn cobs were used to heat the old cook stove oven.

Yeast Foam

1 c. corn meal   1 tsp. sugar
1 c. buttermilk   1/2 tsp. salt
1 cake yeast foam

Bring buttermilk to a boil, add corn meal. Remove from heat, cool until luke warm. Add yeast which has soaked while milk is heating. Pour mixture into a pan, 3/8 inch thick. Cut in pieces and dry in a warm place.

Whole Wheat Bread

2 1/2 c. water   1/4 c. butter (or lard)
2 cakes yeast   4 c. whole wheat flour
3 tsp. salt   2 to 3 c. unbleached flour
1/4 c. molasses

Dissolve yeast in the 1/2 c. water to which 1 tsp. sugar has been added.

Heat water; add salt, sugar, molasses, and butter. Cool to luke warm.

Add whole wheat flour, beat with spoon until light. Add yeast and white flour, using more flour if needed. Knead until dough is light and elastic. Cover, let rise in warm place until double in bulk, about 1 hour.

Knead down and let rise to double in size. Knead, divide dough into 2 equal parts. Shape into loaves and put into well greased pans. Let rise to about double. Bake in preheated oven at 350° for 45 minutes or until done.

Zwieback

2 cakes compressed yeast
1/2 c. warm water
1/3 c. sugar
3 1/2 c. scalded milk

1 c. shortening
3 tsp. salt
10 c. flour

Dissolve yeast in warm water with part of the sugar. Pour milk on shortening. When cool, add salt and rest of sugar. Add the yeast mixture and flour. Let rise until double in bulk (about 2 hours at 80°). Knead down, let rise the second time for 1 hour. Place on greased pans and let stand until about double in bulk. Bake at 375° 20-25 minutes.

Zwieback

2 packages yeast
2 c. milk
2 c. water
1 c. butter and lard mixed

salt
1/2 c. sugar
flour

Scald milk and add butter, salt, and sugar. Dissolve yeast in water. Mix all together and add flour to make a stiff dough. Let rise until double, work down once. Pinch off small balls of dough, placing 2 inches apart on greased pans, put slightly smaller ball on top, pressing down with thumb. Let rise until double in size. Bake at 400° 15-20 minutes.

Nalesniky
(Filled Pancake)

2 eggs   1 1/3 c. milk
1/2 tsp. salt   1 c. sifted flour (approx.)

Beat eggs, add milk, salt, and enough flour to make a thin dough that resembles heavy cream. Mix well. Pour some of the batter into a hot greased pan. Lift the pan so that batter covers bottom. Brown lightly, flip on other side and brown. Remove to flat surface after all pancakes are fried, fill with Cottage Cheese Filling.

Cottage Cheese Filling

2 c. cottage cheese   1 egg
1 tbsp. sugar, if desired   salt and pepper to taste

Mix well, spread on pancake and roll as a jelly roll. Place roll in greased skillet and brown. Applesauce spiced with cinnamon may be substituted for the cottage cheese filling.

Crepes
Pancakes

3 eggs   1 c. milk
1 c. flour   salt
1/4 c. oleo   applesauce
2 tbsp. sugar

Mix all ingredients, except sauce.
  Heat and grease pan.
  Use 3 tbsp. of mixture and spread evenly over pan. (This is a very thin pancake.)
  Brown on both sides.
  As each cake is fried spread with applesauce, roll and put into a pan in warm oven until all are baked.
  Spread sugar on top and heat few minutes longer.
  Serve, adding more apple sauce as desired.

Potato Pancakes

4 large potatoes
1 onion, grated
2 eggs, well beaten

1/2 tsp. salt
1/2 tsp. soda
1 1/2 tbsp. flour

Peel and grate potatoes. Add eggs and onion. Combine flour, salt, and soda. Add to potato mixture. Drop by spoonfuls on hot greased skillet. Brown on both sides. Good served with applesauce.

Sweet Rolls

2 cakes yeast
1/4 c. warm water
1 c. scalded milk
1/4 c. butter
1 tsp. salt

1/2 c. sugar
2 eggs
1 lemon, rind and juice
5 to 5 1/2 c. flour

Soak yeast in warm water. Scald milk; add butter, sugar, and salt. Cool. Add yeast, eggs, lemon rind and juice. Add enough flour to make stiff batter. Beat well. Add remaining flour to form soft dough. Knead well and place in greased bowl. Let rise until double. Punch down and shape into rolls. Let rise until double. Bake at 375° 15-20 minutes, or until brown.

Coffee Cake

Mix together:
3 c. flour
3/4 c. shortening
1/4 tsp. salt

1/2 tsp. each of nutmeg,
cloves, and cinnamon
1 c. sugar

Save 1/2 c. of this crumb mixture for the topping.

Add 2 eggs, 1 c. raisins and 1 c. chopped nuts.

Dissolve 2 tsp. soda in 2 c. buttermilk and add to the mixture, beating well.

Put into a greased and floured 9 by 13 by 2 inch pan, add topping and bake at 350° for 40 minutes or until done.

Serve either warm or cold.

Cropulsha
Fritters

1 c. flour	1/2 c. milk
1 egg	1/2 tsp. salt

Mix and roll out thin (1/4 inch). Cut in squares and fry in deep fat or oil. Eat with watermelon or cherry *moos*.

Roll-Kuchen
Crullers

1/2 c. sweet or sour cream	2 eggs
1/2 c. milk (1 c. half and half	1 tsp. salt
may be substituted for	1 tsp. soda with sour
cream and milk)	cream or 1 tsp. baking
1 tbsp. sugar	powder with sweet cream
3 1/2 to 4 c. flour	

Beat eggs. Add cream and milk.

Sift dry ingredients and add to egg mixture. Use just enough flour to make a soft dough which can be rolled out. When well mixed let stand 2 hours. Roll out 3/8 inch thick and cut into oblong strips, 2 by 7 inches. Prick with a fork.

Deep fry in oil or melted shortening until light brown on both sides. Drain on absorbent paper. While still warm, roll in powdered sugar. Serve with watermelon.

Egg Platts

2 eggs, well beaten	3 tbsp. flour, or enough to
2 tbsp. milk	make soft dough

Drop by spoonful into hot fat, until brown.

Porzelke
(German Fritter)

2 c. milk
3 eggs
1 tsp. salt
1 cake yeast
1/2 c. warm water

1/4 c. butter
1/4 c. sugar
2 c. raisins
4 to 5 c. flour

Mix yeast with 1/2 c. warm water. Scald milk, cool to luke warm, add yeast mixture and remaining ingredients. Add raisins. Use enough flour to make a soft dough. Let rise. Drop by spoonful into hot deep fat and fry until golden brown. Makes 6 dozen.

Porzelke
New Year's Cookies

1 package yeast dissolved
    in 1/4 c. water
2 c. milk
3/4 c. sugar
1 tsp. salt

1 c. raisins, cook a few
    minutes and drain
2 eggs
5 or 6 c. flour

Scald milk, cool to lukewarm. Add the dissolved yeast. Beat the eggs and add to milk and yeast. Add sugar and salt. Then flour and raisins last. With the spoon mix till a medium soft dough. Do not knead. Let rise until double in bulk. Then stir down again and let rise. Drop by tbsp. into deep hot fat, 375°. Fry until golden brown turning once. Drain on absorbent paper. Roll in sugar. Makes 7 dozen.

Pummelches
(Berliners)

1 c. cooled, scalded milk
1 package yeast dissolved
    in 1/4 c. water
1/2 tsp. salt

1 tsp. vanilla
1/2 c. sugar
1 c. melted butter
6 eggs, well beaten

Mix the above ingredients. Gradually add flour until dough is just stiff enough to handle. Care must be taken not to add too much flour. Let rise until double in bulk. Work down and allow to rise again. Stew 2 c. prunes and raisins with 1/4 c. sugar and a little water. Pit prunes.

Roll out dough 1/2 inch thin. Place fruit mounds on half of rolled out dough. Fold other half over and cut out with cookie cutter. Let rise, then fry in deep fat till brown and done.

CAKES AND COOKIES

Applesauce Cake

Cream together 1 c. sugar and 1/2 c. butter or lard. If desired, add 1 or 2 eggs. Sift together 2 c. flour, 1 tsp. cinnamon, 1 tsp. allspice, 1/2 tsp. cloves, 3/4 tsp. salt and add to mixture. Then take 2 tsp. soda dissolved in 2 tbsp. of hot water, and add to mixture. Then fold in 1/2 c. chopped walnuts, 1/2 c. raisins, 1 1/2 c. applesauce, and 1 tsp. vanilla. Bake in a slow oven 45 minutes. Mashed peaches, plums, or almost any kind of cooked fruit may be used instead of apples, if desired.

Bundt Cake

1 c. sugar	1 1/2 c. flour
5 eggs	1/2 tsp. vanilla extract
1 tsp. baking powder	

Beat eggs, add sugar, add the rest of ingredients. Put in tube cake pan and bake at 375° till done.

Molasses Cake

1/2 c. butter	1 c. buttermilk
1 c. sugar	1 c. molasses
2 eggs	1/2 tsp. soda
1/4 tsp. salt	1/2 tsp. baking powder

Add enough flour to stiffen.

You may take 1 c. sour cream and 2 tsp. black strap molasses instead of butter and buttermilk.

Coconut Cake

1/2 c. butter
1 c. sugar
3 eggs, save 2 egg whites
   for frosting
1/2 c. coconut in batter

1/2 c. coconut for frosting
3/4 c. milk
2 c. flour
1 heaping tsp. baking
   powder

Cream butter and sugar, add 2 egg yolks and 1 whole egg. Then add milk, then flour with baking powder. Add 1/2 c. coconut. Bake at 375° in two 9 inch cake pans, about 20 minutes. Make a frosting using 2 egg whites. Beat egg whites until stiff. Add 1/4 c. sugar and beat till of right consistency to spread. Put cake on oven ware plate. Spread on first layer. Put other layer on top and frost top and sides and use the 1/2 c. of coconut for top and sides. Put in oven and brown at 350°.

This was a special cake made for last day of school dinner. This used to be made with fresh coconut.

Prune Coffee Cake

2 dozen large prunes
3/4 c. milk
1/4 c. sugar
3 tbsp. shortening
1 cake compressed yeast

1/4 c. lukewarm water
1 egg
3 1/2 c. flour
1 tsp. salt

Scald milk and pour over the sugar, shortening, and salt in a large mixing bowl. Cool to lukewarm. Soften yeast in warm water. Add beaten egg and mix well. Add to milk mixture. Add half the flour and beat thoroughly. Add rest of flour and mix well. Roll dough out into 2 parts to fit 2 nine inch cake pans. Pit the prunes and arrange halves with cut side up on top of the cake. Let rise until double in bulk with the following Topping.

Topping

1 c. sweet or sour cream
2 tsp. cinnamon

2 egg yolks
1 c. sugar

Mix together.

Pour over the cakes and bake in moderately hot oven, 350°, for 40 minutes. Serve hot.

Ammonia Cookies

2 eggs
2 c. sugar
3/4 c. butter

1 c. milk
5 cents worth of ammonia
flour to make soft dough

This recipe was copied from a small notebook that was dated 1903 and 1904.

Mamma's Cookies

1 1/4 c. sugar
1 c. thick sour cream
1/4 tsp. salt
1/4 tsp. nutmeg
2 tsp. baking powder

2 eggs
1 tsp. soda
1 tsp. vanilla
2 1/2 c. flour

Sift flour, baking powder, soda, salt, and nutmeg together several times. Beat eggs, add sugar and cream. Mix well, add flour mixture.

This is a soft batter. So put lots of flour on the board and roll out 1/4 inch thick. Bake about 7 minutes at 400°.

Soft Molasses Cookies

2 c. sour cream
1 c. lard
3 c. sugar
1 c. molasses
3 eggs

1 level tsp. soda
1 tsp. cinnamon
1 tsp. allspice
3 heaping tsp. baking
   powder
flour enough to handle

Place all ingredients in bowl and mix well. Roll out and cut cookies.
Bake at 400° for 10-15 minutes.

Ginger Cookies

Cream together:
    1 c. sugar   1 c. butter or margarine
Add:
    2 eggs, beat well   1 tbsp. soda dissolved in
    1 c. molasses   1/2 c. lukewarm water
Mix well and add:
    1 tsp. lemon flavor   1 tsp. vinegar
    1 tsp. ginger   pinch of salt

Mix well and add 2 c. flour, or more, until soft dough can be handled.
Roll out and cut in desired shapes. Bake at 375°.

Ginger Snaps

2 c. sugar
2 c. lard
4 eggs
2 c. dark syrup

2 tsp. baking powder
2 tsp. ginger
flour

Cream sugar and lard. Add syrup, eggs, and enough flour to make
a stiff dough. Roll 1/4 inch thick and cut with cookie cutter. Bake
at 375° about 10 minutes.

Grandma's Sugar Cookies

1 c. butter
2 c. sugar
2 eggs
3 tsp. vanilla
5 c. sifted flour

3/4 tsp. soda, dissolve soda
in 2 tsp. vinegar in a
measuring c. Add milk
to make 1/4 c. liquid
1 tsp. baking powder

Sift flour and baking powder together. Cream butter, add sugar, add eggs one at a time and beat. Add vanilla. Then the other ingredients. Stir well. Roll out on floured board, sprinkle with sugar, cut with cookie cutter and bake at 350°. (Edges will be a light brown when done.)

Aunt Anna's Cookies

4 eggs
1 c. butter
4 c. sugar
12 c. flour
1 c. lard
4 tsp. vanilla

1 c. milk
4 tsp. soda, dissolved in
little vinegar
1 c. cream
4 tsp. cream of tartar

Cream butter and lard. Add sugar and cream well. Add the well beaten eggs. Sift dry ingredients and add alternately to the creamed mixture with the liquid. Add the vanilla.

Roll out and cut with a glass or any cookie cutter. Bake at 375-400° until done.

This recipe was brought out to Kansas in the early part of this century when Aunt Anna came from Pennsylvania to visit her relatives in this state. Since then many a delicious cookie has been added to complete the daily lunch box of children attending the rural school.

Sweet Cookies

1 1/2 c. sugar
2 eggs, beat well
1 c. sour milk
3/4 c. sweet cream
2 tsp. baking powder

1 tsp. soda, mix in sour
milk
3 or more c. flour, enough
to make medium dough

Add baking powder to flour. Add any flavor you like.

Roll out—not too thin, and cut out with a cookie cutter. Bake at 375°.

DESSERTS

Bread Pudding

Mix together:

1/2 c. brown sugar	1 1/2 c. milk
4 slices of dry buttered bread	cinnamon or raisins, or both
2 eggs, beaten	1/4 tsp. salt

Bake in 350° oven for 30 minutes.

Gorevey

2 cakes yeast	2 c. sweet cream
1/2 c. lukewarm water	2 c. sugar
7 to 8 c. sifted flour	1 tsp. salt
1/2 c. lard	6 egg yolks
1/2 c. butter	

Dissolve yeast in the 1/2 c. lukewarm water, add 2 c. flour and enough more lukewarm water to make a thick batter. Let stand about an hour, or until spongy. Heat the lard, butter, cream, sugar, and salt together. Cool and add well beaten egg yolks. Add all to the first mixture. Add enough flour, 5 or 6 c., to make a smooth dough and knead. Let rise until dough has doubled, punch down once and let rise again. Form into five large buns, each about the size of a soft ball. Place each in a pie tin and let rise until double in size. Bake in a 375° oven 30 minutes. Frost with cream and sugar icing or a powdered sugar icing and decorate with corn candy.

Cottage Cheese Pie

2 eggs	1/2 tsp. salt
2 c. dry cottage cheese	3/4 c. sugar
1/2 c. milk	pie dough for 9 inch pie

Beat the eggs and mix with the other ingredients. Pour into unbaked pie shell. Sprinkle cinnamon on top. Bake at 350° about 45 minutes.

Old Fashioned Baked Custard Pie

3 c. milk	2 tsp. flour
3 eggs	1/4 tsp. cinnamon or nutmeg
3/4 c. sugar	1 tsp. vanilla
1/2 tsp. salt	1 pastry for 9 inch crust

Combine flour and sugar. Add beaten eggs. Bring milk to boiling point, add egg mixture gradually. Pour into an unbaked pie shell and sprinkle spice over top. Bake at 350° for 40-45 minutes.

Old Fashioned Vinegar Pie

3 eggs	3/4 c. sugar
3 tbsp. butter	1/2 c. flour
2 tbsp. vinegar	pinch of salt
1 1/2 c. hot water	3/4 c. chopped nuts, toasted

Beat eggs until very light, then add the butter and hot water to the combined sugar, flour, and salt and blend smoothly. Cook over hot water, stirring constantly until thick. Add 1/2 c. nuts.

Turn into pie shell and sprinkle remaining nuts over the surface to make one of the most delicious pies.

DUMPLINGS

Beroge-Pirogy

Combine 1 egg, slightly beaten with 3 c. flour and enough water to make a stiff dough. Roll out as for noodles and cut in 3 inch squares. Fill squares with cottage cheese to taste. Fold dough in triangular shape and pinch edges together. Cook slowly in salted water about 5 minutes. Drain. Serve with sauce. Squares may be filled with kraut instead of cheese.

Sauce

Boil together 2 tbsp. lard and 1/2 c. cream.

Bohne Beroge
(Pirogy)

2 c. milk	1/4 c. lukewarm water
1 c. cream	1 tsp. sugar
1/2 c. butter	1 egg, beaten
3/4 c. sugar	9 c. sifted flour
1 cake yeast	1 tbsp. salt

Scald milk and cream. Add butter and sugar. Cool to lukewarm. Dissolve yeast in warm water to which 1 tsp. sugar has been added. Add to creamed mixture. Beat in egg. Gradually add sifted flour and salt. Mix well. Knead dough. Cover and let rise until double in bulk. Punch down and let rise again until double. Form into small buns, size of a walnut or larger if desired. Let rise and flatten with hand. Place heaping teaspoon of filling in center of each bun.

Filling

Cook until soft 1 c. pinto beans. Pour off liquid, mash, then add 2/3 c. sugar, 1/2 tsp. salt, and 1/4 c. cream. Mix well and ' fill dough. Fold dough over and pinch edges together. Place on greased pan and let rise until double in bulk, about 1 hour. Bake in 375° oven until brown, about 20-25 minutes. If desired, the *beroge* may be served with a topping made by combining 6 tbsp. sugar with 1 1/2 tbsp. cornstarch and adding 2 c. cream, scalded, cook over slow heat, stirring constantly, until thickened.

Homemade Noodles

3 eggs	salt
flour	

Break eggs into bowl. Add enough flour to make medium stiff dough. Divide and roll out to paper-thin. Let dry. Roll as for a jelly roll. Slice very thin. Let dry and store.

Summer Noodle Dish

Cook noodles. Drain and cool. When cold put into serving dish. Add sauce made with half cream and half sour, clabbered milk. Delicious for a hot summer evening meal.

Noodles and Bread

Use enough noodles for your family. Cook until done. Drain. Break up bread in 1 inch squares and fry in butter till brown. Pour milk over bread to soften, then pour over noodles. Season with salt and pepper.

Food in Polish Russia

Bread was a staple food in the early years. This was usually dark rye bread, made with sour dough. Lard was spread on this. Potato pancakes or noodles would be served quite often. For these recipes the potatoes would be ground fine and mixed with flour. Noodle dough would be made stiff enough to be rolled into little balls, which would then be cooked in milk or water.

A syrup for table use would be made by cooking carrots, which were grown in the gardens. Other vegetables produced were cabbage and parsnips, which kept good.

Coffee was made in the homes by roasting and then grinding beans or cereal grains.

Hams were salted down or smoked at butchering time, which took place in the early part of winter. These hams could be kept until summer.

Home is not a house alone—It's family and friends.
The warmth that kitchen gatherings and a cup of coffee lends . . .
It's love and understanding blended well with a kindliness that
fills the heart and makes home
A Place of Happiness!

Bedtime Prayer

Part of the bedtime prayer which the father prayed while the family knelt down, each by his or her own chair.

Wenn in dieser bevorstehenden Nacht, einer oder der andre, sein Leben schliessen soll, dann wollest Du uns ein seeliges Ende verleihen, so dass wir von hier in Frieden scheiden koennen, und dort in die ewige Ruhe eintreten, wo wir dich loben und preisen koennen mit allen Heiligen. Dazu wollest Du uns Kraft verleihen durch deine Liebe und Barmherzigkeit. Amen

If it is Thy will, that one or the other should close his life in death this night, then we pray that Thou wilt grant us a holy ending, so that we can depart from this life in peace, and enter into everlasting rest, where we can praise and worship Thee with all the Holy ones. To this end, we pray for strength, through Thy Love and Mercy. Amen.

MEATS

Suppen-Fleisch
Sour Meat
Cook neck of beef till tender. Pick meat off of bones. Add prunes, onion, vinegar, salt, and pepper. Cook together until done.

Fruit Sauce for Ham

1 c. each of prunes, dried pears, peaches, apricots, and raisins	1 c. sugar 1/2 tsp. cinnamon 1/2 tsp. salt

Wash fruit, leave whole. Barely cover with warm water, and let set for several hours. Add sugar, cinnamon, and salt and gently cook on low heat until fruit is done and most liquid absorbed.
Serve with ham.

SALADS

Gurken-Salat
Cucumber Salad

2 cucumbers   1 c. sour cream
1 large sweet onion   salt and pepper

Wash cucumbers and slice very thin into a bowl. Peel and slice onion, paper thin. Add to cucumbers. Add sour cream, salt, and pepper.

Serve with pan fried potatoes.

Sure Komst
Dill Cabbage

The Ostrogers were an especially impoverished group and this was reflected in the frugality of their food habits and recipes. The re-use of ingredients is shown in the dill-cabbage recipe.

After eating all the dill pickles from a crock or jar, use the juice and seasonings, such as leaves, dill, garlic, etc. to pour over cooked wedges of cabbage, (tender but not soft). Let stand over night or longer.

E. Foth

SOUPS

Beet Borsht

Peel 6 or 8 beets, the size of goose eggs. Dice in strips like noodles. Use about half of the stems and cut into inch strips, add 1 tsp. minced onion. Cut about 3 or 4 slices bacon into narrow strips. Boil all together in 1 1/2 quarts water till the beets are done. Make a thin sauce of 2 1/2 tbsp. flour with half and half or cream. Then add salt to taste and add 1/2 c. vinegar, let come to a boil.

Chicken Borsht

1 stewing chicken
2 medium heads cabbage
4 medium potatoes
1 large onion

2 c. tomatoes
salt and pepper to taste
1 c. cream

Boil chicken until tender. Remove meat from bones, dice and return to broth. Add diced fresh vegetables, tomatoes, and seasonings. Simmer until vegetables are done. Just before serving, add cream and reheat but do not boil.

Bean Soup

2 c. navy beans
soup bone, ham
1 onion

2 whole cloves
1/2 c. cream
1/2 tsp. prepared mustard

Put beans, onion, and soup bone in a large sauce pan. Cover with water. Bring to a boil, turn heat down to simmer. Add cloves and mustard. Simmer all day or until beans are done. Before serving, add cream.

Water Dumplings
(Poor Man's Dish)

Cook sausage, bacon, or ham in 1 quart water. (Cut meat in small pieces.) Add a small diced onion, salt, and a few whole allspice.

Make a dough of flour and water. Roll out like noodle dough. Cut into 1/2 by 1 inch wide strips. Add to boiling meat and cook till done. You may use diced potatoes instead of noodles.

Potato Ball Soup

Peel and grate 5 or 6 raw potatoes. Put in a salt cloth bag and squeeze till potatoes are completely dry. Form into small balls, size of marbles, drop into boiling milk. Add salt to taste. Cook until done.

Water Potato Soup

Peel 3 or 4 potatoes, cut in 1/2 inch cubes. Add a little onion. Cook in water till done, mash a little. Fry about 4 or 5 strips of bacon till crisp. If there is too much grease, pour some off. Add to potatoes. Season with salt and pepper to taste.

Chluecka
Rivel Soup
Old Fashioned Polish Dish

Take 1 egg, 3/4 c. flour, and pinch of salt. Stir together and work with fingers so little pieces form. If too thick, add a little milk so all of the flour is used up. Drop into 3 c. boiling milk and bring to a boil. Serve hot.

Short Soup
(Beef Stew with Gravy)

Take a 2 pound beef roast and cut into 1 1/2 inch pieces. Sear in an iron skillet with a little butter. Brown on all sides. Take meat out and put in a heaping tbsp. flour and brown. Add water to make gravy, stirring constantly. Add enough water to cover meat. Salt and pepper to taste. Simmer about 1 hour.
    This was served to a threshing crew at harvest time.

Sauerkraut Soup With Pork

Boil some pork ribs, ham hock, or any other pork meat enough for the family. When the meat is tender, drain off a little juice if it is too soupy. Then add the sauerkraut, as much as needed for the family. Cook till it is done. Make a paste or white sauce with about 2 tbsp. flour and water. Slowly add 1 c. sweet cream and mix well. Slowly pour over the sauerkraut. Keep stirring all the time, till it thickens. If it is too thick, add some sweet milk.

This is good with boiled potatoes.

Plume-Moos

2 c. dried prunes	2 tsp. cinnamon
1 c. dried raisins	3 tbsp. flour
1 c. sweet cream	water
1/2 c. sugar	

Cover dried fruit with water and cook until done. Cool slightly and add cream. Combine sugar, cinnamon, and flour and stir in enough water to make a thin paste. Add to fruit and cook until thick, stirring constantly. Serve either hot or cold.

Kirsche Moos is made in the same manner except that 2 c. of sour cherries with juice are substituted for the prunes and raisins. The sugar is increased to 1 c.

Buttermilk Plume-Moos No. 1

1 quart buttermilk	2 heaping tbsp. flour
1 c. prunes	with 1/2 c. cream to
1 c. raisins	make a thickening
1/2 c. sugar	

Cook the prunes and raisins ahead of time. Heat 2 or 3 sticks of cinnamon slowly in the buttermilk, stirring constantly. Mix sugar with the heated buttermilk, to keep it from curdling. Slowly add the thickening, while stirring. Cook until thickened to about the consistency of thin white sauce or heavy cream. Add prunes and raisins. Heat thoroughly and remove from heat. Serve warm or chilled.

Buttermilk Plume-Moos No. 2

2 c. prunes
1 c. raisins
1 stick cinnamon
1/2 c. cream

1/3 c. sugar
1/2 tsp. salt
2 c. buttermilk
flour paste

Wash fruit. Add water to barely cover. Add cinnamon stick, cook over low heat until almost done. Add salt, sugar, and buttermilk. Bring to a slow boil, stirring constantly. Slowly add flour paste (flour and water). Cook until slightly thickened. Remove from stove and add cream.

Cherry Moos

Heat 1 quart canned cherries. Mix 1 round tbsp. flour, 1/4 c. sugar, and 1 c. cream. Pour on hot cherries and gradually bring to a boil.

Prune and Raisin Moos

2 c. pasteurized, cultured
    buttermilk
3/4 c. raisins
1/2 c. prunes
2/3 c. sugar

2 tbsp. flour
1/2 c. sweet cream
2 c. water or enough so
    fruit will be covered
    when done

Cook raisins and prunes until tender. Make a thickening of flour and a little water. Add cinnamon and cream; add to fruit, stirring constantly. Bring to a boil; add sugar. Let cool. Add buttermilk. (For smooth texture, do not cook the buttermilk.)

Wedding and Holy Day Treats

For special festivals wheat bread would be baked and served with various soups—such as *Pluma Moos*, *Borscht*, beer-honey soup, or milk soups in which barley or oatmeal were cooked.

PRESERVING

Sour Beef

9 pounds beef
3 pounds plums (prunes)
3 pounds raisins
6 onions

2 1/2 c. sugar
1 1/2 c. vinegar
salt to taste

Boil plums and raisins separately. Boil meat until it loosens from the bone. Save broth and put it on the meat again. Put in cans and seal.

Dill Pickles

1 gallon cucumbers
3-4 inches long
1/2 c. salt

4 cloves garlic
3 heads dill
enough water to cover

Use grape leaves, horseradish leaves, and cherry leaves.

Good Dill Pickles

13 c. water
3/4 c. pickling salt

1 c. vinegar

Bring this to a boiling point. Put cucumbers, dill and garlic in jars. Pour boiling brine in jars and seal at once.

Beet Pickles

2 or 3 gallons of beets. Cook beets until tender. Skin.
Make syrup:

2 pints water
2 pints vinegar
3 pints sugar

1 level tsp. pepper
1/2 tsp. each cloves and
allspice, if desired

Let come to a boil. Put beets in and boil 5 minutes. Put into jars. Seal immediately.

VEGETABLES

Baked Sauerkraut

canned sauerkraut   1/2 c. raisins
   (size 2 1/2)   1/2 c. brown sugar
1 c. prunes

Empty kraut into large casserole. Wash fruit. Add to sauerkraut. Add brown sugar, mix well. Bake in moderate oven to brown. Stir as needed so kraut will brown evenly.

Spareribs or sausage may be added while baking.

Preboiled Fried Potatoes

Cook potatoes until almost done. Peel and slice 1/4 inch thick. Melt oleo or butter in skillet. Salt to taste. Fry until just hot.

Pan Fried Potatoes

4 medium potatoes   salt
4 tbsp. fat   pepper

Put fat into a skillet. Heat. Add thin sliced potatoes. Fry on medium heat until golden brown. Turn and continue frying, stirring occasionally, until brown and done.

Buttermilk Potatoes

Peel and cut up about 2 c. potatoes. Cook with salt and little onion. When done pour off water and crush with a fork. Make a thickening of 1 c. buttermilk, 1 c. cream, and about a heaping tbsp. flour. Pour over potatoes and bring to a boil.

Kalesh
Potatoes and Rice

Dice 2 medium potatoes. Add 2 c. water and 1/2 c. raw rice. Add salt, a few peppercorn, and allspice kernels. Add a little onion. Cook together until done.

Fried Onions In Milk

Fry 1 large onion in a little grease in which meat has been fried for better flavor. Brown the onion, then add sweet milk, as much as is needed. Add a little salt. Pour this over the boiled potatoes in a bowl. It tastes good.

Spring Time Garden Hash

Make dumplings with 3 whole eggs, well beaten, to which 1/2 tsp. salt and 1 c. flour have been added. Add more flour if needed to make a soft dough which can be dropped into boiling water to form the dumplings. Boil a few minutes and drain well.

Brown 2 c. diced bacon in skillet. Drain off most of the grease. Add the drained dumplings and 6 fresh onions, tops and all, diced. Season with salt and pepper to taste. Cook until onions are tender.

This may be served this way or placed in a casserole and warmed for a short time.

Serves four.

10

The Russian (Low German) Mennonites

HISTORY

The Low German Mennonites In Russia

The "Low German" people lived in Northern Germany. When the Anabaptists began in the Netherlands in the sixteenth century many were forced to leave their homes due to persecution of their new faith. They settled in West Prussia, in the Danzig area, and along the Vistula River.

In the beginning they had been welcomed as good farmers who drained the undesirable swamp lands of the river area. As Mennonites, however, they were not considered full-fledged citizens. This attitude often caused hardships for them, which were increased when they were prohibited from purchasing new land. Their religious freedom also seemed in danger of being taken from them, and so they began to look elsewhere. When Catherine II of Russia invited them, as well as citizens from other countries, to settle in Russia, many of the Mennonites accepted. They were promised religious freedom, exemption from military service, and self-government. The future looked promising.

For some years these Mennonites prospered and gradually established their own way of life. Four main settlements were established: Chortitiza, Molotschna, Trakt, and Alexandertal. These larger units consisted of a number of villages, which varied in size and numbers. Schools were begun and, although the teachers were often not adequately educated for this task, it was a beginning for later higher education. Mixed farming was encouraged, and winter wheat became a specialty. Primitive agricultural machinery was replaced by advanced implements produced in Mennonite factories.

Gradually the concerns for the poorer people, such as laborers, widows, and orphans, resulted in mutual aid organizations— "*Fuersorge*". Such help enabled daughter villages to be established through cooperative purchase of land and loans to these settlers.

Around 1870, however, it became apparent that they were to lose their special privileges such as: exemption from military service, private schools, local government, and their German language. Some accepted alternative service of a civilian nature, but others felt this would not be a permanent arrangement and so looked to America. Delegates were sent to check into the conditions of both Canada and United States. In 1874, the first group left for America; and by 1880, about 18,000 people left Russia to seek a new life in a new land.

A typical ship load consisted of about six hundred families. Some of these disembarked in Philadelphia, Pennsylvania; and from there took the train to Topeka, Kansas. Others sailed up to Manitoba from Moorhead, Minnesota, along the Red River. Some remained in the eastern part of the country the first winter and then continued in the spring. No beginnings were easy, and many hardships were experienced by these early pioneers.

An interesting story about one group coming to Kansas tells about the people arriving during the 4th of July celebration. When the fire crackers were heard, the new arrivals became dismayed, as they thought that they had landed in the middle of a war zone.

When the Alexanderwohl group landed on the East coast, they had their first introduction to the peanut. Here sacks of these nuts were tossed to them. After the long ocean trip, these peanuts were greatly appreciated.

There was also a second exodus from Russia during the twentieth century. The Mennonites had reached a high stage of development: an advanced educational system, extensive land-holdings, large commercial enterprises, flour mills, etc. The world seemed at peace, and the future looked promising. Then came the 1st World War in 1914, and the 2nd World War in 1945. The Mennonite colonies were overwhelmed, and life and property were unsafe. Suffering, broken families, and brutal murder by roving bands followed the Bolshevik Revolution and thousands fled, finding refuge in Germany and in North and South America.

Although life has not always been easy for these refugees, especially in South America, they have again established prosperous communities and enterprises.

We, the descendants of these refugees from the Lowlands of Europe, are grateful to them for the many religious and economic opportunities we enjoy because of their faith and their sacrifices.

Preparation for Migration

The Mennonite families planning to migrate to America in the 1870's, spent many days in preparations. This undertaking was a heart-breaking adventure for them, as they knew they would never again see their loved ones who remained in Russia. Regardless of this sadness, their preparations continued.

The menfolk were responsible for the building of large chests of wood and of wicker. These were to hold many precious articles which the family would need in the new land. The children, with their tiny fingers, were given the task of sorting the kernels of the Hard Winter Wheat. Other seeds were also gathered—all kinds of tree seeds, especially mulberry, sweet watermelon seeds, dill, and parsley, and many other favorites. Even after a hundred years in the new homeland, the Mennonites raise fine quality products similar to those produced in Russia by their forefathers.

During this time, the women were busy baking and toasting *Zwieback* and many sacks of flour were used. Perhaps some of these *Zwieback* also helped fill the wicker chests! Who can imagine the amount of food it would take to feed a family of six or so for almost two months.

The women also brought their art of cooking with them. Many of the recipes used by the Low German people in America have been handed down from generation to generation. Several of the favorite recipes have a Russian origin but have become accepted as part of the Mennonite heritage. Among these Russian names are: *Vareniky* (a cottage-cheese filled dough), *Piroshky* (a fruit filled pastry), *Paskha* (a Russian Easter bread), *Borsht*, etc.

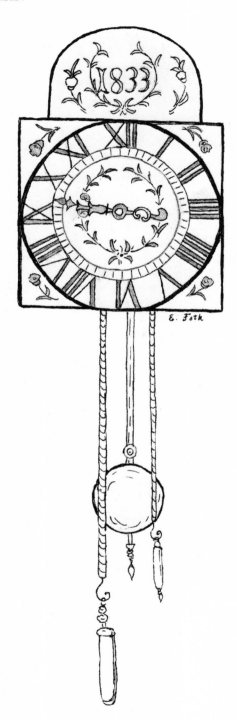

Plautdietsch
J. H. Janzen

Maunch eena kaun keen Plautdietsch mea
en schaemt sich nich emaol.
Em Geagindeel: he meent sich sea
met siene hoage School,
red't hoogdietsch, englisch, rusch — so vael,
daut eenim dieslich woat.
Weat es de gaunze Klaetamaehl
nich eene Schinkeschwoat.

Auls eck noch kleen wea, saut eck oft
bi Mutt're oppim Schoot,
en plautdietsch saed se, — o so oft; —
"Mien Jung, eck sie die goot."
Waut Mutta plautdietsch to mi saed,
daut klung so woarm en tru,
daut eck daut nimmamea vegaet
bat to de latzte Ruh.

A literal translation would be:

Hardly anyone can speak Low German anymore
and isn't ashamed of it.
On the contrary, he thinks he's something
With his advanced education.
He speaks High German, English, Russian, so much
That one gets dizzy
This whole business isn't even worth
A bacon rind.

When I was still young
I often sat on Mother's lap
How often, in Low German, she said to me,
"My boy, I love you."
What mother said to me in Low German
Sounded so warm and true
That I shall never forget it, until I find
My final rest.

MENU

Sunday Morning
    Fresh *Zwieback*
    Cheese
    Coffee or barley coffee (*Prips*)

Other mornings, especially during winter
    Cracklings fixed with stewed dried apples or boiled potatoes
        Some fixed the cracklings plain and ate them with syrup
    Oatmeal was a must
    Bread

Noon meal
    Ham hock with navy or green beans
    Borsht or beef stew
    Canned fruit for dessert

Evening meal
    Fried ham or smoked sausage
    Fried potatoes
    Dill pickles
    Apple, cherry, or gooseberry *moos*

BREADS

Introduction
Zwieback

Zwieback or "Double Buns" are a great favorite among the "Russian" Mennonites, as well as any visiting friend. These buns are usually baked on Saturday to be served for *Vaspa* or lunch on Sunday. The dough for *Zwieback* must be kneaded well to give a good texture to the buns.

Years ago *Zwieback* were always served for weddings and for the fellowship hour following funerals. To some extent, this custom is still kept up in some Mennonite communities, and *Zwieback* are making a "come back" in other circles of Mennonite ethnic groups.

Zwieback are usually served with cheese, lump sugar, and coffee.

Dunking them is also a special treat!

Zwieback No. 1
Double Buns

Dissolve: 2 cakes yeast in 4 tbsp. warm water and 4 tsp. sugar. Let stand 10 minutes.

Add:

3/4 c. melted butter and lard	flour, enough to make
1 1/2 c. warm milk	a stiff dough
4 tsp. salt	

The dough will be softer than bread dough. (When the dough no longer sticks to the bread board on which it is being kneaded, it will have enough flour.)

Let rise until double in bulk. Pinch off small balls of dough and place on a greased baking sheet. Then place a smaller ball on top of each bun. Press down to help seal.

Let rise until double. Bake at 375° about 15 minutes or until nicely browned.

Zwieback No. 2
Double Buns

Scald 3 c. milk. Cool to lukewarm.
Melt 1 c. shortening (1/2 butter and 1/2 lard).
      3 tsp. salt   2 tbsp. sugar
Put above ingredients in large mixing bowl.

Dissolve: 2 packages dry yeast in 1/4 c. warm water to which 1 tsp. sugar has been added. After yeast becomes spongy, add to the milk mixture. Add 3 c. flour, beating until very smooth. Gradually add about 5 c. more of flour and mix well.

Put on a baking board and knead well, about 5 minutes. Return to bowl and let rise until double. Knead down again. Let rise until light. Pinch off small balls of dough. Put on greased pan. Then pinch off a smaller ball of dough and place on top of the other. Press down with finger to hold. Let rise till double. Bake at 425° for 10 minutes.

Paskha
A Russian Easter Bread

Dissolve: 2 packages dry yeast in 1 c. warm water, potato water if available. Add just enough flour to make a very soft sponge. Set aside.

Scald: 2 1/2 c. milk and pour over 1 c. of flour and beat until very smooth. Cool slightly.

Stir in the yeast and mix well.

Beat: 2 whole eggs and 12 egg yolks until light. Add 2 c. sugar and continue beating until creamy. Add to yeast mixture.

Add 1 c. melted butter or margarine, 1 tsp. salt, and 2 tsp. lemon flavoring, or use the grated rind of a lemon.

Mix in appoximately 10-12 c. flour, beating as long as possible; then knead. The dough must be somewhat soft, so do not add too much flour.

Let rise in a warm place until light in texture. Punch down and let rise again until double.

In the meantime grease 6-8 round tins, 3# shortening tins, or tall 48 ounce fruit juice tins which are very good for this.

When the dough has doubled itself, pinch off a small ball and put into the tins. Only a very small amount of dough will be needed, (approximately a piece of dough of about 2 1/2 inches thick when spread over the bottom of the tin will be adequate).

Let rise till almost to the top of the tin and bake in a 325° oven for about an hour. (If tops seem to brown too quickly, cover with a piece of brown wrapping paper so they will not burn.)

When cool, these breads may be iced and decorated. They may be cut in round slices or lengthwise in wedge-shaped pieces. The round slices are delicious toasted when the bread becomes a week old. Although it is not necessary to butter this bread, it does taste very good that way.

This Easter bread was acquired by the Russian Mennonites and so brought to many of our communities over here. The Russian Orthodox woman would ice and decorate these breads very elaborately and on Easter Sunday each one would give this offering to the priest. As the bread is baked in a round tin the dough rises above the top, forming a round "dome", reminding one of the domed Orthodox churches. When served in the home, and company being present, the guest of honor would be offered the iced top, otherwise the oldest member would be honored. If *Paskha* is to be kept somewhat longer than a few days, it is better to omit the icing and the fancy decorations.

Bulke
White Bread

1 package yeast	3 tsp. salt
3 c. water	4 tbsp. shortening
1 c. potato water	flour to make a stiff
4 tbsp. sugar	dough, about 11 c.

Dissolve yeast in a little of the warm water to which a little sugar has been added. When spongy, put into the warm liquid and add the sugar and just enough flour to make a soft sponge. Beat well. Cover and let rise until light.

Add the salt and the melted shortening.

Add the remainder of the flour, kneading it in, using as much as needed to have a stiff dough.

Cover and let rise until double. Knead down and let rise again.

Working on a bread board, knead the dough a little, and let it rest for a few minutes. Then cut into 3 or 4 even pieces. Shape into loaves. Place in greased loaf pans and let rise until almost double.

Bake in 350° oven until done, about 1 hour.

A. Brandt

Sweet Zwieback
Zdibnoy

Dissolve 1 package of dry yeast in 1 c. warm water. Scald 2 c. milk, and cool to lukewarm. Beat until light: 1 c. sugar and 4 egg yolks. Melt 1 c. shortening, part butter.

Mix the above ingredients and add the stiffly beaten egg whites. Gradually beat in enough flour to make a soft dough. Knead lightly. Let rise until double and knead down. Let rise again.

Pinch off small balls of dough and place on a greased pan. Let rise until double. Bake at 325° until a golden brown.

These may be dipped into sugar or brushed with lightly beaten egg yolk before baking.

Schnetke
Biscuits

1/2 c. lard	1 c. milk
1/2 c. margarine	1 c. cream
2 1/2 tsp. baking powder	1 tsp. salt
4 to 4 1/2 c. flour	1 egg may be added

Sift dry ingredients and cut in shortening. Add the beaten egg, if used, and the liquid. Turn out on floured board and roll out 1/2 inch thick.

Cut into squares or rectangles. Bake at 400° until browned, about 15-20 minutes.

Good served with *Borscht*.

Porzelky
A New Year's Doughnut

Dissolve 1 package yeast in 1/2 c. warm water to which 2 tsp. of sugar have been added. When sponge-like, pour into a large mixing bowl in which 2 1/2 c. warm milk have been cooling.

Beat 3 eggs and add 3/4 c. sugar, 1 1/2 tsp. salt, and 1/4 c. melted shortening. Add to the yeast mixture. Gradually add about 3 1/2 c. flour, beating well after each addition. Add 2 1/2 c. raisins before the last amount of flour is to be added. Add more flour if needed.

This will be a fairly stiff dough but one that is not to be rolled out or worked by hand.

Let rise in a warm place. When double, cut off pieces of dough with a spoon dipped in hot fat, and deep fry (like regular doughnuts).

Roll in powdered sugar or sprinkle with white sugar.

In some homes these are made somewhat stiffer and the dough is rolled out and cut in rounds. Place on floured board and let rise until light. Deep fry. This method makes more even sized doughnuts.

These are a specialty for New Year's Day.

New Year's Wish With Porzelky

Eck sach den Schornsteen roake
Eck wisst woll waut jie moake
Jie bake Niejoasch Koake.
Gew jie mi eene
Dann bliew eck stoane,
Gew jie mi twee
Dann fang eck ann to goane,
Gew jie mi dree, fea, fief toa glick
Dan wensch eck ju
daut gaunze Himmelrick.

I saw the chimney smoking.
I knew very well what you were making,
You are baking New Year cookies.
If you give me one,
I stand still,
If you give me two
I'll start to go,
If you give me three, four, five for luck
Then I wish you the
Whole Heavenly kingdom.

Rollkoake, Crullers No. 1
Served with Watermelon

Beat 2 eggs, add 1/2 c. melted shortening, 1/2 c. milk, and 2 tsp. salt. Add enough flour to make a soft dough, about 3 c. Place dough on a floured board and roll out very thin. Cut into 5 inch by 2 inch pieces. Cut a slit in the center and fry in deep, hot fat, 375° until done.

Tjleene Tjinje, Tjleene Sorje:
Groote Tjinje, Groote Sorje.

Small children, small worries;
Big children, big worries.

Crullers No. 2

1 c. sour cream
1/2 c. sweet milk
4 eggs
4 c. flour, approx.

1/2 tsp. salt
1 tsp. baking powder
1 1/2 tbsp. sugar, if desired

Sift dry ingredients into mixing bowl and make a well in the center of the flour. Add the beaten eggs with the liquid and put into "well"; mix well, using fork or your hands.

Roll out fairly thin on a floured board and cut into oblong pieces. Deep fry in hot fat. If these are pushed down into the fat at the beginning of being fried, they will puff up and fry better.

Rogge-Brot
Rye Bread

Cook a potato in about 2 c. water. When done, mash. There should be 2 c. of liquid, and if more is needed to make this amount, add either milk or water.

Dissolve 1 cake of yeast in 2 tbsp. molasses and add to the liquid.

Add:

1 heaping tbsp. lard
1 c. rye-graham flour

2 tsp. salt

Mix well and gradually add enough white flour to make a fairly stiff dough. Knead well and let rise.

When the dough is light, knead again and divide into two equal parts. Form into loaves and put into greased bread pans.

Let rise. Bake in moderate oven until done, about 1 hour.

Sour Dough Rye Bread

6 c. white flour
3 c. rye flour
2 tbsp. lard
    sour dough "bun"

2 c. warm water
1 package yeast
1 c. potato water
1 tbsp. salt

Dissolve yeast in a little warm water. Add to remainder of the warmed liquid, lard, salt, and sour dough. Beat in the rye flour and gradually add enough white flour to make a stiff dough, about 5 c. Knead well. Cover and let rise until light.

Knead down and let rise again until double in bulk. Form into loaves and put into greased loaf pans. Let rise until almost double.

Bake in moderate hot oven until done, 50-60 minutes.

The Making of Yeast and "Sour Dough"

Hops were planted along a fence, since they were vines. When the hops were in pods, a handful was taken, put into a bag and boiled in 2 quarts of water with 4 cut up potatoes (grated). This mixture was cooked until the potatoes were done; the bag was removed, but squeezed dry. The potatoes were mashed and the mixture of hops, water, and potatoes was allowed to cool. A c. of sugar was added, also 1/4 c. salt and 1 c. of old yeast (left over from the previous time). This was allowed to stand for several hours and then used as yeast for baking.

CAKES AND COOKIES

Obst Plautz No. 1
Coffee Cake

Mix a soft dough of:

1/2 c. cream	1/2 c. sugar
1 egg, beaten	1 1/3 c. flour (approx.)
1 tsp. baking powder	

Pat into a cake pan, having a fairly thin layer. Place cut fruit on top of dough; any tart fruit is good: apples, cherries, apricots, etc. Mix 2 tsp. flour to 1/2 c. sugar and sprinkle over fruit.

Top with a crumb mixture:

1/2 c. sugar	3/4 c. flour
1/4 c. butter	

Mix these together by hand until crumbly.

Bake at 350° until lightly browned, about 45 minutes.

Plautz may also be made using a regular pie dough for the base and using the same method; a *zwieback* dough is also good. If this is used, allow the *Plautz* to rise until light before baking.

Kracktichkeit es daut haulva leve.
Kinya, fecht den desh auf.

Cleanliness is half of life.
Children, sweep off the table.

Obst Plautz No. 2
Fruit Coffee Cake

Sift:

2 c. flour	1/2 tsp. salt
2 tsp. baking powder	1/3 c. sugar

Add: 1/4 c. margarine and rub into dry ingredients.

Beat: 1 egg and add 6-7 tbsp. milk and stir into crumb mixture. Mix well.

Press into a large baking sheet, pushing up the edges. Put fruit on the top, using apples, cherries, plums, apricots etc.

Top with a crumb topping:

1 1/2 c. flour	1 c. sugar
1/2 c. butter	

Mix with hands until crumbly.

Bake in moderate oven until golden brown, about 30 minutes.

Pfeffernuesse
Little Spiced Buns

Dissolve: 3 packages yeast in 1/2 c. warm water and 2 tbsp. sugar. Then add dissolved yeast to:

2 c. warm water	1/2 c. molasses
3/4 c. sugar	2/3 c. shortening, melted

Sift:

9 c. flour	3 tsp. cinnamon
3/4 tsp. pepper	1/2 tsp. nutmeg
1 tsp. salt	

Add to liquid, beating well. Use another c. of flour, if necessary, to make a fairly stiff dough. Let rise 30 minutes and knead down. Let rise again until double.

Pinch off small pieces of dough about size of a walnut and place on greased pans, about 1 inch apart. Let rise till double in bulk. Sprinkle sugar over the top of the "buns" and bake in a hot oven, 375°, until brown, about 20 minutes.

A good "snack at bedtime".

Knack-Soat
Sunflower Seed Snack

Several outstanding features marked the village farms of the "Russian" Mennonites in their new homes in America. The buildings were patterned after those of the old country, with the house and barn together or separated by a narrow passage—a great convenience during the blustry winter weather! Then there were the picket fences lining the village street, separating each home, and usually painted white, giving a sense of neatness and well-being. Behind these fences clusters of brightly colored hollyhocks bloomed during the summer months. Lastly in the garden, the bright yellow sunflowers added their touch of beauty to the whole. These not only seemed ornamental, but were also very important during the long winter days when they were used as "snacks" or treats by young and old.

When the sunflower was ripe, it was picked and stored in a dry place, most likely in the attic of one of the farm buildings. Here it would be "threshed" by knocking or scraping off the seeds, which would then be placed in sacks and stored. Needless to say many of these seeds never got this far. What young fellow could resist eating handfuls of these morsels as he worked. No need to store all of them!

Then often in the afternoon, especially on Sundays, when the oven was still warm from the noon meal, a large pan of these seeds would be shoved into the oven and roasted a little. Now they were really delicious; and, when guests arrived in the evenings, or Sundays after church, it was not unusual to see the menfolk sitting in the kitchen chewing sunflower seeds. It really was quite an art to eat these. Not one seed at a time! A handful would be quickly put into the mouth and soon a stream of empty shells would be seen flowing out the other side. Through it all the conversation never slackened, and many hours of good fellowship were enjoyed.

Needless to say before the coffee kettle could be heated and lunch served, the kitchen floor had to be swept. This job did not take long, and soon all were seated around the table enjoying an early *Vaspa*, lunch.

These sunflower seeds were, and still are, called *Knack-Soat*, or cracking seeds, and are a popular treat among our "Russian" Mennonites today. Often now, however, sunflower seeds can be bought in little packages and enjoyed by everyone; but the art of eating these seeds "properly" is not known or readily acquired by anyone not raised with this specialty.

Russian Peppermint Cookies

Cream: 3 c. sugar and 1 c. butter.

Add: 5 eggs, one at a time; beat well after each. Then add 2 c. sweet or sour cream and 10 drops of peppermint oil.

Dissolve 2 tbsp. baking ammonia in 2 tbsp. hot water. Slowly add 8 c. unsifted flour.

Roll out fairly thin and cut with 2 1/2 inch cutter.

Bake at 375° for 9 minutes. Cookies will be almost white.

Makes 8 dozen cookies.

Mother's Molasses Cookies

3 c. sugar	1 tsp. star anise
1 1/2 c. lard	1/2 tsp. pepper
1 1/2 c. molasses	1/2 tsp. cloves
4 tsp. soda	1 tsp. baking powder
4 c. buttermilk	flour to make soft dough

Cream sugar and lard. Add molasses and buttermmlk. Dissolve soda in 1/4 c. of the buttermilk and add to the mixture. Mix spices and baking powder with the flour and add enough flour to make a soft dough, just firm enough to roll out and cut.

Bake at 425° for about 7 minutes, or until done.

Makes about 2 gallons of cookies.

Honey Cookies

2 2/3 c. honey	4 eggs
4 tbsp. soda	8 c. flour
rinds of 2 lemons or	pinch of salt
2 oranges	

Melt honey over a slow fire. Add grated rinds. Dissolve soda in a little vinegar and add to honey mixture. Let this stand an hour or two, stirring often. Then beat eggs well and mix with honey.

Add flour and salt. Let batter set for 3 days in a warm place. Roll out and cut. Bake at 425° for 5 minutes. Use orange or lemon juice and powdered sugar to frost while cookies are still hot. Large recipe.

CHEESE AND DUMPLINGS

Dwoy
(Stinky Cheese)

Take a pound of dry curd cottage cheese, drained until dry.

3/4 tsp. salt	6 tbsp. country sour cream
1 tsp. caraway seed	

Mix thoroughly and put into a crock. Let it ripen 4 or 5 days, stirring once or twice daily, depending on warm or cool weather. Cover with damp cloth. Roll into balls and let dry until ripe, 5 to 7 days. Store in refrigerator in airtight container.

Vareniky
Cottage Cheese "Pockets"

2 to 2 1/2 c. dry curd cottage cheese	1/4 tsp. salt 2 egg yolks

Mix these ingredients and set aside while the dough is being rolled out.

Dough:

1/2 c. milk or water 1/2 tsp. salt	2 egg whites

Beat lightly with a fork and gradually add enough flour to make a soft dough which can be easily rolled out, approximately 1 1/2 c.

Roll dough out quite thin and cut into circles about 3 inches in diameter. Place a tsp. of cottage cheese mixture on each circle, fold over and pinch the edges together, or cover with another circle.

When all the dough has been cut, drop the *Vareniky* into boiling, salted water. Boil 5-8 minutes. Drain in a colander. Serve with:

1. Cream gravy made by bringing 1 c. cream and 3 tbsp. butter to a boil and serving over the *Vareniky*.
2. Add the cream to fried ham drippings and heat thoroughly.
3. Slowly brown butter fat until a golden brown and pour over the *Vareniky*.

Dumplings
Kielke—Homemade macaroni

Mix:

3 eggs, lightly beaten 1 1/2 tsp. salt 1/3 c. milk	2 3/4 c. flour or enough to make a stiff dough

Knead dough well. Then roll out quite thin. Cut into 2 inch wide strips and stack several strips, putting flour between to prevent sticking. Cut the dough into narrow strips, or noodles. Toss to separate on lightly floured board.

Cook in boiling salted water for a few minutes, until *Kielke* are done. Strain.

Serve with: onions sauted in butter to which the *Kielke* are added or with a hot cream sauce made by melting 3 tbsp. butter in a pan and adding 1/3 c. cream. Onions may also be added to this cream sauce, or brown 1/4 pound butter slowly in a pan until a golden color.

Making Molasses

In September or October when the sugar cane was ready, it was cut down, the leaves chopped off and the seed part topped. Each was put in a stack. The leaves and seed were used to feed the cattle. The stocks were taken to the press. This press was horse drawn, the horse going round and round while someone fed the four-roller press. The juice was then strained before it went into four pans. It was cooked and skimmed until clear and just the right color and consistency.

Farmers would bring their cane to the press, and the cost of making the molasses would be one half of the finished product. The farmer who owned the press always raised cane for molasses which was then sold.

DESSERTS

Gries Pudding
Cream of Wheat Pudding

3 3/4 c. milk	4 eggs, separated
2/3 c. Cream of Wheat	pinch of salt
3/4 c. sugar	1 to 1 1/2 tsp. vanilla or
	lemon flavoring

Bring milk to a boil and slowly add the cream of wheat, stirring constantly. Add salt. Beat the egg yolks until light and add the sugar. Slowly stir this into the hot milk, stirring. Cook for 5 minutes.

In the meantime beat the egg whites until fairly stiff. Add 2 tsp. extra sugar for each egg and beat well.

Add the flavoring and lastly fold in the beaten whites.

Pour into a serving bowl and cool.

Delicious served with fruit juice or cream.

Waut de Mann met dem Ladawoage nen bringe kaun
Kaun de Fru met dem Schaldok rut droage

That which a man brings in with his farm wagon,
His wife can carry out with her apron.

Gretti Malkschi Moos
Barley Soup or Porridge

3 c. buttermilk   1 1/4 c. pearl barley
1 quart sweet milk

Add the barley to the heated milk and set on low heat. Stir occasionally and cook until barley is tender and the "porridge" thick.

To serve, cool the porridge and add sweet milk. If desired this may be served hot; but, in most cases, it was served cold for supper. Sweeten to taste.

MEATS

Golubtsy
Cabbage Rolls

Remove the core of 1 large head of cabbage with a sharp knife. Place cabbage in a deep pan and pour boiling water into the hollow of the core. Cover completely with boiling water. Let stand until leaves are pliable. Drain off the water.

Take the cabbage leaves apart, one at a time. Cut off the hard stem from the bottom.

Wash thoroughly 2 c. rice and add to 2 c. boiling water to which 1 tsp. salt has been added. Bring to a boil. Cover and turn off heat allowing the rice to absorb all the water.

Saute 1 large onion, minced, in 4 tbsp. bacon fat or shortening. Add 1 c. cooked meat, ground.

Combine with the rice and season to taste with salt and pepper. Cool mixture.

Place a spoonful of rice mixture on each cabbage leaf and roll up. (Tooth pick may be used to "tie" leaf together.)

Place cabbage rolls in baking pan, sprinkle with salt.

Mix together 1 1/2 c. tomato juice and 1/2 c. sour cream. Pour over the cabbage rolls. Cover tightly and bake at 350° for 2 hours or until both cabbage and rice are done.

Bubbat With Sausage

1 cake yeast	3 1/2 to 4 c. flour
3 tbsp. sugar	1 tsp. salt
1 1/2 c. milk	1 lb. of smoked sausage
1 egg	(approx.)

Scald the milk and cool to lukewarm. Add the dissolved yeast and sugar. Add the beaten egg, salt, and flour (enough flour to make a soft dough). Let rise until light and double in bulk. Place one layer of dough into a greased pan; then put a layer of cut sausage on top of the dough and cover with another layer of dough.

Let rise about 1 hour.

Bake at 350° for at least 1 hour or until done.

Cracklings and Eggs

Fry 2 c. cracklings until somewhat crisp. Drain off excess fat. Form into 5 or 6 little "clusters" or circles. Flatten out. Break an egg into each cluster. Cover pan with a lid and fry slowly until eggs are done. Add salt and pepper to taste.

Adding just a little water to the cracklings prevents them from getting hard.

Cracklings are also very good when fried with diced apples. Fry slowly until the apples are tender.

Cracklings are usually eaten with brown bread. Some people enjoy syrup with this, while others like a tart plum jam.

In whatever way cracklings are served, much of the fat or lard should be drained off.

Sauerkraut and Spare Ribs

Cook spare ribs or back bone in enough water to cover, until meat is done. Add sauerkraut. Heat thoroughly.

For variation add several tbsp. rice, a little onion and sauerkraut; or cook potatoes with jackets and at serving time pour kraut over peeled potatoes. Add a little cream to kraut before serving.

Pirozhky With Meat

Make a regular *Pirozhky* recipe or use a *Zwieback* dough recipe. Instead of a fruit filling add a meat mixture which can be made from left-overs.

Saute 1 small onion and add 1 1/2 to 2 c. left-over meat, ground, and about the same amount of left over mashed potatoes. Add salt and pepper to taste. Mix well. Place by heaping spoonful on dough similar to fruit *Pirozhky*.

Meat *Pirozhky* may be used as part of the main course of a meal instead of dessert, as is the case of a fruit *Pirozhky*.

Fried Ham and Onion Gravy With Cooked Navy Beans

Sliced ham for 4 to 6 people. After frying ham, remove and add 3 sliced onions. When onions are slightly browned, add enough flour, salt, pepper, and milk to make a gravy. Pour gravy mixture over hot cooked beans.

Ruehrei
Scrambled Eggs

For each egg used add:
    2 tbsp. flour   salt and pepper to taste
    3 tbsp. milk

Mix the flour and milk until smooth.

Beat the eggs until light and add to the paste mixture.

Add the seasoning. Melt a little lard or shortening in a frying pan. When hot, add the egg mixture. Do not have the heat turned up too high. When the eggs begin to thicken, turn with a spatula to keep pieces rather large. Brown other side. Serve hot.

Stelle Wota ranne deep.
Still waters run deep.

Stewed Squabs or Young Fryers

Cut up chicken, but leave squabs whole. Put in a kettle with two c. water, 2 tbsp. butter, salt, and pepper to taste and 1/4 tsp. anise seed. Bring to a boil, turn to simmer and cook for about 2 1/2 hours or until done. The liquid is then used to put over potatoes that have been cooked with jackets on.

Old Fashioned Mustard Recipe

1 tbsp. dry mustard	1 tsp. bacon fat
3 tbsp. sugar	1/4 c. boiled vinegar
3 tbsp. flour	

Mix the above. Add a little tumeric powder for color. Keeps indefinitely. Good with ham!

PASTRY

Pirozhky No. 1
Made with Yeast

1 cake yeast dissolved in 1/2 c. warm water to which 1 tsp. sugar has been added.

Melt 1/2 c. butter or margarine and add to 1 c. scalded, cooled milk. Add 1/2 c. sugar. Gradually sift in a little flour, beating well after each addition. Add enough flour to make a soft dough which can be rolled out, about 3 c.

Roll out smaller pieces of dough 1/4 inch thick. Place dabs of fruit, about 2 heaping tbsp., along the dough—but not quite to the edge. Fold the bare dough over the fruit part and cut off half circles of dough which are over the dabs. The straight side of the fold should be placed down on the greased tin, not too closely together. Let rise for a few minutes until rather light.

Bake in medium oven until done, about 25 minutes.

Any fruit may be used which is not too juicy, as this would be difficult to keep sealed. Apples, apricots, prunes, etc. are good.

Pirozhky
Apple Dumpling

1/2 c. shortening	2 c. flour
1 tsp. salt	milk to make a soft
1 tsp. baking powder	dough, like pie pastry
1 egg	

Sift dry ingredients into mixing bowl and cut in the shortening. Add the beaten egg and just enough milk to be able to roll out the dough, approximately 5 tbsp.

Roll out the dough like for a pie. Cut into 4 inch squares. Place a tbsp. of cut-up apples in center of square and add 1 tsp. of sugar. Bring the 4 corners of dough together in the center and press together. The edges may be moistened to stick better.

Bake in moderate hot oven, 375°, until light brown.

E. Foth

Warkentin Mill, Halstead, Ks.

Kingya en Kalva Moat
Motte ole Leed Veate.

Children's and calves portions
Older people should decide.

Dried Apples

Mennonite immigrants were favored with rich virgin soil. Orchards of one acre consisted of apples, apricots, and cherries.

My paternal grandmother and two aunts would dry apples and store them in wooden barrels in the attic of the old sod house. One barrel contained apples that were sugared down. This was our "candy". Grandpa's contribution was sweet wood and St. John's bread. We grandchildren loved to get into this barrel of sugared apples. A box was placed near the barrel so as to better reach the apples. Whenever we had eaten too many with the result of a tummy ache, we had another treat coming, namely a cube of sugar with a few drops of peppermint on it.

A. Brandt

My grandparents had a long mulberry hedge, which was always neatly trimmed. They put up yards of mosquito netting on this hedge on which the apples that had been peeled and cut were placed to dry.

Pioneer women were never idle, especially during apple *schnitzing* time. Very often neighbors of the village came in to help. They came not in a horse drawn carriage or a car but on foot.

I loved my grandmother's dried apple pie. Apples were cooked until done, sugar added, shoved to the back of the stove and stewed until a dark brown. They were baked in large black pans, maybe 18 by 18 inches square. It was delicious hot or cold. It took a bushel of apples to make 1 1/2 gallons of dried apples. In pioneer days they must have dried wagon loads of them. Sharing with others was common practice.

Today we enjoy dried apples, peaches, and apricots dried in a fine wire frame put on top of the airconditioning unit. With the hot air from the bottom and the sun from above, it is a quick process.

PRESERVING

Russian Watermelon Pickles

Fill a 50 gallon barrel at the end of the season with partly ripe melons that have been washed in cold water. Add 10 pounds of butchering salt, the pulp of about a dozen or more larger melons, dill and grape leaves, and fill barrel with cold water. This barrel was placed in the woodshed. It was covered with a slightly smaller round top than the opening of the barrel. It was then weighted down with a large rock. After a month or 6 weeks melons are ready.

We, today, use a 10 gallon crock, and 2 pounds salt. Be sure and weight melons down. Some put green tomatoes in with the melons to pickle.

Sauerkraut

To every 5 pounds of shredded cabbage add 3 tbsp. salt. Mix with hands or with potato masher until juicy. Put in stone jar, press down, cover with cloth, top with a plate and weight down. A smaller jar filled with water makes a good weight. Let this stand for 2 or 3 weeks. Wash cloth or change to a fresh one every few days. When ready to pack in jars press down, add boiled, cooled water to fill jar, and process in a 250° oven for an hour.

Leberwurst
Liver Sausage

6 lbs. pork, using part of the cooked meat from pig's head	2 lbs. pork liver 1 to 2 onions salt and pepper to taste

Cook pork until done, about 1 hour. Grind the meat and the raw liver. Saute the onions until tender but still white in color. Add salt and pepper to taste and mix thoroughly.

Put mixture into prepared casings and tie off with a string into desired sizes. Pierce casings with a sharp pointed fork or needle to prevent their breaking during cooking.

Cook 1 hour in the broth in which meat was boiled.

Leberwurst may also be put into pint jars and processed 1 hour in boiling water. Leave 1/2 inch head space in jars for this.

Leberwurst is "delicious" spread on brown bread, especially home made bread.

Butchering Time

In the good old days it was the custom to set a date for butchering. Relatives and neighbors were asked if they could help. Then you returned the favor. For us, when I was a girl, it was the usual thing to call on our grandparents, aunts, and uncles to help.

There was a great stir of activity at our farm as early as 4:30 or 5:00 a.m. The stars were still out and the air was oh! so crisp and pure. Lanterns were lit and the chores done in a hurry. Also the big iron kettle, hung in our outer kitchen, was filled with water and a roaring fire was built underneath. This water was later used for scalding the hogs.

Our helpers were all invited for breakfast. Mother had a bake day preceding this day. For breakfast, she made a large pot of freshly ground Arbuckle brand coffee. Coffee cake, white and dark bread, real butter, jams and jellies, canned fruit and sometimes scrambled eggs were served. After a ride, either by buggy or Model T Ford in the cold morning air, a hot breakfast tasted super good. The ladies brought dark aprons for outside work and nice clean ones for inside. The men bundled up and went to kill the first hog. It was then lowered into a trough of scalding hot water. The hair was then removed with sharp scrapers. The carcass was pulled up with a winch and hung in a tripod. The 'master dresser' slit it open. The entrails were removed and carried to the outer kitchen.

Here is where the ladies and the older girls went to work. They chose the sunny or sheltered side of the outer kitchen. Here they turned the intestines inside out and scraped and scrubbed them thoroughly. Then they were put into warm water till needed.

After one or more hogs had been killed and dressed and cut up, it was dinner time. Mother had killed several plump chickens and roasted them to perfection. There were potatoes, gravy, vegetables, relishes, pickles, chilled stewed fruits, and pies for dessert. What lively conversation went on around the table.

Then the men and some ladies bundled up and went out to the shed to grind meat for sausages and to chop the fat for rendering lard. This was put into the iron kettle and stirred constantly with large wooden paddles. After the fat had melted down, the ribs were gently lowered into this and fried till the bones turned easily. That was the cue to take the ribs out into a drip pan. Later the lard was strained into crocks and the little shrivels called cracklings were put into smaller crocks.

We had some expert sausage makers in the family. These sausages were cut into lengths and smoked in Grandfather's smokehouse. The hams and sides of bacon were salted down and later smoked, also. The rinds, jowls, and head were boiled till well done. The meat was picked off; the meat and juice were then pressed into large pans and chilled. Later the cooled mass was called 'head cheese'.

Mother fried meat balls and served fruit soup *(Moos)* and other goodies for supper. Then everybody hurried home to do their chores. We also did ours. After washing dishes we were glad to go to bed. Next day, with the help of hot water and scouring powder, we cleaned everything and put the tools away.

Grandparents, parents, and most uncles and aunts are gone now. It is good to recall the happy times we had.

Reetja Worscht
Summer Sausage

Grind 50 pounds of beef very fine, season with 4 handfulls salt, 4 tsp. black pepper, and 8 tsp. white pepper.

Stuff this meat mixture into muslin "jockers" and place on a flat surface. Rub with the following mixture:

1 1/2 lbs. brown sugar	2 1/2 lbs. salt
2 ounces saltpetre	

Place board on top of sausage and put a weight on top. About every 2 or 3 days, rub in more of the salt mixture and replace under the board. Continue until all this mixture has been used.

Smoke the meat now, either with a smoke solution or in a smoke house. Let dry and then paint with paraffin wax. Hang meat in a dry place until used.

Serve this sausage with raw onions and fried potatoes.

"Jockers" are home made casings. A piece of unbleached muslin is sewn together to form a "bag" 4 by 18 inches, into which the meat is put.

Sill-Flaesh
Head Cheese

The cleaned pig's head, ears, and nose—with a little of the rind— are put into salt water and cooked until done, about 2 hours.

Remove meat from the bones, discarding the rind, and put through a meat grinder, having the meat as hot as possible. Add salt and pepper to taste.

Put into a cloth sack and weigh down in a pan or stone crock in order to squeeze out the fat. When the ground meat is drained, cover with the broth in which the meat was cooked. When the meat is cool, place the formed meat into a vinegar solution made by boiling 1 pint vinegar and 3 pints water for a few minutes, letting it cool before adding the meat. Meat must be covered.

The meat should remain in brine for 2 or 3 days after which it is ready to be used. Slice to serve.

Head Cheese is good served with raw sliced "Spanish" onions and vinegar; and fried potatoes are a "must".

The cooked pig's feet, heart, and tongue are also very tasty if put into the same brine.

SALAD

Schmauntsupp
Sour Milk Salads

Allow 1 quart of raw milk to thicken in a warm room. When the milk is clabbered, add 1/3 c. sour cream, a dash of salt and pepper and beat all together.

1 tbsp. vinegar and 1-2 tbsp. sugar may be added to the above.
Serve this as a "thin" salad to be eaten with spoons.
Use the following:
1. Thinly sliced cucumbers
2. Lettuce, cut, with hard cooked eggs
3. Cook *kielke* or home made noodles until tender, drain and cool in cold water.

All of these dishes are very good but they taste best when everything is cold. A real treat for a hot summer day.

SOUPS

Moos
Fruit Soup

Moos is a fruit soup made from either canned or dried fruits. Almost any combination of different fruits is good. *Moos* may also have just one fruit, such as Apple *Moos*, Rhubarb *Moos*, Gooseberry *Moos*, etc., or there may be 2-6 different fruits.

Moos is usually thickened with cornstarch or flour, served with or without cream. Some cooks also add *Kielke* to *Plume-Moos*, which adds a different flavor. (For quick cooking add some macaroni.)

Moos is often served on Sundays or special holidays. It can be prepared the day before and so be ready to serve should company be invited for Sunday dinner. Fried ham and fried potatoes, pre-cooked in their jackets, are usually served with a *Moos*.

Plume-Moos

No. 1

1 1/2 c. raisins	1 c. sugar
1 c. prunes	1 cinnamon stick

No. 2

3/4 lb. prunes	3/4 lb. raisins
1/4 lb. dried apricots	1 can cherries
1 c. dried apples	1/2 lb. sugar

No. 3

1 package mixed dried fruit	1 c. sugar, or to taste
1 c. raisins	3 quarts water

Cover dried fruit with water and cook until tender.

Make a thickening of either flour or cornstarch using: 4 tbsp. cornstarch for 10-12 c. water or 1/2 c. flour for 8-10 c. water.

Add the sugar to the starch or the flour and make a paste with a little water or cream. Add slowly to the cooked fruit and bring to a boil. Stir constantly.

This *Moos* is usually served cold.

For variety when cornstarch is used as a thickener, add a package of cherry or raspberry gelatin.

Plume-Moos

makes 2 gallons of *Moos*

1 1/2 lb. raisins	water to cover fruit or
1 1/2 lb. prunes	about 4 quarts
1 star anise	

Cook until done. Cool.

Mix 1 1/2 c. sugar, 1 1/4 c. flour, and 1 tsp. cinnamon with a little water to make a paste, add 2 c. sweet cream. Add the juice of one lemon or a little vinegar. Add to fruit mixture and let come to a boil, stirring gently.

Variations: Add several c. of buttermilk instead of lemon or vinegar and less water. For a real treat add dates after the sugar-flour mixture has been added.

Gooseberry Moos

2 c. canned gooseberries   3 tbsp. flour
1 c. water   2 c. milk
1 c. sugar

Bring gooseberries and water to a boil. Make a thin paste with the sugar, flour, and part of the milk. Add slowly to the gooseberry mixture and add alternately with the remainder of the milk. Good served hot or cold with fried ham and fried potatoes.

Mom's Green Bean Soup

1 1/2 pounds of country ribs
   Boil until tender in water with a little salt added (about 2 hours).
   Peel 2 potatoes, 2 carrots and cut into small pieces. Add some whole pepper (10 seeds), allspice (5 seeds), and a little bay leaf, also half of a small onion, and 1/4 tsp. summer savory. Cook for 30 minutes. Add one can of string beans and one soup ladle of cream, and bring to a boil. Serve.

   Soup ladles were often used as a measuring device. They were found in every home, and the cook would know just how full to make the ladle for her different recipes. This ladle would also be used to "skim" the cream off the milk. It was a good measuring cup. As these ladles were quite a good size, we could say that they contained 3/4 to 1 c. of liquid.

Green Bean Soup

Use either a ham bone or a piece of smoked ham. Cover with water and cook over a medium low heat for about 3/4 hour. Add a sprig of summer savory and a small onion, sliced fine.
   Cut up 3 medium potatoes, 3 carrots, and 1 1/2 c. green beans sliced in 1/2 inch pieces. Cook until vegetables are done.
   Just before serving add 1/2 c. of sweet or sour cream.
   If fresh beans are not available, use canned beans but add these just a few minutes before serving as they only need to be thoroughly heated.

Summer Borscht

2 1/2 qts. soup broth, cooked
  ham hock until done
8 sorrel leaves
1 stalk dill
1 1/2 c. sour cream

2 1/2 c. beet greens, chopped
2/3 c. chopped onion greens
  or winter onions
5 potatoes, diced
12 green pea pods

Add prepared vegetables with the soup stock and boil until done.
Add salt and pepper to taste and gradually add the cream.
Serve hot.

Borscht

2 to 3 lbs. soup meat, with
  some bone (briskets
  are good)
1 tsp. salt

1 small bay leaf
sprig of parsley
little dill or dill seed
1/4 tsp. pepper

Cook the above ingredients in water to cover meat completely.
When meat is almost done add the vegetables:
  1/2 onion
  1 small head cabbage, sliced
  5 potatoes, cubed
  3 carrots, diced

Add additional water to make at least 2 quarts liquid. Add 1 1/2 c.
canned tomatoes; or, if raw tomatoes are used, add with other
vegetables. Simmer a few minutes.
  If cream is used, add about 2/3 c. just before serving. (Canned
evaporated milk may also be substituted.)
  Some cooks add 1 tbsp. of vinegar before the cream is added.
Schnetke are good served with *Borscht!*

Borscht
large quantity: 10 gallons

100 lb. bones for broth
20 lb. cabbage
1 1/2 lb. onions
2 tsp. pepper
1/3 c. sugar
2 qts. sour cream

10 lb. meat, diced
1 peck potatoes
5 gal. water
1 c. salt
dill and parsley

Fish Soup

2 1/2 lbs. mild fish, approx.	1 large onion
1/2 tsp. peppercorns	sprig of parsley
1 bay leaf	salt to taste

Cover fish with cold water and bring to a boil. Add the seasoning and onion. Cook until fish is tender; carefully lift it out of the soup and put into large soup bowl or on a platter.

Add 2 potatoes, diced, which have been cooked separately, to the strained soup. Bring to a boil again and add a ladle of sour cream and a small piece of butter.

Chopped green parsley leaves may be sprinkled on top of soup to add color.

The fish may be served in individual bowls with the soup or served separately as the "meat" dish for the meal.

Some cooks also thicken this soup with a paste made with a little flour and the cream. Either way is good.

VEGETABLES

Peas

Cook the amount of peas needed, until done.

Add salt and pepper to taste.

Chop a sprig of parsley into fine pieces and sprinkle over the peas. Dot with butter.

Geschmoade Grene Schauble
Green Beans

Pick fresh garden green beans and prepare for cooking.

Cover with cold water, add 1/2 tsp. salt and bring to a boil. Cook a few minutes. Add about 1 pound of cubed pork and cook beans and meat together until both are done.

Add salt and pepper to taste and just before serving add 1/2 c. sour cream.

For variety: Fry 6 slices of bacon, cut into smaller pieces and add both bacon and drippings; or cube cooked ham and add after beans are almost done.

Schmoor-Kohl or Komst
Stewed Cabbage

6 c. sliced cabbage	1/2 bay leaf
10 prunes	1/2 c. raisins or
	1 c. dried apples

Melt 1/4 c. shortening in heavy saucepan and add the cabbage and fruit. Cook with a tight fitting lid over a low heat, about 1-1 1/2 hours. Stir occasionally. Cabbage shoud become a golden brown. When tender add about 1 tsp. salt, a little pepper, 1 tbsp. sugar, and 1 tbsp. vinegar.

(Should there be difficulty in cabbage sticking to pan, add just a little water.)

Sauerkraut With Prunes and Raisins

1 no. 2 1/2 can sauerkraut	1/2 c. sugar
1/2 c. raisins	2 tbsp. butter
1 c. prunes	1/2 c. water, more if needed

Stir all together, cook slowly until brown, 1 1/2 hours.

The Silkworm Industry

One of the most interesting, yet unprofitable and short-lived experiments which took place was the raising of silk. The Marion County Record, in 1881 wrote: "It is reported that a large group of Mennonites in Marion and McPherson counties now have on hand about a carload of cocoons for silk production. These people did the same thing in Europe." Interest in raising silk became strong enough to obtain subsidies from the Kansas State Legislature in 1887. A silk station was established at Peabody in 1887 and proved to be quite popular with persons who came for silkworm eggs, took them home and returned the cocoons. The Kansas Legislature supported the industry until 1895. The station lost money, the promoters died, and the legislature lost interest.

Although there was interest among the Mennonites in raising silk, cold rainy weather, constantly changing management, and cheap foreign silk made silk-raising in Kansas unprofitable. The silk station was abolished by legislative enactment in 1897.

There was for a time a Kroeker Silk Station at Hillsboro, operated by a Helen Kroeker, who received her training in the Peabody Silk Station. She developed the mill until it employed more persons than the one in Peabody. Many farmers took the opportunity to supply cocoons for the mill for an additional income. Peter L. Janzen, for instance, planted four rows of Mulberry trees around his four acre orchard, using the mulberry leaves to feed the silkworms.

Low German In America

In the great Mennonite migration from Russia to North America in 1874 the Chortitza, or Old Colony Mennonites, went to Manitoba, and later some to Mexico and South America. They had preserved the original Low German in its purest form, although it also shows Russian and English influences. They have only a very limited mastery of High German and English, and of Spanish in Mexico and South America.

Among the Mennonite groups of Russian background in the United States, Low German is still spoken or understood in solid Mennonite Communities such as Goessel, Buhler, Inman, and Hillsboro in Kansas, Henderson in Nebraska, and Mountain Lake in Minnesota. However, few young people are able to converse in Low German. It can be expected that Low German will gradually disappear among the Mennonites in the United States, but will likely remain in use for some time to come in Canada and particularly in Mexico and South America, where the bearers of this language are living in much greater isolation.

Low German Mennonite Literature

Among the Mennonites of Russia, J. H. Janzen was the first to write Low German plays. They were primarily designed to be given in schools and deal particularly with questions pertaining to education. He continued his writing in Canada and was suceeded be Arnold Dyck, who wrote *Dee Fria*, a comedy, *"Wellkaom op'e Forstei!"* and a number of other Low German plays and numerous narratives and short stories, such as *Koop enn Bua op Reise; Koop enn Bua faore nao Toronto; Die Millionaea von Kosefeld;* and *Onse Lied*. These plays are still being given in Mennonite communities of North and South America where Low German is spoken. This is generally the case in Canada, Mexico, Brazil, and Paraguay.

Appendix

Storage of Eggs

Eggs were often very scarce by mid-winter, especially for town people. In order to have plenty on hand for baking, dozens of eggs would be stored in the fall when they were plentiful. One of the methods used for this was simply greasing the eggs well with lard, wrapping them in a piece of newspaper, and then placing them in layers in a sturdy box. This container was then stored in a cool, frost free, corner in a storage closet, or basement.

Some families stored their eggs in chopped straw, or even grain. A solution of sodium silicate, called "water glass", was also used later and could be obtained at the drug store. This was mixed with water and poured into a stone crock. Only clean eggs that had not been washed were used for this. From time to time more eggs were added but the liquid always had to be above the egg level. The crock was covered with a wooden lid. Eggs would keep for six months by this method.

When eggs were stored by these various methods, they were usually used for baking and cooking purposes. For eating, such as fried or boiled eggs, fresh ones could be purchased in limited quantities in the local stores.

Yeast Starter

Take 1/2 c. of hops or peach leaves and boil in 1 quart water. Take 2 medium potatoes and grate. Add these to strained hop water. Add 1 tbsp. salt and 1 tbsp. sugar to liquid.

When cool add about 3/4 c. flour and mix till smooth. Set aside until it bubbles. Keep in cool place. Ready for use.

Granulated Soap

1 can lye	3/4 c. Borax
3 c. cold "rain" water	4 1/2 lbs. melted, strained fat

Dissolve lye in cold water in a stone jar or granite kettle. Stir in Borax with wooden spoon or paddle. When Borax is dissolved, slowly stir in melted fat. Stir slowly for 10 to 15 minutes. Then stir off and on for the next 24 to 36 hours. It will be white and granular. Spread out on clean surface to dry.

May be used for all household tasks.

Soap Making

E. Foth

Wall Paper Paste

Dissolve 3 pints flour in 2 quarts cold water.

Gradually add 8 quarts boiling water and boil slowly for 10 minutes, stirring constantly.

When cool, add 1 tsp. alum.

Weather Wise

Grain for future use or seed should be harvested at the increase of the moon.

Avoid the first day of the new moon for planting, also the days on which it changes quarters.

Harvest all crops when the moon is growing old — they keep better.

Don't butcher hogs in the waning moon. If you do, the pork will shrink in the skillet.

Graft and prune trees in the increase of the moon. Leave three buds on the grape vine when pruning.

Timber cut in the full of the moon will be sappy and will soon rot.

Potatoes and other root crops should be planted in the dark of the moon.

How to Preserve a Husband

1. Be careful in your selection.
2. Do not choose too young.
3. When once selected, give your entire thought to preparation for domestic use.

Some insist on keeping them in a pickle, others are constantly getting them into hot water. This makes them sour, hard and bitter. Even poor varieties may be made sweet, tender, and good by garnishing them with patience, well sweetened with love, and seasoned with kisses. Wrap them in a mantle of charity, keep warm with a steady fire of domestic devotion, and serve with peaches and cream.

Thus prepared, they will keep for years!

Cleaning Tableware

Tableware was made of steel with wooden or bone handles. To scour, ashes were used until shiny. The articles were then washed in hot suds, rinsed well, and dried. If left wet, the tableware would rust. Wood ashes did about the same job that cleansing powders do today.

"The Home Doctor"
Home Remedies

Tie a strip of bacon over a boil or thorn puncture.

For a sore throat, prepare a mixture of turpentine and lard in a cloth and tie around the neck.

For a bee sting, apply the juice of an onion; or apply ammonia diluted with 1 tsp. to 1 c. of water.

For a boil, make a poultice of soap and sugar and wrap over the boil.

Rendered mutton suet, formed into small cakes, is good for parched lips and chapped hands.

"Eat pumpkin seed for a wet bed."

A few drops of peppermint oil in 1 tsp. sugar will ease a stomach. Also drinking camomile tea is good for this.

For severe coughs grind slightly browned sunflower seeds to make a tea. Drain and add a little sugar. This tea loosens the cough. Another syrup for this malady was to cut up a large onion and cover with water and 3 tbsp. sugar. Simmer for about 30 minutes until it is syrupy. Take as needed.

If your hands get dark from canning vegetables or fruit, use lemon juice.

Heat bags filled with sand in the oven and lay it to your ear for an earache.

Mustard Plaster for chest congestion: 1 tbsp. dry mustard, 4 tbsp. flour, 1 egg white. Mix dry ingredients. Add beaten egg white. Spread on cloth and place next to skin 15 to 20 minutes. Be careful not to burn chest!

For minor burns or scalds, place a wet tea bag on the burned spot to ease and remove the sting. Another method is to soak a clean cloth in a solution made of 2 tbsp. baking soda to 1 quart of warm water. Place the pad over the burn and bandage loosely. If skin is not broken, apply clean cold water to relieve pain.

Hot Lemonade for the sniffles: Heat 1 c. water, juice of 1 lemon, and 2 tbsp. honey, but do not boil. Drink it steaming hot and strong enough to "wrinkle up" your face.

Eierbier
Beer with Egg

Beat 2 to 3 eggs, add 3 to 4 tbsp. sugar and continue to beat until creamy. Gradually add 1 quart beer.

This was used for "upset" stomachs and seemed to be a simple remedy for this problem!

"Grog"
(A Hot Toddy)

Boil 2 c. water and 2 tbsp. sugar until blended. Add 1 c. rum or red wine. If wine is used, add a few cloves.

Drink hot for colds, fever, flu, etc.

Grandpa's Salve
RX dated 1880, Elkhart, Indiana

3 oz. beeswax	3 oz. burgundy pitch
3 oz. lard	

Melt together. Take from stove and add:

2 drams balsam peru	2 drams turpentine
2 drams oil of juniper	

Mix together then add:

1 oz. gum of camphor

Mix well. Store in small sealed jars. Use on wounds. Keeps well.

Hand Lotion

10 cents worth of gum of tragacanth (4 oz.)	8 oz. rose water
1 pint soft water	8 oz. glycerine
	rubbing alcohol

Soak gum of tragacanth overnight in water in a crock and cover with a plate. In the morning beat with a wooden spoon until smooth. Slowly add rose water and glycerine. Keep stirring. When all is added and smooth, thin down with alcohol.

A pioneer mother wrote her daughter telling her how to wash clothes.

Receipt

1. Build a fire in backyard to heat kettle of rain water.
2. Set tubs so smoke won't blow in eyes if wind present.
3. Shave whole cake lye soap in boiling water.
4. Sort things, making three piles, one pile of white, one pile of colored, and one pile of rags and britches.
5. Stir flour in cold water to smoothe for starch and then thin down with boiling water.
6. Rub dirty spots on board, then boil. Rub colored but don't boil.
7. Take white things out of kettle lifting with broom handle, then rinse, blue and starch.
8. Spread tea towels on grass.
9. Hang old rags on fence.
10. Pour rinse water in flower bed.
11. Scrub porch with soapy water.
12. Scrub privy seat and floor with soapy water caught from porch floor scrub.
13. Turn tubs upside down.
14. Go put on a clean dress. Smooth hair with side combs. Brew up tea, set and rest a spell and count your blessings.

Wash Days

The black cookstove was heated up and the copper boiler put on to heat the water with the homemade soap slivered in to make good suds. Clothes were sorted and put into the washer that was run by hand. A wheel with a handle on it operated the plunger up and down. The faster we turned the wheel, the cleaner the clothes got. After about ten to fifteen minutes, the clothes were run through the wringer, also operated by hand, and the white clothes put on to boil in another batch of soapy water, washed again, rinsed, and hung out to dry. For our family, it was a half-day's work for two people.

"If a girl wasn't able to bake with sour dough, she wasn't ready for marriage."

Sour Dough
(Sauerteich)

Breads were often made with a "sour" dough, which was started in several ways. This bread had a sour taste and was very delicious.

No. 1—No yeast needed.

A c. of flour and a c. of water was beaten until very smooth. This paste was put into an earthenware bowl and placed in a draft free cupboard for about two weeks or until it was "fermented". When needed, 2 c. warm water and 2 c. flour were beaten into the sponge and allowed to stand overnight. (Half of this mixture would be saved for the next starter.) About 2 c. of sponge would be used for 4 c. of flour when mixing the bread.

No. 2—With yeast.

To a flour-water mixture one cake of dry yeast would be added and put into a bowl, which was covered with a thin cloth, and set aside in a cool place. Off and on it would be stirred. When fermented or spongy, it was ready for use. Part of the sponge would be left in the jar and flour and water, in equal parts, would be added and mixed until smooth. This "sour" sponge could be kept active for a long time, provided the starter was replenished after being used.

No. 3

For sour dough rye bread a piece of dough the size of a bun, would be set aside and allowed to sour for a few days until a hard crust would cover the whole piece. This would then be buried in the sack of rye flour until needed. When baking time came around, the bun would be soaked in lukewarm whey made from buttermilk. When it had softened, it would be treated like other yeast. This method was somewhat slow but the rye bread was very tasty.

No. 4—Hop yeast.

In many of the pioneer gardens, hops were planted in order to have a basis for bread making. The hops were dried and stored for use during the winter. Some of the early settlers in America were able to get dry compressed yeast which was used with the hops. The yeast cake was soaked in warm water to which a little sugar had been added. A large potato was grated or sliced thinly and cooked in 1 quart of water to which the hops had been added. When the potato slices were done the mixture was cooled to lukewarm. The dissolved yeast mixture would then be added and the sponge put into a glass jar to rise. Some of this yeast sponge would always be left in the jar as a starter. When bread needed to be baked, a potato and hops would again be boiled, added, and allowed to rise overnight.

Loaf of Bread With Hop Yeast

1 1/2 c. of yeast sponge	1 1/2 c. warm water
2 tbsp. lard	1 1/2 tbsp. sugar
1 tsp. salt	flour to make fairly stiff dough

Add the warm water to the sponge. Melt lard and add. Add salt and sugar and gradually beat in flour, enough to make a dough which can be kneaded. Let rise. Knead down, form into a loaf and put into a greased pan. Let rise until almost double and bake in moderate oven about an hour.

Sour Dough Bread

To 2 c. of sour dough sponge, add 1 tsp. salt, 3 tbsp. sugar and 2 tbsp. melted lard.

Gradually add about 4 c. flour, beating well. Add flour enough to make a smooth, fairly stiff dough. Cover and let rise until double. Knead a little and form into loaves. Put into greased pan and let rise again until light. Bake in moderate oven about 50 minutes.

Names of Foods of Dutch Descent

English	Netherlands	West Prussian High German	Polish Low German	Molotchna-Chortitza Low German
apples	appel	Aepfel	Appel	Aupel
beans	boonen	Bohnen	Schable	Schauble
bread	brood	Brot	Brot	Bulke (Brot)
butter	boter	Butter	Botta	Botta
cabbage	kool	Kraut	Komst	Komst
cherries	kersen	Kirschen	Tjorsche	Tjorsche
cheese	kaas	Kaese	Tjees	Tjees
dumpling		Kloesse	Kielke	
eggs	eieren	Eier	Eia	Eia
flour	meel	Mehl	Meel	Mehl
grapes	druiven	Weintrauben	Wiendruwe	Wiendruwe
jam	jam	Confiture	Appel-Botta	Schmeasel
lettuce	sla	Salat	Salat	Salout
meat	vleesh	Fleisch	Fleesch	Fleesch
milk	melk	Milch	Meltj	Maltj
onions	uien	Zwiebeln	Tzipple	Tzipple
pears	peren	Birnen	Beere	Beere
pepper	peper	Pfeffer	Pepa	Pepa
potatoes	aardappelen	Kartoffeln	Toefcha	Eadschoke
salt	sout	Salz	Solt	Solt
sugar	suiker	Zucker	Zocka	Zocka
soup	soep	Suppe	Supp	Supp
tomatoes	tomaten	Tomaten	tomatoes	Bocklezhane
pickles	augurken	Saure Gurken		Sure Gurke

Names of Foods of Swiss Descent

English	Pennsylvania German	Hutterite	Swiss	Swiss Galician	Swiss Volhynian	South German
apple	Appel	Apful	Aepfel	Eppel	Eppel	Appel
beans	Bohne	Bohnen	Bohnen	Bohne	Bohne	Bohne
bread	Broot	Brot	Brod	Brot	Brot	Brot
butter	Butter	Booter	Butter	Butter	Butter	Butter
cabbage	Kraut	Kraut	Kraut	Kraut	Kraut	Kraut
cherries	Kersche	Wiksilen	Kirsche	Kersche	Kersche	Kersche
cheese	Kaese	Kaes	Kaes	Kaese	Kaes	Kaes
dumplings	Dampfnudeln	Knoodel	Knepp	Knodel	Pirogi (Knep)	Knepp
eggs	Eier	Ahlen	Eijer	Eier	Eier	Eier
flour	Mehl	Mael	Mehl	Mehl	Mehl	Mehl
grapes	Trauben	Winegrapen	Dreeba	Trawe	Weintraube	Trauwe
jam	Psaa(s)fs	Chelly	Gschmier	Lestwerch	Latwerk	Ladwerk
lettuce	Salat	Salat	Salat	Salat	Salat	Salat
meat	Fleisch	Fleisch	Flasch	Fleisch	Fleisch	Fleisch
milk	Milch	Milch	Milch	Milch	Milch	Milch
onions	Zwiewel	Zwefre	Zwiebel		Zwible	Zwieble
pears	Beere	Pearn	Beere	Beeren	Beeren	Beere
pepper	Pfeffer	Pfeffer	Pfeffer	Peffer	Peffer	Pfeffer
potatoes	Grumbeere	Kartufl	Herraepfel	Kartoffel	Krumbere	Grumbere
salt	Salz	Salz	Salz	Salz	Salz	Salz
sugar	Zucker	Zucker	Zucker	Zucker	Zucker	Zucker
soup	Suppe	Suppe	Supp	Supp	Supp	Supp
tomatoes	Tomaten	Buglezhna	Tomatis	Tomato	Tomato	Tomato
pickles	Gumere	Kratzuitz	Gumere		Saure Gumere	Gumere

Names of Some Immigration Ships

Colina

Cimbria

City of London

City of Richmond

Elbe

Holsatia

Nederland

Teutonia

Vaderland

In 1874, a total of 5,039 Mennonites arrived in America. Ten years later, the total had reached 13,172.

Mennonite Life, June, 1973, p. 40.

Immigration Song

Ein Auswanderungs-Lied	Immigration Song
Jetzt ist die Zeit und Stunde da,	The time and hour is now at hand,
Dass wir ziehn nach Amerika,	We're moving to a foreign land.
Viel tausend Seelen geht's dort gut,	Where souls by thousands prosper well,
Dass troestet uns und gibt uns Mut.	Dauntless with tears, we say farewell.
Jetzt ist die Zeit und Stunde da	The time and hour is now at hand,
Dass wir ziehn nach Amerika	We're moving to a foreign land;
Die Wagen stehen schon vor der Tuer,	Our wagons loaded stand in row
Mit Weib und Kinder ziehen wir.	With wives and children we shall go.
Jetzt ist die Zeit und Stunde da	The time and hour is now at hand,
Das wir ziehn nach Amerika	We're moving to a foreign land;
Die Pferde stehn schon angespahnt,	Our horses hitched to wagons stand,
Wir ziehen in ein fremdes Land.	We're leaving for an unknown land.
Ihr alle die mit uns verwandt,	To our beloved ones and our kin;
Reicht uns zum letzten mal die Hand.	We say farewell and sigh within;
Ihr Freunde weinet nicht zu sehr.	Weep not so hard that we must part,
Wir sehn uns nun, und nimmer mehr.	It grieves our weary saddened heart.
Seid alle maennlich, und seid stark,	Be manly and renew your strength,
Macht uns den Abschied nicht zu hart.	As time goes on we'll meet at length.
Wir ziehen ja nicht aus der Welt,	We still remain upon this sphere
Auch da ist Gott, der uns erhaelt.	Where God's protection will be near.
Wenn unser Schiff zur See einschwimmt,	When we embark the ship at sea
Dann werden Lieder angestimmt.	We'll join in songs of jubilee;
Wir fuerchten keinen Wasserfall,	We fear no water and no wave,
Der Liebe Gott ist ueberall.	For God is here and His love saves.
Und kommen wir gen Baltimore,	When we'll arrive on yonder shore,
Dann haben wir das Land empor,	God's holy name we will adore;
Und rufen laut "Victoria"!	We'll shout when we step on the strand,
Jetzt sind wir in Amerika.	America, thou blessed land!
Willkommen fremdes Vaterland,	Welcome, thou fatherland, afar,
Wo sich mein Herz hat hingewandt,	Where favored gates stand wide ajar;
Du Land wo ich geboren bin,	We now our land of birth disown,
Muss meiden und muss weit dahin.	We've chosen a home in lands unknown.
Leb wohl du altes Vaterland,	Farewell, farewell, my fatherland,
Lebt alle wohl die uns gekannt.	Farewell, again, my kindred band;
Wir werden uns einst wiedersehn,	Some day we'll meet on heaven's shore,
Dort wo die Friedens Palmen wehn.	'Neath peaceful palms forever more.

This immigration song was written on July 30, 1874 by Jakob Stucky, elder of the Mennonite congregation at Kotosufka, Zhitomir district in Volhynia, western Russia, and printed in America in April 1875. The English translation is by Abe J. Unruh, Montezuma, Kansas.

Metric Conversion Chart

Approximate Conversions
TO Metric Measures

When You Know	Multiply by	To Find
LENGTH		
inches	2.5	centimeters
feet	30	centimeters
yards	0.9	meters
miles	.6	kilometers
AREA		
square inches	6.5	square centimeters
square feet	0.09	square meters
square yards	0.8	square meters
square miles	2.6	square kilometers
acres	0.4	hectares
MASS (weight)		
ounces	28	grams
pounds	0.45	kilograms
short tons (2,000 lb)	0.9	tonnes
VOLUME		
teaspoons	5	milliliters
tablespoons	15	milliliters
cups	0.24	liters
pints	0.47	liters
quarts	0.95	liters
gallons	3.8	liters
cubic feet	0.03	cubic meters
cubic yards	0.76	cubic meters
TEMPERATURE (exact)		
Fahrenheit temperature	5/9 (after subtracting 32	Celsius temperature

Approximate Conversions
FROM Metric Measures

When You Know	Multiply by	To Find
LENGTH		
millimeters	0.04	inches
centimeters	0.4	inches
meters	3.3	feet
meters	1.1	yards
kilometers	0.6	miles
AREA		
square centimeters	0.16	square inches
square meters	1.2	square yards
square kilometers	0.4	square miles
hectares (10,000 m²)	2.5	acres
MASS (weight)		
grams	0.035	ounces
kilograms	2.2	pounds
tonnes (1,000 kg)	1.1	short tons
VOLUME		
milliliters	0.03	fluid ounces
liters	2.1	pints
liters	1.06	quarts
liters	0.26	gallons
cubic meters	35	cubic feet
cubic meters	1.3	cubic yards
TEMPERATURE (exact)		
Celsius temperature	9/5 (then add 32)	Fahrenheit temperature

Index

Sketches

Index